Anglican Religious Life

2016-2017

A Year Book of
Religious orders and communities in
the Anglican Communion,
and tertiaries, oblates, associates and companions

Published by
Canterbury Press Norwich
a publishing imprint of The A & M Group Ltd *(a registered charity)*
Invicta House, 108-114 Golden Lane, London EC1Y 0TG
www.scm-canterburypress.co.uk

ARLYB 2016-2017 published August 2015

A catalogue record for this book is available from the British Library.

ISBN: 978-1-84825-776-4

Agents for Canterbury Press outside the UK:

Australia	Rainbow Book Agency	www.rainbowbooks.com.au
Canada	Novalis Books	www.novalis.ca
Europe (continental)		c/o marketing@hymnsam.co.uk
Ireland	Columba Bookstores	www.columba.ie
New Zealand	Church Stores	christianbooksnz.com/churchstores
South Africa	Methodist Publishing House SA	http://methodist.org.za/work/publishing/methodist-publishing-house
USA	Westminster John Knox	www.wjkbooks.com
West Indies		c/o marketing@hymnsam.co.uk

The Editorial committee of ARLYB and the publishers wish to thank
The St Andrew's Trust and **Anglican Religious Communities (ARC)**
for supporting the publication of this *Year Book*.

Drawings by Alison Finch
The cover design is by Leigh Hurlock

The photographs on the cover are from:
CSS in Bangladesh, CHC in the UK, CCSB in Cameroon, SLG in the UK, LBF in Australia, OSB Malling in the UK, OSB Mucknell in the UK, the Sisters of Jesus Way in the UK, SHC in Korea, SSJD in Canada & SSAP in the USA.

Contents

Foreword
by The Most Revd Justin Welby,
Archbishop of Canterbury

Life in Religion is the ultimate wager on the existence of God. The Church should always be engaged in doing things that make no sense if God does not exist. This is the reason why I hold the Religious life in the highest esteem. Through the commonality of goods, the life of obedience and above all the commitment to shape life around the *Opus Dei* (that is, prayer), the monastic life models for all Christians what it means to live fully and abundantly, with and for Christ. In my own Christian living, I am very grateful to have discovered the *Rule of St Benedict*, which has probably shaped me more than any other text besides the Bible.

Without prayer, the Church is in danger of being indistinguishable from any other NGO. It is through the action of praying that the Church demonstrates it is no mere organisation for 'doing good' (as one prominent political leader put it to me recently) – but the channel of God and God's action. The self-giving of prayer opens the doors to eternity, for us and for all those around who care to see and hear the call and light of Christ through that very self-giving. As Karl Barth put it, 'Prayer is the most intimate and effective form of Christian action… all other work comes far behind it … and is doing the will of God only to the extent that it derives from prayer. The greatest Christian busyness is only idleness if the proper work [of prayer] is not done' (*Church Dogmatics* III.3).

When appointed as Archbishop of Canterbury, I committed to seek a renewal of prayer and Religious life as my first priority for the Church. This is because of my conviction that if any renewal is to happen in the wider Church, it will not be the result of better structures or more gifted leaders. It will follow because there are disciples who follow Jesus with all their being, setting the gospel fully into practice, laying down their lives in prayer and in action – such as the kind of disciples who are consecrated to God through Religious vows. Religion has provided the engine room of conversion and renewal throughout the history of the Church. It is hard to find an example of renewal anywhere in God's Church since the end of the Roman Empire that has not been preceded and accompanied by a renewal of prayer, usually within flourishing Religious communities.

In my own encounters with Religious communities, usually from times of retreat, I have experienced a palpable combination of vulnerability and joy that is a hugely powerful witness to Jesus Christ. Such witness is counter-cultural for the world and prophetic for the church – and a visible sign of the greatness and goodness of God. Blessed be God! And blessed be all those represented in the pages of this *Year Book*.

+ JUSTIN CANTUAR

4 December 2014, Feast of St John of Damasus (8th C) and Nicholas Ferrar (17th C)

In his journeys through the Anglican Communion in these first years of his time in office, the Archbishop has included communities in his visits. Above he is with the Society of the Holy Cross in Korea and below on a visit to SSJD & CSC in Canada.

A Prayer for Vocations to the Religious Life

Setting a particular Sunday each year as a Day of Prayer for Vocations to the Religious Life was begun in 1992. This is currently the **Fourth Sunday after Easter**. All are also invited to pray each Friday for the life and work of the Religious communities in the Church, using the following prayer, written by a Little Brother of Francis, originally for communities in Australia and New Zealand.

Lord Jesus Christ
in your great love you draw all people to yourself:
and in your wisdom you call us to your service.
We pray at this time you will kindle in the hearts of men and women
the desire to follow you in the Religious life.
Give to those whom you call, grace to accept their vocation readily
and thankfully, to make the whole-hearted surrender
which you ask of them, and for love of you, to persevere to the end.
This we ask in your name. Amen.

A NOVENA OF PRAYER FOR RELIGIOUS LIFE

Day 1: 2 Thessalonians 1: 3
We give thanks for Religious communities throughout the world.

Day 2: Romans 14: 7-9
We give thanks for members in our communities who have died.

Day 3: Acts 15: 36-40
We pray for those who have left our communities.

Day 4: Ephesians 4: 1-6
We give thanks for our own vocations.

Day 5: 1 Thessalonians 5: 12-14
We pray for our leaders and for all who make decisions.

Day 6: Titus 2: 7-9
We pray for novice guardians and all who teach in our way of life.

Day 7: 1 Corinthians 12: 27-31
We pray that we will be faithful to our vows.

Day 8: Acts 2: 44-47
We pray for all who seek to know and to do your will and that men and women will be led to join our communities.

Day 9: 2 Corinthians 4: 16-18
We recognize that the future is in God's hands. We pray that the Holy Spirit will help and support us as we live in the Light of Christ.

We give thanks for the Religious Life in all its forms in the Church, and today we pray especially for:

1 Community of All Hallows *in the UK*
All Saints Sisters of the Poor *in the UK*
Society of the Precious Blood *in southern Africa & the UK*

2 Community of the Holy Spirit *in the USA*
Holy Spirit Sisters (Alsike kloster) *in Sweden*
Community of St Mary *in Malawi, the Philippines & the USA*

3 Community of the Resurrection *in the UK*
Community of the Resurrection of Our Lord *in South Africa*
Communities in the Mar Thoma Church *in India*

4 Community of Saint Francis & Society of Saint Francis & the Third Order SSF *throughout the world*
Little Brothers of Francis *in Australia*
Sisters of St Francis *in Sweden*
Society of the Franciscan Servants of Jesus & Mary *in the UK*

5 Community of the Servants of the Will of God *in the UK*
Community of the Sisters of the Church *in Australia, Canada, Solomon Islands & UK*

6 Brotherhood of St Gregory *in the USA and elsewhere*
Sisters of St Gregory *in the USA*
Christa Sevika Sangha *in Bangladesh*
Church Mission Society *throughout the world*
The Order of Mission *throughout the world*

7 Community of Jesus' Compassion *in South Africa*
Order of Women in the Church of South India *in India*
Community of the Holy Name *in Lesotho, South Africa, Swaziland & the UK*

8 Society of the Servants of Jesus Christ (FMJK) *in Madagascar*
Order of Julian of Norwich *in the USA*
Society of Our Lady of the Isles *in the UK*

9 Community of St Denys *in the UK*
Society of the Sacred Advent *in Australia*
Christian ashrams *in India*

10 Community of St Laurence *in the UK*
Chita che Zvipo Zve Moto (Community of the Gifts of the Holy Fire) *in Zimbabwe*
Chita che Zita Rinoyera (Holy Name Community) *in Zimbabwe*

We give thanks for the Religious Life in all its forms in the Church, and today we pray especially for:

11 Order of St Benedict *in independent Abbeys and Priories throughout the world*
Benedictine Community of Christ the King *in Australia*
Benedictine Community of the Holy Cross *in the UK*
Benedictine Community of Our Lady and St John *in the UK*
Congregation of the Companions of St Benedict *in Cameroon*

12 Community of the Holy Transfiguration *in Zimbabwe*
Community of the Transfiguration *in the Dominican Republic & the USA*
Oratory of the Good Shepherd *throughout the world*

13 Community of the Glorious Ascension *in the UK*
Brotherhood of the Ascended Christ *in India*
Sisters of Jesus' Way *in the UK*

14 Order of the Holy Cross *in Canada, South Africa & the USA*
Society of the Holy Cross *in Korea*
Society of the Sacred Cross *in the UK*

15 Community of St Mary the Virgin *in the UK*
Society of Our Lady St Mary *in Canada*
Evangelical Daughters of Mary's Way *in Sweden*

16 Community of the Companions of Jesus the Good Shepherd *in the UK*
Community of the Good Shepherd *in Malaysia*
Society of St Anna the Prophet *in the USA*

17 Melanesian Brotherhood *throughout the Pacific region*
Community of the Sisters of Melanesia *in the Solomon Islands*
Devasevikaramaya *in Sri Lanka*

18 Companions of St Luke - OSB *in the USA*
Company of Mission Priests *in the UK*
Society of St Luke *in the UK*

19 Order of the Holy Paraclete *in Ghana & the UK*
Order of the Community of the Paraclete *in the USA*
Community of the Holy Name *in Australia*

20 Society of St Margaret *in Haiti, Sri Lanka, the UK & the USA*
Community of Nazareth *in Japan*
Contemplative Fire *in the UK*
Single Consecrated Life *in the UK*

21 Community of St Clare *in the UK*
Little Sisters of St Clare *in the USA*
Order of St Helena *in the USA*

We give thanks for the Religious Life in all its forms in the Church, and today we pray especially for:

22 Community of the Sacred Passion *in the UK*
Community of St Mary of Nazareth and Calvary *in Tanzania & Zambia*
Community of Ss Barnabas and Cecilia *in Australia*

23 Community of Celebration *in the UK & the USA*
Community of St John the Evangelist *in the Republic of Ireland*
Order of the Teachers of the Children of God *in the USA*

24 Community of St John Baptist *in the UK & the USA*
Order of Anglican Cistercians *in the UK*
Worker Brothers & Sisters of the Holy Spirit *in Australia, Canada, Haiti & USA*

25 Community of St Paul *in Mozambique*
Society of St Paul *in the USA*
Sisterhood of the Holy Nativity *in the USA*

26 Order of St Anne *in the USA*
Community of the Sisters of the Love of God *in the UK*
Church Army *in the UK*

27 Community of St John the Divine *in the UK*
Sisterhood of St John the Divine *in Canada*
Society of St John the Divine *in South Africa*
Brothers of St John the Evangelist *in the USA*
Society of St John the Evangelist *in north America & the UK*
Sisters of Charity *in the UK*

28 Society of the Sacred Mission *in Australia, Lesotho, South Africa & the UK*
Sisters of the Incarnation *in Australia*
Sisters of Jesus *in the UK*

29 Community of St Michael & All Angels *in South Africa*
Community of St Peter (Woking) *in the UK*
Community of St Peter, Horbury *in the UK*
Society of the Sisters of Bethany *in the UK*
Benedictine Sisters of Bethany *in Cameroon*

30 Community of St Andrew *in the UK*
Community of the Sacred Name *in Fiji, New Zealand & Tonga*
Community of the Gospel *in the USA*

31 Congregation of the Sisters of the Visitation of Our Lady *in PNG*
Community of the Blessed Lady Mary *in Zimbabwe*
Sisterhood of St Mary *in Bangladesh*

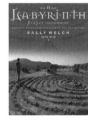

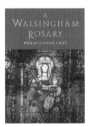

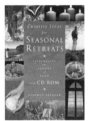

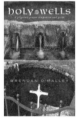

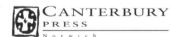

News of Anglican Religious Life

Pilgrimage

Come, dip a scallop shell into the font
For birth and blessings as a child of God.
The living water rises from that fount
Whence all things come, that you may bathe and wade
And find the flow, and learn at last to follow
The course of Love upstream towards your home.
The day is done and all the fields lie fallow
One thing is needful, one voice calls your name.

Take the true compass now, be compassed round
By clouds of witness, chords of love unbound.
Turn to the Son, begin your pilgrimage,
Take time with Him to find your true direction.
He travels with you through this darkened age
And wakes you everyday to resurrection.

Malcolm Guite

Community in the Heart of the Church

Archbishop Justin has made the revival of Religious life in all its forms a goal of his time in office. This is because the vision of a renewed Church cannot come to fruition without a renewed commitment to prayer. Here the role of Religious communities is important. To foster this aim, the Archbishop called a meeting at Lambeth Palace on 28 March 2014, inviting representatives of many different types of community to listen to talks and have much discussion. Participants came away feeling that this was an impetus for new initiatives.

The Archbishop's own innovative idea was soon announced. He wished to open up Lambeth Palace for no fewer than 56 young people each year (age-range 20-35) from right across the Christian family tree to share in a transformative experience, defined by a monastic round of prayer, study and service to the poor. Members are either resident (16) or integrate their commitment to Lambeth Palace with a working life in and around London (40). The new venture will be known as the Community of St Anselm. The intention is to give the members a formation in a disciplined life of prayer that will inform their work for Christ in the future, wherever that mission may be or whatever form it takes. The vision is an affirmation of the Religious life as being at the heart of the Church and its mission.

The prior of the Community is Revd Anders Litzell, who was brought up in Sweden and who was ordained in the Church of England in 2012. He and his young family will also be living at Lambeth Palace. He will be accompanied by members of the ecumenical community Chemin Neuf, some of whom live at Lambeth Palace (and have written for this *Year Book* – see the articles section). The St Anselm study programme will include Scripture, Ethics and Church History along with reflection, week-long retreats and accessing the wisdom of great exponents of the Religious life such as Ss Benedict, Francis and Ignatius of Loyola.

On his appointment Father Anders said: "We pray that the community will be identified by prayer, by learning, by love for each other and of the poor – all with one intention above all others: to become more like Jesus."

News from Korea

Sister Catherine SHC writes:

We have three Burmese postulants who came to Korea in June 2013 and were admitted as postulants at Michaelmas 2014. We are working to train and nurture them

for opening a Religious community in Myanmar in future. They are learning Korean and also about Korean culture while they live with us in Seoul and until they make their profession. It will take 2-3 years in the novitiate and a further 3-4 years for junior and final profession. Novice Oi Lan of the Community of the Good Shepherd in Malaysia returned home after a year's training. A few Sisters made a pilgrimage to England and Taize in France in June 2015.

Centenarians

Sister Dorothea CSC of St Michael's Convent, Ham Common, celebrated her 100th birthday in December 2014. A former superior of the community, she has continued to be active in community and ministry long past what would usually be a retirement age. Here Dorothea is seen with her telegram from Her Majesty Queen Elizabeth II.

Alongside her is Sister Scholastica CSC who had received a similar telegram of congratulations in 2012. Schol went on to celebrate her 103rd birthday on 3 February 2015 but sadly died soon after.

You can read more about Schol in the Remembering and Thanksgiving section.

A Good Read!

Quite a number of new books on Anglican communities have been published since the last edition of the *Year Book*. Several community histories have found their way into print and are all full of fascinating stories and photographs of the communities concerned. The **Community of Transfiguration** produced a history in 2014. Written by their Sister Monica Mary, called *Women of Devotion*, it follows the Sisters' work through 125 years of service, including the unusual story of a group of Anglican Sisters in China (mentored by CT) who flourished until the advent of the Communist government of 1949.

The **Sisterhood of St John the Divine**, whose main house is in Toronto, Canada, published *A Journey Just Begun: The Story of an Anglican Sisterhood* in early 2015, co-edited by Jane Christmas & Sister Constance Joanna. This chronicles 140 years of Anglican Religious life in Canada and the wide influence this dynamic community has had over their years of service.

Later in 2015, it was the turn of the **Community of the Holy Name in the UK**, Lesotho and South Africa, whose 150th anniversary of foundation was celebrated in August 2015 with a great thanksgiving service in Derby Cathedral, UK. Most of the text was written by the late Sister Constance CHN but had not been published in its entirety before, but, with some editing and an added section by Sister Julie to bring the story right up-to-date, it has now been issued with the title *What's in a Name?: Portrait of a Community*. This is an in-depth study of how an Anglican sisterhood survived difficult beginnings in the 19th century before flourishing in the 20th both in the UK and overseas. The **Community of the Holy Name in Australia** was founded in 1888 quite separately from its UK namesake and its own rich history is captured by Sister Sheila's 2014 book *Some suitable women*. CHN Australia has also pioneered for the faith and the Religious life in more than one country and so this too is an international story. The fifth history scheduled for 2015 publication is about the **Community of St Francis**, a group of sisters who remained small and hidden for many years after their foundation, before expanding from the 1960s. The book is by Helen Stanton and called *For Peace and Good,* the publisher being Canterbury Press.

For those who like their history in an autobiographical form, they need look no further than a new book by **Father Ralph Martin SSM**. It was published early in 2015 under the title *Towards a new day: a monk's story*. The first half is an engaging narrative telling of his personal journey from home in Canada to the old UK mother-house of the Society of the Sacred Mission at Kelham, through the early 1960s, when the Society was confident and flourishing, to its struggle to re-establish a new purpose once its theological college closed a decade later. The personal perspective on those extraordinary events makes for a gripping read. The second half of the book traces his journeys and ministries from Japan to Ghana, Teeside (UK) to Kuwait, from Rome to Lesotho, and then Australia.

Eldridge Pendleton SSJE has published a book on Charles Grafton, one of the early members of the **Society of St John the Evangelist** from the USA: *On the Kingdom: The life of Charles Chapman Grafton, Society of Saint John the Evangelist*. Although Grafton did not stay in the community, and eventually became Bishop of Fond du Lac, he was influential in the development of SSJE and in particular was a strong voice for the

Religious life at the 1897 Lambeth Conference.

In 2014, a striking contribution came from the Minister-General of the Anglican Franciscans, **Brother Clark Berge SSF**. He produced a succinct and lovingly-crafted book on the vows, simple enough in its vocabulary to be used even by those for whom English is not a first or even second language, yet so profound and thought-provoking in its insights that it has something to say to the scholarly. Unadorned by long theological words or concepts, it has an accessible depth of teaching about the Christian life as well as the Religious life. If you have ever wanted a straight forward explanation of the relevance and the power of the vows of Poverty, Chastity and Obedience, here is a book that will help you. Published as *The Vows Book: Anglican Teaching on the Vows of Obedience, Poverty and Chastity,* it is a significant text for anyone thinking about the Christian faith.

Malling Abbey

Abbess Mary David OSB writes:

During 2016, the Community will celebrate two significant anniversaries: the centenary of our arrival at Malling Abbey and the fiftieth anniversary of the consecration of the church. On 15 December 1916, our sisters arrived at West Malling from the remote village of Baltonsborough in Somerset and became tenants of this historic Abbey where generations of Benedictine nuns had prayed and worked from 1090 to 1538. On 20 June 1966, the new church, built on the site of the crossing of the medieval church, was consecrated.

Our thanksgiving for past milestones is augmented by our hope for the future as our present guest accommodation is altered to become a non-residential Diocesan Centre for Spirituality and Theological Education. We would value prayers as we begin a new century of Benedictine life here, and a new chapter in our history. During the time of alterations and building work, we shall be able to offer only limited hospitality. We hope to use the interlude for refreshment, renewal and communal reflection on our Benedictine heritage. It is a time of challenge and opportunity as we consider how we may best pass on our monastic tradition to those who will live it out in the coming generations.

Love Fulfilled

The Community of the Servants of the Cross came to an end in 2014-15 when the last two surviving sisters died. Mother Angela died aged 92 on 17 April 2014, after 60 years of profession. Sister Jane died on 31 January 2015, also aged 92, after 52 years in profession.

The Community was founded following the rescue work with vulnerable girls undertaken by the Wantage sisters (CSMV) in Fulham, London. Reflecting the attitudes of the Victorian era, it was felt appropriate by CSMV to create a 'daughter community' for women who might not meet their rigorous entry standards. The work of the Servants of the Cross would be to care for aged and infirm women as an act of reparation. The first professions were in 1882 and in 1893 the growing group of CSC sisters moved to Worthing in Sussex. They also cared for a while for invalid children and at one time some sisters helped at a hospital in South Africa.

However, their main work became the care of the seriously ill, often terminally so, and to this end a new convent and nursing home was built at Findon, Sussex, opened in 1934. In the centre of the impressive complex was a fine chapel. At this stage, the community began to attract more vocations, peeking at around thirty professed by the 1950s, and in due course a convalescent home at Lindfield was added to their work.

In the 1960s, fewer vocations were being received and the demands of nursing were requiring more high-level qualifications and more financial investment to bring the nursing home up to the latest standards. As a result, in 1967 the Findon property was sold and the community gathered at Lindfield, with those sisters wishing still to nurse doing so outside the convent. The Sisters had always had a Wantage sister as their superior, but in 1976 were allowed to elect from their own number. Three sisters took this role: Dorothea 1976-85, Doris 1985-95 and Angela 1995-2014.

As numbers dwindled, the remaining sisters moved from Lindfield to several locations. With the deaths of Angela and Jane, the Community's work has been accomplished and, in the 130 years of service and prayer, love has found fulfilment.

Love ignited

As some communities die, others emerge to give new expression to the Religious life. This *Year Book* has a number of new entries. Two Anglican communities have emerged in French-speaking Cameroon in the past decade and both are now sufficiently established to be included. There is a group of brothers called the **Congregation of the Companions of St Benedict** at Yaoundé. In 7 years, they have grown to 9 brothers with a further 8 currently in the noviciate and they hope to found a women's branch of the Congregation in years to come.

The **Benedictine Sisters of Bethany** based at Bamenda, run orphanages and are helping over 150 children who would otherwise be homeless.

We are pleased also to have two more communities from the Church of Sweden to add to section 4. These Religious are in communion with Anglicans through the Porvoo Agreement and their presence in this *Year Book* is a contribution to the ecumenical journey of growing together.

There are six new entries in the Acknowledged Section, representing a wide range of new forms of the Religious life, from a dispersed group of **Anglican Cistercians** to the network of **Contemplative Fire** and the missional leadership of **The Order of Mission**. The **Society of Saint Anna the Prophe**t is drawn from the older generation of women, showing that age is no barrier to catching the enthusiasm of a Religious vocation.

The **Community of Saints Barnabas and Cecilia** is our new entry from Australia, and the **Community of the Gospel** is from the USA, both foundations being open to both men and women, and witnessing to the values of the Christian life in their members' varied locations.

A retreat group of the Community of Ss Barnabas & Cecilia

Thanks to Malcolm Guite

In a new departure to celebrate the tenth edition of the *Year Book*, we are thrilled that Malcolm Guite has given us permission to reprint some of his poems, which you can find on several title-pages through the book. Malcolm is the Chaplain at Girton College, Cambridge, and the author of books on religious themes as well as books of poems. The latter include *Sounding the Seasons, The Singing Bowl, Word in the Wilderness* and *Waiting on the Word*, all published by Canterbury Press. He is the author of *Faith, Hope and Poetry,* published by Ashgate in 2012. He is also a singer-songwriter and fronts the Cambridge-based band Mystery Train. Visit www.malcolmguite.com where you can read Malcolm's blog, some of his poetry, or find out more about his music and media appearances. We are very appreciative of his generosity in sharing some of his poetry in this *Year Book*.

Articles

Benedict

You sought to start a simple school of prayer,
A modest, gentle, moderate attempt,
With nothing made too harsh or hard to bear,
No treating or retreating with contempt,
A little rule, a small obedience
That sets aside, and tills the chosen ground,
Fruitful humility, chosen innocence,
A binding by which freedom might be found

You call us all to live, and see good days
Centre in Christ and enter in his peace
To seek his Way amidst our many ways
Find blessedness in blessing, peace in praise
To clear and keep for Love a sacred space
That we might be beginners in God's grace.

Malcolm Guite

Why Community?

Three members of the Chemin Neuf Community give their personal answer to the question, "why community?". Chemin Neuf, whose French name means "New Way", is a Roman Catholic community with an ecumenical vocation. It has members from many denominations and is made up of couples, families and celibates.

The Chemin Neuf Community's spirituality draws from the Ignatian tradition and from the charismatic renewal. Founded in 1973, Chemin Neuf is now present in some 30 countries and has about 2000 members. Since January 2014, four members have been living at Lambeth Palace, among whom are the three authors.

For more information, see www.chemin-neuf.org.uk

A sign of God's Kingdom

by Oliver Matri

At Easter 1986, the first life commitments in the Chemin Neuf Community were celebrated in St John's Cathedral in Lyons. On that occasion, a document rather provocatively titled "Community Manifesto" was published. It gave the following answer to the question 'why community?':

"Because divisions between Christians are the greatest obstacle to evangelisation; because we believe that the prayer of Jesus Christ for unity will be fulfilled: 'that they may all be one so that the world may believe', together, Orthodox, Protestants, Catholics, without waiting any longer, we follow the humble path of shared daily life."

This expresses very well the heart of our calling to community life: it is a prophetic sign of the Kingdom of God, 'so that the world may believe'. In an increasingly individualistic society, freely choosing to give up one's comfort and independence in order to live in community is deeply counter-cultural and does not go unnoticed.

In the case of Chemin Neuf, our ecumenical vocation means that we live this community life with men and women of all Christian denominations, seeking to witness to the unity that is possible through the 'humble path of shared daily life', despite the doctrinal and theological differences that remain. While we live, pray and evangelise together, the brothers and sisters fully retain their own identity and remain in communion with their respective churches. Being a Lutheran, I have always felt the deep respect that this implies.

As anybody who has lived in community knows, sharing one's daily life is all but easy. On the contrary, it is a way of life that makes us realize our call to – and need for – reconciliation: with one another among fellow community members, and also as a ministry to couples and individuals.

This is why, in all of our community houses and most of our sessions, we regularly have dedicated times of reconciliation. These are usually calm times of prayer where one can ask God and one another for forgiveness and be reconciled. For some people, this will simply be through silent prayer in front of the cross or through a one-to-one conversation. For others, it might involve confession (depending on their denomination), writing a letter to someone, etc. Many other communities have similar practices, in obedience to the biblical command: 'do not let the sun go down on your anger' (Ephesians 4:26). By living reconciled, we hope to be a reconciling leaven in the dough of our different churches and of the world at large.

Sharing our weaknesses
by Ula Michlowicz

I am a Roman Catholic and a consecrated celibate. Very early in my life, as a young deeply committed scout, I had this conviction that to change the world I have to do it with others. The fact that the world had to change was obvious for me, growing up in Poland under a communist regime. We had this dream of living together, welcoming the poor, then the 'adult life' took over …

Having been living in community life for almost twenty years I still have this desire of being a world changer, but my intimate discovery is that it begins by being changed myself.

I entered into community life persuaded that I was bringing so much to the people I lived with; then, very quickly I discovered my poverties, defences and resistance to others. The narrow and painful way of sharing our weakness is what makes community life possible. We experience that the community is not built by sharing our strengths and abilities, but by sharing our weaknesses. This was my fundamental discovery and the beginning of the adventure of changing the world around me.

The people we live with are different.

They are the best way of becoming more aware of who we are, the best way of going to Christ (*Le sacrement du frère*, the brother's sacrament, as they say in French) and the best way of being changed. Not only morally (becoming more Christlike etc.) but as human beings as well. Coming from different races, different Churches and sharing daily life leads, through a lot of mercy and 77 times of asking for forgiveness, to being able to welcome the other, not with a sort of condescension but as an equal brother or sister for whom Christ has died.

Open to others – depending on God
by Alan Morley-Fletcher

I am married to Ione, and we are both Anglican. So for us the idea of living in a Community, and specifically in a Roman Catholic Community, was a big question. Why give up our independence as a couple with a family to join others? Our first experience of the Chemin Neuf Community was in a "Cana" week-long session for couples and families – so here already was something that spoke to us: care for marriage and the family, and deep care for the relationship between husband and wife. In addition we found a Community that was open to Christians of all denominations, and this echoed our own desire for Christian Unity.

But to think about living in Community required more than interest in a mission and the ecumenism of a Community, it needed a deep personal conversion, to prepare me to love others in a new way.

To live in a Christian Community requires me to love the Church, the whole church, and not just my own little familiar bit, and live that out in my everyday life. It is easy to say, but living with others even of my own denomination, but then also alongside those of other denominations, and with cultural differences on top of that, confronts me with my own lack of acceptance of others. It shows me my own prejudices and propensity to judge, and brings up all the baggage and history that I unconsciously have within me that tempts me to think that my way is right and good and that other people's ways are strange or not so good. To go beyond this I have had to learn to accept and love and live with people I have not myself chosen.

But there are big pluses too in Community. There is the support that I and we as a couple and family receive from others. The openness that is essential to good community life allows me a space to bring to others my struggles, my fears, my weakness. And this in turn helps me to come to God and deepen my relationship with him in that greater openness and realisation that I must depend on his strength.

Why a Rule of Life?

by Canon Patrick Woodhouse

Each spring, one of my favourite jobs in the garden is putting up the frame of poles to support the climbing French beans that can go on cropping for week after week through the high months of summer. Having manured the ground, and planted the seed, long poles are carefully selected and bound together into a long A frame. To simply build it is a promise of what is to come. For weeks this stark edifice dominates the garden, but then as summer draws on, gradually the stems and leaves of the growing, flowering, and then fruiting beans entirely cover it, until it becomes completely hidden from sight. Still of course it is there, a firm structure, largely hidden, but utterly essential if the rich abundance of life is to continue even into October.

It is perhaps a well-worn analogy, but this image does suggest something of what a Rule of Life is about. The providing of a structure which is essential but hidden in the sense that it can so deeply become part of us that we no longer, as it were, notice it; a structure without which there is little chance of any genuinely spiritual life emerging.

It is extraordinary just how unskilled we human beings can be at handling our own complex lives, how little we can really know ourselves. And how easy it can be to spiral into addictive and destructive behaviour patterns and get trapped in them again and again as old wounds, forgotten hurts, and damaging ingrained ways of behaviour assert their dominance and direct – often disastrously – how we behave. Or sometimes people try to escape the muddle of who they are by losing themselves in something else – in an addiction to work perhaps – and so become driven people, no longer really in charge of their own direction, but driven by some kind of compulsive need, the need to succeed, the need to be recognised, the need to be admired and loved.

There is a well-known Zen story about a man on a horse. The horse is galloping along at a great speed, and it appears that the man on the horse is going somewhere really important. Another man, standing alongside the road, shouts to him as he gallops by, "where are you going?" and the first man shouts back, "I don't know! Ask the horse!" Why a Rule of Life? Because we need so often to be saved from the confusion and muddle and worst tendencies of ourselves. Because we need to get off the horse of our own drivenness, and discover the wonderful surprise of who, created in the image of God, we truly might be.

Or, perhaps, we might say that we need a Rule of Life because we need some shelter, some protection from the stress and 'multiple overwhelmings' of our times. We need a framework, a shape for our living, which can - amid the distractions and confusions and noise of our very anxious world – create some space, and enable us to see.

But how to construct a Rule of Life that is appropriate and right? That, in itself, requires skill. And, if it is going to be the right kind of shape that will enable growth, a depth of sensitive self-understanding, which is why it is best crafted with someone else who is skillful in spiritual discernment, and who can give us the space and encouragement to explore what might be the right kind of pattern and balance for us.

In the Christian tradition the best known Rule was crafted for his monks by St Benedict around the year 530. It has been astonishingly influential down the centuries and it continues to offer a shape for living the Gospel of God into our own times. It is called the *Rule of St Benedict*, but interestingly, it begins with the simple word 'Listen'. 'Listen carefully my son to the master's instruction' are Benedict's opening words, 'and attend to them with the ear of your heart'.

Though these evocative words were written for monks something like 1500 years ago, they can speak powerfully to lay people today, for they point to the kind of spiritual attitude that needs to be cultivated if we are to construct a Rule of Life that will be genuinely helpful and appropriate.

Each one of us needs to learn to listen to 'the master's instruction' for us, and how best we can attend to that 'instruction.' That may require a degree of self-understanding that we may not initially have. People can be very adept at understanding the complexities of the world around them, and be remarkably blind as to who, at a profound level, they really are. That is why a good spiritual guide can be important. Someone who can help us understand the complexities of our own story, can help us comprehend its many ups and downs, can help us make sense of our shifting moods, can help us acknowledge our fears, value our dreams, and help us identify not just what we may superficially want, but what are our deeper needs and longings. Most important of all, it will be someone who can help us begin to really value and love ourselves, created as we are, in the image of God.

All this, and more, is part of beginning to listen to what may be the master's very particular 'instruction' for us and how we can best follow that instruction. Once that kind of attitude of *attending with the ear of the heart* has begun to be grasped, then the different areas that go to make up a Rule of Life can be fruitfully explored.

Any Rule that is going to embrace all that a person is, and is called to become, is likely to cover, first, the practice of praying. What habits and disciplines need to be cultivated so that a person's life is anchored ever more deeply, every day, in the mystery of God? Second, what kind of work can best use and develop a person's gifts, and does that work need clear boundaries? Third, a rule needs to insist on times for rest and holidays. Fourth, there should be some reference to study and reading that stretches the mind and takes the person into new areas of understanding. Fifth, Christian faith is about belonging to others, so a Rule should refer to the communities of faith and life that the person shares in. And then a Rule must refer to the wider world, to working for justice and peace, to engagement in care for the earth, and to the costly giving of resources.

But discerning and building a structure of life covering all these areas, must begin with listening, and continue with deeper listening; and always accompanied by kindness and gentleness towards oneself. If a Rule of Life ever begins to breed guilt and failure, then it would be better to completely re-work it.

In one of her last letters written on the 18th August 1943 to her friend Henny Tideman from the Dutch transit camp of Westerbork before she was taken on the train to Auschwitz, the young Jewish diarist Etty Hillesum wrote: 'Things come and go in a deeper rhythm, and people must be taught to listen; it is the most important thing we have to learn in this life.' (Etty, *Letters & Diaries of Etty Hillesum 1941-1943*, edited by Smelik, translated by Pomerans, Eerdmans, 2002, 640.)

To listen. To listen and to attend with the ear of the heart. It is only out of such profound attentive listening that any Rule will emerge that is really going to serve and not oppress a person. For, in stark contrast to the frame of poles which is fixed in place before the beans can grow, a Rule does need to emerge out of the needs and longings of the individual as they feel their way towards their ever loving, beckoning God. It cannot be imposed. And so their Rule of Life, shaped in conversation with their soul friend, will, as it were, move just ahead of them on their journey, stretching them, encouraging them, challenging them, that they might find and dwell ever more deeply in the love of God, and so find abundant life.

Why Vows?

by Father George Guiver CR

Any thought of making vows for life is an enormous challenge for anyone today and this is worth probing into. We can start by looking back in history. We find no mention of vows or profession amongst the 4th-century Desert Fathers. Candidates would simply be clothed after sufficient entreaty and most of the formation for the monastic life followed after. If in early Egyptian monasticism the candidate was not a Christian, the preparation for baptism and monastic profession would be done together, and the two rites done at the same time too. There were no promises - in the beginning monastic profession was simply a giving of one's whole self. Amongst the Orthodox Churches even today there are no vows as such.

Communities however did begin to feel their way to something more structured. By the time Saint Benedict (c. 480-547) wrote his *Rule* the candidate promised obedience, stability and conversion of life. These are not described as vows, and are mentioned almost in passing at the beginning of the rite. They also overlap, conversion of life summing them all up. In the *Rule of St Benedict* chapter 33 we also read: "no one may presume to give, receive or retain anything as their own ... Monks may not have free disposal even of their own bodies and wills." There we have in effect the Evangelical Counsels of poverty, chastity and obedience. It was however only from the 12th/13th century onwards that these three came to be spoken of explicitly as vows, something that has remained with us till today.

The main argument for having vows, whatever form they take, is that such a formula, recited in the form of a solemn promise, greatly helps concentrate the mind and bring out the deeper meaning of the profession rite. Obviously, we do not vow ourselves simply to three aspects of the life – it is presupposed that we also vow ourselves to our community, to love and service, to prayer, the daily liturgy, silence and solitude, study, work, integrity (seeking to be our true self), responsibility, enclosure (for some), prophetic living, and so on – in other words, to all the aspects of the monastic way of living the gospel.

If that is the history of vows, what do we find in the scriptures to justify them? It might be thought we should search for examples of vows, of which there are plenty in the Old Testament and quite a few in the New. However, if the early tradition simply understood monastic profession as a total giving of ourselves for life, then a quest for scriptural examples of making of vows might be irrelevant. We should instead look for examples of total giving of ourselves in response to God's call. Abraham is an obvious example, leaving everything and setting off without knowing the end of the journey. In the New Testament we have James and John leaving their nets, boats and father to follow Christ. Religious Life is a particular form of this, responding to Christ's call to 'leave everything and follow me'.

The second scriptural basis, just as important, is baptism. Monastic profession is baptismal, a re-entering into our baptismal commitment and transformation, in order to enable it to take us further. At Mirfield we now have a large total-immersion font in our church, and we begin profession rites at the font. Mediaeval monasteries often had an area called 'Galilee' – an example can be found in Durham Cathedral. From ancient times until the modern era there was an Eastertide tradition in cathedrals and parish churches of a daily procession to the font after Vespers. The font was seen as Galilee – 'there you will see him'. The monastic alternative was to process to the Galilee.

Behind monastic profession, then, stand scriptural stories of completely giving ourselves and also there stands the model of baptism. But a need did grow up for more specific promises of commitment in order to focus the mind, and this led to the inclusion of vows in the profession rite.

For anyone exploring the possibility of Religious community life the vows, or even the simple idea of giving ourselves completely away, can seem very daunting. We have to remember that we can only begin to understand the vows as we get nearer to them. A novice who is cut out for the life will so grow into the community that the vows when the moment comes will happen so naturally as almost to be unremarkable, simply a statement of what has become the case (rather than an 'experience' which makes you swoon, which we can be tempted to want in worship today). The life is one continuous growth from the point where you started. And there is something else: we have to un-learn our individualism. Religious profession is a big moment in the life of an individual, certainly, but it is a passing from being an individual to being individual-in-community. Monastic profession is first and foremost a corporate act, made by the community, of which I am now a part. And the main actor is neither me nor the community, but God. Discerning a vocation is not so much a difficult personal decision leading to my promise, but rather a difficult personal discernment of God's promise.

The vows, then, are a powerful sign and seal of an act that is bigger – the total giving of ourselves to the Love we have discerned to be calling us. Why vows? Why give yourself totally and utterly to the love at the heart of all things? Well – that's what love is, and that's what faith is.

Why Hospitality?

by Sister Annaliese CSC

"You have become family to me"

"You saved my life" "This has become my home"

"I've never had a room of my own before"

These moving words are just a few of the comments we are so privileged to hear from some of the beautiful women who have come to live with us.

Jesus said : "Knock and the door will be opened for you"(Matthew 7:7). For most of the women who have come to live with us at CSC Ham Common, they have had to knock on many, many doors before one opened for them.

For us, sharing our home with women who have suffered extreme exclusion is a natural extension of our ministry of hospitality. It is also part of our Christian stewardship - we had some empty rooms while there are any number of women who are suffering on the streets or in very unsafe accommodation.

We linked in with a wonderful, well-established Charity called 'Praxis - the Place for People Displaced' who we have been working in partnership with for over four years.

As Religious Communities many of us are needing to rethink what to do with our spacious buildings. It is possible to offer hospitality via Praxis to individuals suffering from extreme exclusion, on a short term or long term basis. Praxis is sensitive to the needs of Religious Communities and gives ongoing support and advice to the 'Host' as well as the guest.

Jesus also said that by welcoming the stranger we are welcoming him (Matthew

25:35). Over the last four years we have welcomed eleven (mostly young) women as a type of Alongsider. The majority have stayed with us for several years. We of course, had all sorts of ideas about how this was going to work out but much has needed to develop and adapt as we have gone along. We have seven women living with us at the moment plus two toddlers and another baby on the way! We had not planned on having children living with us and they do pose some challenges to a Convent offering retreats(!) but they bring so much joy and fun and are very loved indeed.

Each of these Alongsiders has a precious and unique story - some are refugees or asylum seekers, while others have been here since childhood originally staying with friends or distant relations and have all but lost touch with their country of origin. Those women who have been here since they were children, had been in paid work or at University until they were suddenly told that they hadn't got the right papers and were not allowed to work, receive student grants or benefits. Waiting in 'the system' for years is what all of our women have in common.

We have been able to access funds through a local charity and other trusts which has made it possible for most of our women to attend courses, have English tuition, study with the Open University and cover extra expenses for them and the babies. This has made a huge difference to the quality of their waiting.

As a Community we responded to a need but could have no idea how many blessings we would be given in return - our hearts have been widened along with our horizons. Their youthful energy is a real tonic, and I like to think that these women help keep us our spirits young! We have been very grateful for help around the house, enjoyed all sorts of exotic foods, hosted a large wedding blessing in our garden - (followed by a disco on the grass) and at times had our Midday Office transformed by some rather more modern Christian music than we have been used to! It was very moving to be able to help one woman when she couldn't go to her mother's funeral by holding a memorial service in our Chapel, and this and the feast afterwards was attended by many of her friends. There have also been delightful parties for the children's first and second birthdays; but for the most part, our lives interweave (relatively) quietly as Grace moves gently between us.

Why Silence?

by Bonnie Thurston

On an ordinary day, when or where does one experience silence? Noise is ubiquitous. We have become a people who spend enormous amounts of time, energy and money making noise. Why have we become people who cannot bear silence? Could it be because we are afraid?

We protect ourselves from things we fear. We protect ourselves from serious illness with doctor's visits, vitamins, and insurance policies (in case the other two do not work). We protect ourselves from injury with bicycle helmets and automobile seats belts. From what are we protecting ourselves by constantly manufacturing noise, including speech? We go shopping, and there is music in the background. We get in the car and turn on talk radio or pop a disc in the CD player. In many homes, the television is seldom off. It forms the constant undercurrent of noise in domestic life. I know a man who can't go to sleep without the telly on in his bedroom. Even in our worship and liturgies there is precious little silence. We protect ourselves from silence by making noise. What are we afraid of in silence? Truth be told, I think this noise making is about not wanting to know things about ourselves. If we are quiet, we might have to listen to voices from deep within ourselves. If we inhabit a quiet environment, messages from inside we have been marking "return to sender" might be delivered.

Some of us chatter constantly. This reminds me of what the American Trappist monk, Thomas Merton (whose birth centenary is 2015), wrote in his book *Thoughts in Solitude*: "We put words between ourselves and things." (NY: Farrar, Straus & Giroux, 1956/1977, 85) We also put words between ourselves and other people and between ourselves and ourselves. I wonder if some of us manufacture so much language noise because we are afraid that if we are silent and listen inwardly…we won't hear anything at all, that we will discover "nobody's home."

In *No Man is an Island*, Merton suggests people can hide behind language, that they can use words to hide from each other and from God. They "… resist the fruitful silence of their own being by continual noise." Thus they "… never discover that their hearts are rooted in a silence that is not death but life. They chatter themselves to death…". ((NY: Harcourt, Brace and Co., 1955, 261-262) Some folks talk incessantly to assure themselves that they exist. Talking is a way of asserting self in the world. Obsessive talking is sign of personal insecurity. The perhaps unconscious and certainly false reasoning is "If I'm not talking, maybe I'm not."

People who can be silent are those who know that authentic identity comes from another place, another Person, from God Who can be known in silence. In a chapter in *New Seeds of Contemplation* entitled "Pray for Your Own Discovery," Merton wrote, "God utters me like a word containing a partial thought of himself." (NY: New Directions, 1961, 37) We are "partial thoughts of God." God "utters us," speaks our being as God spoke everything else into being. But how will we hear God's affirming and identity creating voice, the voice that says "I love you," if we keep our ears constantly full of noise and our mouths constantly full of meaningless chatter?

Unremitting noise and chatter is a barrier between us and the world, between us and God. The noise-addicted make it very hard for God to get a word in edgewise. The chatter-addicted are less likely to hear God's voice, that "still, small voice" or "sound of sheer silence" (NRSV) Who addressed Elijah on Mount Horeb (1 Kings 19:12), the "sound" which conveys the secure identity of knowing oneself eternally loved.

A created thing, sound is not evil. A few minutes of Bach or a few Psalms from the KJV prove the point. But, like many things, sound and words are wonderful servants and terrible masters. Merton (an articulate promoter of silence if ever there were one!) understood that authentic language, language that communicates, arises from silence. "Words stand between silence and silence: between the silence of things and the silence of our own being." "Truth rises from the silence of being to the quiet tremendous presence of the Word. Then, sinking again into silence, the truth of words bears us down into the silence of God." (Merton, *Thoughts*, 86) "Be still and know that I am God" the Psalmist reminds us. (Psalm 46:10) Perhaps people who feel estranged from God, who haven't "heard" or "experienced" God, or who have and now don't, are listening in the wrong directions or are so assaulted by noise that they can no longer really hear. No wonder Jesus commands "listen!". (Mark 4:3)

Christian spirituality bears witness that the ability to be silent and to listen are primary requisites for intimacy with God. In our world, one of the few places we can go to be silent and listen are monasteries or religious houses. Silence and listening are reasons we go there as guests or postulants, and why some of us remain to become Religious or monastics. But all of us can take 4th Century Desert Christian Abba Pomen's advice to be silent and have peace where ever we live. And some of us will be called to make our lives a listening for God in silence, to be, like Abbot Bessarion's monk, "as the Cherubim and Seraphim: all eye."

Why the 'border lands'?

by Sister Katharine, novice SSC

In the Remembering and Thanksgiving section of this Year Book *there is an obituary of Wendy Robinson. Sister Katharine reflects on how Wendy fulfilled God's calling and mission in her life.*

It was a mission made possible by a life of prayer, silence and profound trust in the promise of Jesus Christ that He would be with us. At heart it is our mission as Religious communities: to dare to live lives that witness to the presence of God at the heart of the affliction of our world. I have used Wendy's own words to summarise the essence of her life and work. (All the quotations are taken from 'The Lost Traveller's Dream', a talk given to [1994] and subsequently published by the Oxford Christian Institute for Counselling [1995]).

Throughout the life story of Wendy there are strong and mysterious threads that weave themselves back and forth – the wide open spaces of the north Yorkshire moors and the Kalahari desert; the silence of waiting upon God; the holding steady of antinomies; the riding of the boundaries with people in their suffering; the world of metaphor in the visual arts, in myth and poetry that both pushes the boundaries to new possibilities, and new understandings, whilst also embracing the fragments of broken boundaries; the allowing for 'soundings across' the plenitude of variety and difference. Central to her life was the presence of God – a God she encountered in Jesus Christ. A God that was there at the heart of affliction or seeming absence.

To encounter Wendy was to meet with a robust humanity; an embodied love rooted in her relationship with God. Her life task was to listen, to wait passionately with the other, to "consent to become incarnate for each other, to embody Love and let Love be present through us. That is the only way people can often experience it, through our embodiment of it. Our task is to help people "to bear the beams of Love" instead of tescaping from them into some terrible form of suffering."

Wendy was an inhabitant of the 'border lands' and a 'boundary rider'. As a psychotherapist she lived with a great question: " How do we keep carrying the divine dimension, the Beyond in the midst, in spite of all the deep and dark things we have to enter into, so that we do not bring about that state of terrifying ontological collapse?" She believed that if she and her colleagues did not allow for the divine, something about what was denied and unacknowledged collapses its weight onto the other things that are there. "The weight of Love falls on human relationships, which are carrying too much and break under the strain. Or it falls on individuals, who cannot carry it all and end in despair and frustration, in woundedness."

She knew from her work that those who are most seriously damaged and afflicted live in the borderlands, on the boundaries of existence. In order to live with the mortal wounds of others and to dwell in those "lonely, dark, deep places of unknowing of the human heart", Wendy saw the need for "a theology for boundary riders, wayfarers, those who have to stay out in those places with others, where God, if God is experienced at all, is usually incognito, in disguise; where He is spoken of, if at all, with great care; and where to live the questions of suffering which people endure, is to do theology. They are places of sudden encounter and exchange, which can be surprising, or shocking; where suddenly there is a meeting or encounter in Love and in Truth, so that one can't get outside it and wonder what is happening. It is not possible to know which is God and which is us, and what exactly is going on in theological terms, but only that there is Love and there is Truth, there is meeting: something has happened between two people. We have to stay there, and learn to speak of You, the eternal You, coming to meet us. Those places where God is experienced as Beyond in the the midst – so deeply in the midst as to be inseparable from it."

To choose to live with affliction is to live in "places of terror and devastation" where the edges of existence are also the edges of language but are also places of "rare, unique, shy and heart rending beauty". Wendy learned much from her relationship with contemplative communities about the patient enduring of silence and the vital need to wait on God. " We have to learn to be silent, and to know that presence in the place of stillness where, at first, there seems to be nothing, but in the end it may prove to be God. ... So often we have to wait with people in that frightening interval between death and resurrection, where the only chance of growing up, of surviving, of going on, depends on our capacity to wait in that kind of emptiness." At the same time she was a 'bricoleur', someone who could suddenly see "something in a gutter that was worth picking up and using somewhere." She sought "to live with brokenness, to know that the broken whole is still a potential whole, and that the great art of healing will always involve, this side of eternity, that brokenness taken into the body, my body, broken for you; our body, broken in terms of all that we can give to others in relationships, held in Christ's body, 'Broken for you ...'".

Wendy, still present to us in the Communion of Saints, left us with a question: "The God who is less easily named is the God who is mysteriously there in the borderlands we have to share with people. Named or unnamed, God is present. Are we?"

Directory of traditional celibate Religious Orders and Communities

Francis

'Francis rebuild my church which, as you see
Is falling into ruin.' From the cross
Your saviour spoke to you and speaks to us
Again through you. Undoing set you free,
Loosened the traps of trappings, cast away
The trammelling of all that costly cloth
We wind our saviour in. At break of day
He set aside his grave-clothes. Your new birth
Came like a daybreak too, naked and true,
To poverty and to the gospel call,
You woke to Christ and Christ awoke in you
And set to work through all your love and skill
To make our ruin good, to bless and heal
To wake the Christ in us and make us whole.

Malcolm Guite

Section 1

Religious communities in this section are those whose members take the traditional vows, including celibacy. For many, these are the 'evangelical counsels' of chastity, poverty and obedience. In the Benedictine tradition, the three vows are stability, obedience and conversion of life, celibacy being an integral part of the third vow.

These celibate communities may be involved in apostolic works or be primarily enclosed and contemplative. They may wear traditional habits or contemporary dress. However, their members all take the traditional Religious vows. In the Episcopal Church of the USA, these communities are referred to in the canons as 'Religious Orders'.

There are at least 1,776 celibate Religious in the Anglican Communion, (801 men and 975 women). There are no statistics currently available for some orders (so they are not included here) and therefore these figures are a minimum number.

The approximate regional totals are:

Africa:	322	(Men 43, Women 279)
Asia:	69	(Men 12, Women 57)
Australasia & Pacific:	757	(Men 558, Women 199)
Europe:	409	(Men 108, Women 301)
North & South America & Caribbean:	219	(Men 80, Women 139)

International telephoning

Telephone numbers in this directory are mainly listed as used within the country concerned. To use them internationally, first dial the international code (usually 00) followed by the country code (see list below).

Australia	+ 61	India	+ 91	Solomon Islands	+ 677
Bangladesh	+ 880	Republic of Ireland	+ 353	South Africa	+ 27
Brazil	+ 55	Japan	+ 81	Sri Lanka	+ 94
Canada	+ 1	Korea (South)	+ 82	Spain	+ 34
Fiji	+ 679	Lesotho	+ 266	Swaziland	+ 268
France	+ 33	Malaysia	+ 60	Tanzania	+ 255
Ghana	+ 233	New Zealand	+ 64	UK	+ 44
Haiti	+ 509	PNG	+ 675	USA	+ 1

Society of All Saints Sisters of the Poor

ASSP

Founded 1851

All Saints
15A Magdalen Road
Oxford OX4 1RW
UK

Tel: 01865 249127
(Voicemail is checked regularly.)

Email:
leaderassp@socallss.co.uk

Website:
www.asspoxford.org

Mattins	6.30 am
Eucharist	Variable
Vespers	5.30 pm
Compline	8.00 pm

Variations on Sun, Sat, & major festivals

Office book
Own Office book, based on Anglican Office Book 1980

As a small Community, we have the God given opportunity to recognise the very diverse gifts and callings of each individual. Returning to the charism of our Founder, we believe that God calls us to be channels of love to those in need, however the Spirit may move us.

Freed from management responsibility, Sisters continue to be involved in St John's Home for frail and elderly people, Helen and Douglas House, Hospices for children and young adults, and the Steppin' Stone Centre for adults who are homeless or vulnerably housed.

We now have the freedom to take an active part in the life of the parish and the wider community, just as our founding Sisters did. Today this includes preaching, ministry and spiritual accompaniment.

Our guest house gives a warm welcome to those needing retreat or spiritual refreshment.

The heart of our Community life is the worship of God in the daily Office and Eucharist, and our personal commitment to prayer and spiritual reading.

God renews our calling day by day, both as a Community and as individuals and we welcome any who are discerning God's will for them.

SISTER JEAN RAPHAEL ASSP
(Community Leader, assumed office 18 October 2010)
SISTER FRANCES DOMINICA ASSP
(Assistant Community Leader)

Sister Helen Mary
Sister Ann Frances
Sister Margaret Anne *(priest)*
Sister Jane

Obituaries
3 Mar 2014 Sister Margaret, aged 87, professed 62 years

Companions
Those who want to commit support for the community and, where possible, practical help may be invited to become Companions.

Guest and Retreat Facilities
Brownlow House, our guest house with six en-suite rooms. Self-catering.
Email: guestsister@socallss.co.uk

Bishop Visitor: Rt Revd Bill Ind

Registered Charity: No. 228383

St John's Home (for elderly people), St Mary's Road, Oxford OX4 1QE, UK Tel: 01865 247725 Fax: 01865 247920
Email: admin@st_johns_home.org Website: www.stjohnshome.org
Registered Charity No: 228383

Helen and Douglas House, 14a Magdalen Road, Oxford OX4 1RW, UK Tel: 01865 794749 Fax: 01865 202702
Email: admin@helenanddouglas.org.uk
Website: www.helenanddouglas.org.uk
Registered Charity No: 1085951

The Porch Steppin' Stone Centre, 139 Magdalen Road, Oxford OX4 1RL, UK Tel: 01865 728545
Email: info@theporch.fsbusiness.co.uk
Website: www.theporch.org.uk
Registered Charity No: 1089612

Community History & Books

Peter Mayhew, *All Saints: Birth & Growth of a Community,* ASSP, Oxford, 1987.

Kay Syrad, *A Breath of Heaven: All Saints Convalescent Hospital,* Rosewell, St Leonard's on Sea, 2002.
[This is the history of All Saints Convalescent Hospital, Eastbourne, started by our Mother Foundress in 1869 and run by the community until 1959.]

Sister Frances Dominica ASSP, *Just My Reflection: Helping families to do things their own way when their child dies,* Darton, Longman & Todd, London, 2nd ed 2007.
Available from Helen & Douglas House, £6.50.

Behind the big red door: the story of Helen House, Golden Cup, Oxford, 2006, £6.00.

All Saints Convent
PO Box 3127
Catonsville
MD 21228-0127
USA

Tel: 410 747 4104
Fax: 410 747 3321

Three All Saints Sisters went to Baltimore, Maryland, and the community house they began became an independent house in 1890.

In September 2009, the majority of the members of this American community of All Saints Sisters were received into the Roman Catholic Church.

Whilst still living at the Convent in Catonsville with the rest of the community, one sister remains in the Anglican Communion.

Sister Virginia of All Saints *(sometime Mother)*

Website: www.asspconvent.org

Benedictine Sisters of Bethany

Founded 2002

PO Box 975
Bamenda
North-West Region
CAMEROON

Email:
jmankaa@
hotmail.com

Morning Prayer
5.00 am

Midday Office
12.00 noon

Vespers
5.00 pm

Compline
8.00 pm

Eucharist
Every first Sunday of the month.
(We are desperately in need of a Chaplain priest.)

The Benedictine Sisters of Bethany were founded by Sister Jane Manka'a in June 2002. The sisters operate the Good Shepherd Home, an orphanage that is in two locations: Bamenda and Batibo North West Region. These two homes have over 150 orphan children ranging between the ages of 0 to 18 years. The Homes operate farms, bakery, agriculture, fish farming, chicken farm and crafts as a source of self-sustainability.

The Sisters follow the Benedictine Rule of life. Our Community has a companionship with the Community of St John the Baptist, an Episcopal sisterhood in the USA.

REVD SISTER JANE MANKA'A
(Mother superior and founder, assumed office 2002)

Sister Mary Lawrence
Sister Benedict Bih
Sister Rose Tah

Novices: 2 *Postulants:* 1

Other Address
Good Shepherd Home annex, Batibo, PO Box 975, Bamenda, North-West Region, CAMEROON

Community Wares
Chicken farm, bakery, agriculture, piggery, fish farming, African dolls and crafts.

Office Book: Book of Common Prayer

Bishop Visitor: Bishop Thomas Dibo

Sister Jane Manka'a

Brotherhood of the Ascended Christ

BAC

Founded 1877

Brotherhood House
7 Court Lane
(Rustmji Sehgal Marg)
Delhi 110054
INDIA
Tel: 11 2396 8515
or 11 2393 1432
Fax: 11 2398 1025

Email:
delhibrotherhood@gmail.com

Website: http://delhibrotherhood.org

Morning Worship & Eucharist 7.00 am

Forenoon Prayer (Terce) 10.00 am

Midday Prayer (Sext) 12.45 pm

Afternoon Prayer (None) 3.50 pm

Evening Worship 7.30 pm

Night Prayer (Compline) 8.30 pm

Today, the Brotherhood has one bishop (retired) and four presbyters, who belong to the Church of North India. Since the earliest days, the Brotherhood has had a concern for serving the poor and underprivileged. In 1973, the Delhi Brotherhood Society was set up to organise social development projects in the poorer parts of Delhi. The work and social outreach of the Brotherhood is with and not for the poor of Delhi. The Brotherhood has initiated programmes of community health, education, vocational training and programmes for street and working children.

MONODEEP DANIEL BAC
(Head, assumed office 27 November 2013)
RAJU GEORGE *(Deputy Head)*

Collin C. Theodore *(bishop)* Jai Kumar
Solomon George

Associates and Companions
There are twenty-six Presbyter Associates and eight Lay Companions who follow a simple Rule of Life adapted to their individual conditions.

Community Publication
Annual Newsletter and Report (free of charge).

Community History
Constance M Millington, *"Whether we be many or few": A History of the Cambridge/Delhi Brotherhood,* Asian Trading Corporation, Bangalore, 1999.
Available from the Brotherhood House.

Guest and Retreat Facilities
The Brotherhood House at Court Lane has a large garden and well-stocked library. It is used as a centre for retreats, quiet days and conferences. The small Guest Wing receives visitors from all over the world. There are four rooms. Both men and women are welcome.

Most convenient time to telephone:
7.30 am - 8.30 am, 4 pm - 5 pm (Indian Standard Time)

Office Book: The Church of North India Book of Worship & Lesser Hours & Night Prayer (BAC)

Bishop Visitor: Most Revd Dr P P Marandih

Blog: http://delhibrotherhood.blogspot.in

Facebook: http://facebook.com/delhibrotherhood

Chama cha Mariamu Mtakatifu (Community of St Mary of Nazareth & Calvary)

CMM

Founded 1946

The Convent
Kilimani
PO Box 502
Masasi, Mtwara
TANZANIA
Tel (mobile):
0784 236656 or 0756 988635 (Mother)

Email:
masasi_cmmsisters@yahoo.com

Morning Prayer 5.30 am

Mass 6.30 am

Midday Prayer 12.30 pm

Evening Prayer 3.00 pm

Compline 8.30 pm

The Community was founded in 1946 by the Community of the Sacred Passion (CSP). Bishop Frank Weston is the Grandfather Founder of CMM, while Bishop William Vincent Lucas is the Father Founder of CMM. Both were Universities' Missionaries to Central Africa. The CMM Sisters are trying their best to keep the aims of the founders: to serve God, His Church and His people.

There are eleven Houses in Tanzania and one in Zambia.

SISTER DOROTHY CMM
(Mother Superior, assumed office 14 June 2014)
SISTER HELEN CMM (*Sister Superior*)
SISTER MARTHA BRIJITA CMM
(*Sister Superior, Northern Zone*)
SISTER REBECA CMM
(Sister-in-charge, Mother House)

Sister Magdalene
Sister Rehema
Sister Cesilia
Sister Ethel Mary
Sister Neema
Sister Esther
Sister Tabitha
Sister Eunice Mary
Sister Joy
Sister Franciska
Sister Anjela
Sister Gloria
Sister Anna
Sister Prisca
Sister Nesta
Sister Bertha
Sister Aneth
Sister Mary
Sister Agatha
Sister Lucy
Sister Berita
Sister Mercy Neema
Sister Lyidia
Sister Stella
Sister Agnes Margreth
Sister Merina Felistas
Sister Jane
Sister Anjelina
Sister Perpetua
Sister Julia Rehema
Sister Joyceline Florence
Sister Jane Rose
Sister Anna Beatrice
Sister Mariamu Upendo
Sister Josephine Joyce
Sister Skolastika Mercy
Sister Mary Prisca
Sister Paulina Anna
Sister Janet Margaret
Sister Theckla Elizabeth
Sister Janeth Elizabeth
Sister Edna Joan
Sister Josephine Brijita
Sister Dainess Charity
Sister Agnes Edna
Sister Jane Felistas
Sister Asnath Isabela
Sister Ethy Nyambeku
Sister Vumilia Imelda
Sister Anna Mariamu
Sister Foibe Edina
Sister Veronica Modesta
Sister Harriet Helena
Sister Hongera Mariamu
Sister Lulu Lois
Sister Lucy Lois
Sister Penina Skolastika
Sister Anet Oliver
Sister Rhoda Rachel
Sister Judith Natalia

Sister Harriet
Sister Deborah Dorothy
Sister Nesta Sophia
Sister Hongera Elizabeth
Sister Bernadine Jane
Sister Phillipa Sapelo
Sister Antonia Thereza
Sister Violet Monica
Sister Beata
Sister Hope
Sister Erica Mary
Sister Mariamu Elizabeth
Sister Joyce Agnes
Sister Mariamu Stella
Sister Merina Maria
Sister Lizzy
Sister Veronica
Sister Juliana
Sister Merina Happy
Sister Rehema
Sister Hariet
Sister Valiet

Novices: 19
Postulants: 2

Obituaries

27 Nov 14 Sister Christine Madeline, aged 61, professed 41 years

Community Wares

Vestments, altar breads, agriculture products, cattle products, crafts, candles & poultry.

Office Book: Swahili Zanzibar Prayer Book & The Daily Office SSF

Bishop Visitor: Rt Revd Patrick P Mwachiko, retired Bishop of Masasi

Other addresses

P.O. Box 116
Newala, Mtwara Region
TANZANIA

P.O Box 162
Mtwara
TANZANIA
Tel: 023 2333587

P.O. Box 45
Tanga Region
TANZANIA
Tel: 027 2643245

P.O. Box 195
Korogwe, Tanga Region
TANZANIA
Tel: 027 2640643

The Convent
P.O. Kwa Mkono
Handeni, Tanga Region
TANZANIA

P.O. Box 25068
Dar-es-Salaam
TANZANIA
Tel: 022 2863797

P.O Box 150
Njombe TANZANIA
Tel: 026 2782753

P.O. Box 6
Liuli
Mbing Ruvuma Region
TANZANIA
Sayuni Msima

P.O. Box 150
Njombe
TANZANIA
Tel: 026 2782753

Fiwila Mission
P.O. Box 840112
Mkushi
ZAMBIA

Mtandi
Private Bag
Masasi
Mtwara Region
TANZANIA
Tel: 023 2510016

Chita Che Zita Rinoyera (Holy Name Community)

CZR

Founded 1935

St Augustine's Mission
PO Penhalonga
Mutare
Zimbabwe
Tel:
Penhalonga 22217

Bishop Visitor:
Rt Revd
Julius Makoni

Our Community was started by Father Baker of the CR Fathers at Penhalonga, with Mother Isabella as the founder. The CZR Sisters were helped by CR Sisters, and later by OHP Sisters. When they left, Sister Isabella was elected Mother. Today the CZR Sisters work at the clinic and at the primary and secondary schools. Some do visiting and help teach the catechism. We make wafers for several dioceses, including Harare. Some of the Sisters look after the church, seeing to cleaning and mending of the church linen. We have an orphanage that cares for thirty children, with an age range of eighteen months to eighteen years.

In 1982, half the Sisters and the novices left CZR and created another community at Bonda. Six months later, some of those Sisters in turn went to found Religious Life at Harare. So CZR has been the forerunner of other communities in Zimbabwe. Please pray that God may bless us.

MOTHER BETTY CZR
(Reverend Mother, assumed office 2006)

Sister Stella Mary	Sister Emelia
Sister Anna Maria	Sister Annamore
Sister Hilda Raphael	Sister Sibongile
Sister Felicity	Sister Francesca
Sister Elizabeth	

Community Wares:
We sell chickens, eggs, milk, cattle (2 or 3 a year) and wafers.

Community of the Blessed Lady Mary

CBLM

Founded 1982

The Sisters care for orphans on St John's Mission, Chikwaka. One sister works for the diocese of Masvingo and one is working in Harare.

MOTHER SYLVIA CBLM
(Reverend Mother)

Sister Dorothy	Sister Faustina
Sister Anna	Sister Praxedes

**Address: Shearly Cripps Children's Home,
PO Box 121 Juru, ZIMBABWE**

Bishop Visitor: Rt Revd Chad Gandiya

Chita che Zvipo Zve Moto (Community of the Gifts of the Holy Fire)

CZM

Founded 1977

Convent of Chita che Zvipo Zve Moto
PO Box 138
Gokwe South
ZIMBABWE
Telefax: 263 059 2566

House Prayer 5.00 am

Mattins followed by meditation 5.45 am

Holy Communion 6.00 am

Midday prayers 12 noon

Evensong followed by meditation 5.00 pm

Compline 8.30 pm

Office Book
BCP & CZM Office Book 2002

Bishop Visitor
Rt Revd Ishmael Mukuwanda, Bishop of Central Zimbabwe

The Community is a mixed community of nuns and friars, founded by the Revd Canon Lazarus Tashaya Muyambi in 1977. On a visit to St Augustine's Mission, Penhalonga, he was attracted by the life of the CR fathers and the CZR sisters. With the inspiration of the Spirit of the Lord, he believed it was of great value to start a Religious community. The first three sisters were attached to St Augustine's for three months, Sister Gladys being the first admission on 14 May 1978. The first convent was officially opened in 1979 and the initial work was caring for orphans at St Agnes Children's Home.

In January 2000, Canon Muyambi stepped down from leadership, believing the Community was mature enough to elect its own leaders, which it did in March 2000. The Community have a Rule, Constitution and are governed by a Chapter. They take vows of Love, Compassion and Spiritual Poverty. The Community is progressing well with young people joining every year.

SISTER TERESAH CZM *(Archsister, assumed office 2014)*
FRIAR JOSHUA CZM *(Archfriar, assumed office 2006)*

Sister Gladys A	Sister Juliet
Sister Eugenia	Sister Tirivatsva
Sister Elizabeth	Sister Lilian
Sister Eustina	Sister Cynthia
Sister Phoebe	Sister Precious
Sister Lydia	Sister Joyline
Sister Anna Kudzai	Sister Vongai
Sister Vongai Patricia	Friar Tapiwa Costa
Sister Gladys B	Sister Violet
Sister Alice	Sister Blessing
Sister Tendai A	
Sister Itai	*Novices:* 2 *Postulants:* 3

Other addresses in Zimbabwe:

St Patrick's Mission Branch House, Bag 9030, Gweru

St James Nyamaohlovu Bulawayo P. Bag, Matebeleland

No 9 Coltman Close, Mt. Pleasant, Harare

Community Wares
Sewing church vestments, school uniforms, wedding gowns; knitting jerseys; garden produce; poultry keeping.

Christa Sevika Sangha (Handmaids of Christ)

CSS

Founded 1970

Oxford Mission
Barisal Division
Uz Agailjhara 8240
BANGLADESH

Email:
christasevikasangha@gmail.com

Oxford Mission,
Bogra Road
PO Box 21
Barisal 8200
BANGLADESH
Tel: 1715 211821

Morning Prayer

Holy Communion

Midday Prayer

Quiet Prayer together

Evening Prayer

Compline

The Community was founded in 1970 and was under the care of the Sisterhood of the Epiphany until 1986, when its own Constitution was passed and Sister Susila SE was elected as Superior. At Jobarpar, the Sevikas supervise a girls' hostel, a play-centre for small children and help in St Gabriel's Primary School. At Barisal, the Sevikas supervise St Mary's Asroi (Home) and St Agnes's Hostel. The Community also produces for sale a wide variety of goods and produce.

SISTER JHARNA CSS
(Sister superior, assumed office June 2011)
SISTER RUTH CSS *(House Sister, Jobarpar)*

Sister Sobha
Sister Agnes
Sister Dorothy
Sister Margaret
Sister Kalyani
Sister Shefali
Sister Shalomi
Sister Shikha

Postulants: 1 (Rebecca)

Community Wares
Vestments, children's clothes, embroidery work, wine, wafers, candles.
Farm produce: milk, fish.
Land produce: rice, fruit, coconuts & vegetables.

Community Publication
The Oxford Mission News, twice a year. Write to Oxford Mission, 18 Markert Place, Romsey, Hampshire SO51 8NA. Tel & Fax: 01794 515004 Annual subscription: £4.00.

Community History
Brethren of the Epiphany, *A Hundred Years in Bengal,* ISPCK, Delhi, 1979.
Mother Susila CSS, *A Well Watered Garden,* (editor: Mabyn Pickering), Oxford Mission, Romsey, 2000 available from Oxford Mission address above, £5 including p & p.

Guest and Retreat Facilities
Two rooms for men outside the Community campus. One house (three beds) for women. Donations received.

Office Book
Church of Bangladesh BCP & Community Office Book (all Offices are in Bengali)

Bishop Visitor: Most Revd Paul S Sarker, Bishop of Dhaka

Community of All Hallows

CAH

Founded 1855

All Hallows Convent
Belsey Bridge Road
Ditchingham
Bungay, Suffolk
NR35 2DT
UK
Tel: 01986 892749 (office) Mon-Fri

01986 895749 (Sisters)

Email:
allhallowsconvent @btinternet.com

Website
www.all-hallows.org

Lauds 7.30 am

Eucharist
8.00 am (9.30 am Sat, 10.00 am Sun)

Sext 12.15 pm

Evening Prayer
5.30 pm

Compline 8.00 pm

We are a group of women with diverse personalities and gifts called together in a common commitment to prayer and active work under the patronage of the Saints. Central to our life are the daily Eucharist and the Divine Office, combined with time for personal prayer, meditation and spiritual reading. Together they draw us deeper into the desire to "serve Christ in one another and love as He loves us". This overflows into our active works - particularly in our ministry of hospitality, expressed mainly through our Guest Houses, Spiritual Direction, and leading Retreats for individuals and small groups. It also includes some pastoral ministry at our All Hallows Hospital and Nursing Home, which were founded and developed by us, but now form a separate Charity. In addition there is a large Conference Centre and a Day Nursery within our grounds. Our former convent building opposite is now home to an Emmaus community for the homeless.

The ministry of hospitality and prayer continues to flourish at our house in Rouen Road, Norwich, which is closely linked with the adjacent Julian Shrine and Centre.

All enquiries about the life and work of CAH should be directed in the first place to the leaders at the Convent.

SISTER RACHEL CAH & SISTER SHEILA CAH
(Joint Leaders, assumed office June 2013)
SISTER ELIZABETH CAH (*Assistant Leader*)

Sister Violet	Sister Edith Margaret
Sister Margaret	Sister Pamela

Obituaries
26 Dec 2014 Sister Jean, aged 78, professed 50 years

Companions, Oblates, Associates, Contact Members
COMPANIONS, OBLATES, ASSOCIATES and CONTACT MEMBERS offer themselves to God within the community context with a varying degree of 'hands-on' experience. Some experience of the Community 'alongside' can also be offered. Apply to the Convent for details.

Community Publication
A newsletter is circulated yearly at All Saints tide. To be included on the mailing list, please write to All Hallows Convent at the address above.

Community Wares
A wide selection of photography cards, as well as some others.

Other addresses and telephone numbers

Lavinia House (address as All Hallows Convent above)
Tel: 01986 892840

All Hallows House, St Julian's Alley, Rouen Road, Norwich NR1 1QT, UK Tel: 01603 624738

Community History and books

Sister Violet CAH, *All Hallows, Ditchingham,* Becket Publications, Oxford, 1983.

Mother Mary CAH, *Memories,* privately published 1998.
(A collection of memories and reflections primarily intended for friends and associates but available to all.)

Sister Winifred Mary CAH, *The Men in my Life,* privately published 2009.
(reminiscences of prison chaplaincy)

Sister Violet CAH, *A Book of Poems,* privately published 2011.

Guest and Retreat Facilities

Suitable for individuals, couples or small groups. Other details available on request. Enquiries about staying at our guest houses should be addressed to Barbara Pascali, Lavinia House (address as above) or to The Guest Sister (Norwich address as above).

Most convenient time to telephone:
9.00 am - 12 noon; 2.15 pm - 4.30 pm; 7.00 pm - 7.45 pm (any day)

Bishop Visitor: Rt Revd Graham James, Bishop of Norwich

Office Books: Daily Prayer and Common Worship.

Registered charity : No 230143

Benedictine Community of Christ the King

CCK

Founded 1993

344 Taminick Gap Road
South Wangaratta
Victoria 3678
AUSTRALIA
Tel/Fax:
61 3 57257343
Email: cck94 @bigpond.com

Monastic Mattins & Prayer Time 4.30 am
Terce 7.40 am
Eucharist 8.00 am
Sext 12 noon
None 1.15 pm
Vespers & Prayer Time 5.00 pm
Compline 7.15 pm

Office Book
The Divine Office is based on the Sarum Rite, using AAPB for the Psalms. Whenever the Office is sung, it is in Plainsong using BCP Psalms.

The Community of Christ the King is a Traditional Anglican Benedictine order, enclosed and contemplative. Its members endeavour to glorify God in a life of prayer under the threefold vow of Stability, Conversion of Life and Obedience. They follow a rhythm of life centred on the worship of God in the Daily Eucharist and sevenfold Office. The convent, on a 37 hectare property, provides agistment for Dorpor sheep. It is surrounded by attractive flower gardens, a citrus orchard and a kitchen garden. The fruit and vegetables ensure a certain amount of self-sufficiency, and afford the opportunity and privilege of manual labour, essential to the contemplative life. Hospitality aimed at helping visitors deepen their spiritual lives through prayer is a feature of the life. The property, with its extensive views, bush walks and seclusion, is ideally suited to relaxation, quiet reflection and retreat. It is ringed by fourteen large crosses providing opportunity for meditation on the way of the cross, and for prayer in solitude.

MOTHER RITA MARY CCK
(*Revd Mother, assumed office 31 July 1997*)
SISTER PATIENCE CCK (*Assistant*)

Oblates: An Order of Benedictine Oblates has been established, open to women and men, clerical and lay.

Community Publication
The Community publishes a letter twice a year, sent free of charge to all interested in CCK (approximately 300 copies).

Community History
Dr Lesley Preston, *Called to Pray: Short History of the Community of Christ the King*, Benedictine Press, Camperdown, VIC., Australia, 2009. Available from Dr E. M. Crowther, 31 Hazlewood Close, Kidderminster, Worcs., DY11 6LW (for the price of the postage).

Guest and Retreat Facilities
We cater for those who want to deepen their life in Christ. There is a guest house which can accommodate three people (women or men): a self-contained cottage. There is no charge. A flat is attached to the chapel. A large fellowship room provides for parish quiet days and study groups. The original farmhouse is also available.

Most convenient time to telephone:
10 am - 12 noon, 2 pm - 4 pm, 6.45 pm - 7.40 pm.

Visitor: Rt Revd John Ford **Chaplain:** Revd M. Crawley

Community of the Companions of Jesus the Good Shepherd

CJGS

Founded 1920

Harriet Monsell House
Ripon College
Cuddesdon
Oxfordshire
OX44 9EX
UK
Tel: 01865 877103
Email:
cjgs@csjb.org.uk

Morning Prayer
7.30 am

Eucharist 9.30 am
(usually after Morning Prayer in term time)

Midday Office
12.30 pm

Evening Prayer
5.00 pm

Compline 8.30 pm

(all subject to variation in term time)

When the Community was founded, the first Sisters were all teachers living alone or in small groups but coming together during the school holidays. In 1943, West Ogwell House in South Devon became the Mother House and the more usual form of conventual life was established as well. The work of Christian education has always been of primary concern to the Community, whether in England or overseas, although not all the Sisters have been teachers.

In 1996, the Community moved to Windsor to live and work alongside the Community of St John Baptist, while retaining its own ethos. The Community aims 'to express in service for others, Christ's loving care for his flock.' At present, this service includes offering help and encouragement to those seeking to grow in the spiritual life through spiritual direction and prayer, and especially the befriending of the elderly, lonely, and those in need.

In 2012, the Community moved with CSJB to Ripon College, Cuddesdon.

MOTHER ANN VERENA CJGS
(Mother Superior, assumed office 20 March 1996)
Sister Florence

Obituaries

8 Jan 2015 Sister Kathleen Frideswide, aged 98, professed 55 years

Associates

Associates of the Community are members of the Fellowship of St Augustine. They follow a rule of life drawn up with the help of one of the Sisters. They give support to the Community through their prayer, interest and alms, and are remembered in prayer by the Community. They and the Community say the 'Common Devotion' daily. They are truly our extended family.

Community Publication

Newletter of CSJB & CJGS. Contact the Sister Jane Olive CSJB.

Office Book: Common Worship with additions from the old CSJB Office.

Bishop Visitor: Rt Revd Dominic Walker OGS

Registered Charity: No. 270317

Community of the Glorious Ascension

CGA

Founded 1960

Brothers:
The Priory
26 Helmers Way
Chillington
Kingsbridge
Devon TQ7 2EZ
UK

Tel:
01548 580127

Email:
ascensioncga
@fsmail.net

Sisters:
38 Green Park Way
Chillington
TQ7 2HY

Tel:
01548 580939

Email:
jean.pwll
@gmail.com

The Community seeks to live a common-life centred upon daily work, prayer and worship. The corporate pattern of the monastic life is at the heart of our life together; which aims to be informal and inclusive both in worship and hospitality. From its beginning, CGA has had a vibrant sense of mission which we try to maintain through our friendship with those who stay or visit, and also through involvement with people in the local area.

BROTHERS

BROTHER SIMON CGA
(Prior, assumed office 20 May 1993)
Brother David
Brother John

SISTERS

SISTER JEAN CGA *(Prioress)*
Revd Sister Cécile

Bishop Visitor: Rt Revd Richard Hawkins

Registered Charity: No. 254524

Community of the Good Shepherd

CGS

Founded 1978

Christ Church Likas
PO Box 519
88856 Likas
Sabah
MALAYSIA

Tel: 088 383211

Residential address:
MQ8, Jalan Teluk Likas
Kota Kinabalu
88400 Likas
Sabah
MALAYSIA

Email:
sacgs8@gmail.com

Morning Prayer
6.30 am

Evening Prayer
4.30 pm

Compline
8.00 pm

Holy Communion
8.00 am
(1st & 3rd Thu of month)

The CGS Sisters in Malaysia were formerly a part of the Community of the Companions of Jesus the Good Shepherd in the UK *(see separate entry)*. They became an autonomous community in 1978. Their Rule is based on that of St Augustine and their ministry is mainly parish work.

In October 2000, the Sisters moved from Sandakan in the East Coast to Kota Kinabalu, the Capital in the West Coast. Here a new building was put up in the year 2007 to replace the temporary one. With the kind assistance of Associates, the Community continues to serve the Diocese through sewing, making a range of items from altar cloths to palls. Another group makes and supplies altar bread for the whole diocese. Our present chaplain is Revd Canon Chak Sen Fen, Dean of All Saints Cathedral. He is a great support to the Community.

SISTER MARGARET LIN-DIN CGS
(Sister-in-charge, assumed office 1978)

Associates
In Kota Kinabalu, some committed Christian women from the three Anglican Churches join in fellowship with the Community and have become associate members. They follow a simple rule of life to support the Community through prayer and to share in the life and work of the Community. Whenever they can, they come to join the annual retreat.

Community Wares
Altar breads, stoles for clergy, scarves for pastors and lay readers.

Office Book: ASB & the Service Book of the Province of the Anglican Church in S E Asia.

Bishop Visitor
Rt Revd Melter Jiki Tais, Bishop of Sabah

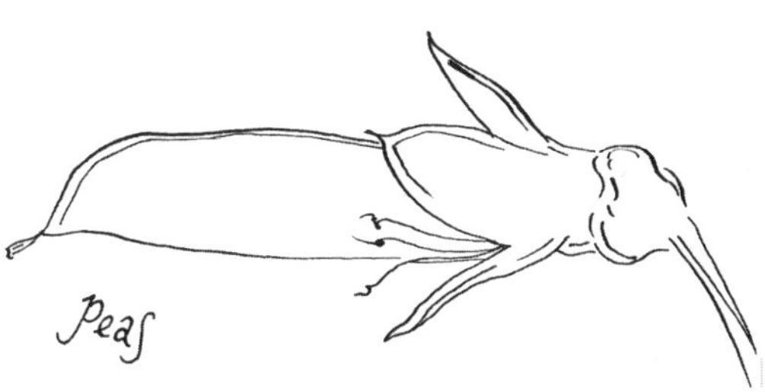

Benedictine Community of the Holy Cross, Costock

CHC

Founded 1857

Holy Cross Convent
Highfields
Nottingham Road
Costock
LE12 6XE
UK
Tel: 01509 852761
Email: sisters@holycrosschc.org.uk

Website: www.holycrosschc.org.uk

(SOUTHWELL DIOCESE)

Matins 6.15 am

Lauds 7.30 am

Terce 9.15 am

Mass 9.30 am (subject to change)

Sext 12.15 am (subject to change)

None 1.30 pm

Vespers 4.30 pm (4.00 pm Thu)

Compline 8.00 pm

Office Book: CHC Office

The Community of the Holy Cross was founded in 1857 by Elizabeth Neale (sister of John Mason Neale, the hymnographer), at the invitation of Father Charles Fuge Lowder. The foundation was intended for Mission work in Father Lowder's parish of London Docks, but succeeding generations felt that the Community was being called to a life of greater withdrawal, and in the twentieth century the Benedictine Office, and later the *Rule of St Benedict*, were adopted. The Community aims to achieve the Benedictine balance of prayer, study and work. All the work, whether manual, artistic or intellectual, is done within the Enclosure. The daily celebrations of the Eucharist and the Divine Office are the centre and inspiration of all activity.

The Community also provides hospitality for retreats and quiet days, deals with a large postal apostolate and produces greeting cards and publications as described below.

The care of the grounds and conservation work in the woodland, old orchard and fields ensures a flourishing of the wildlife much enjoyed by visitors.

SISTER MARY LUKE WISE CHC
(Mother Superior, elected 8 November 1991)
SISTER MARY JULIAN GOUGH CHC *(Assistant Superior)*
Sister Mary Michael Titherington
Sister Mary Bernadette Priddin
Sister Mary Joseph Thorpe
Sister Mary Cuthbert Aldridge
Sister Mary Hannah Kwark
Sister Mary Catherine Smith

Oblates and Associates: The Community has women & men Oblates who are attached to it in a union of mutual prayer. Each has a rule of life adapted to his or her particular circumstances. Oblates are not Religious but they seek to live their life in the world according to the spirit of T*he Rule of St Benedict.* There are also Associates who have a much simpler rule.

Community Wares: A great variety of prayer and greeting cards are available for sale. Many are produced by the sisters and others are from a number of different sources.

Community Publications: A yearly Newsletter published in Advent. Available free from the Publications Secretary.

Bishop Visitor: Most Revd Dr David Hope

Registered Charity: No 223807

Community History

Alan Russell, *The Community of the Holy Cross Haywards Heath 1857 - 1957: A Short History of its Life and Work*, 1957.

A leaflet: A short history of the Community of the Holy Cross.
Available from the Publications Secretary.

Guest and Retreat Facilities

There is limited accommodation for residential, private retreats. The Community also provides for Quiet Days for individuals or groups up to 20. The Guest House is closed after Christmas and Easter.

Community of the Holy Name

CHN

Founded 1888

Community House
40 Cavanagh Street
Cheltenham
Victoria 3192
AUSTRALIA
Tel: 03 9583 2087
Fax: 03 9585 2932

Email: chnmelb @bigpond.com

Website: www.chn.org.au

Eucharist
7.30 am / 5.30 pm

Mattins 9.00 am

Midday Office
12.45 pm

Vespers 5.30 / 5.00 pm

Compline 7.30 pm

The Community of the Holy Name was founded in 1888 within the Diocese of Melbourne by Emma Caroline Silcock (Sister Esther). The work of the Community was initially amongst the poor and disadvantaged in the slum areas of inner-city Melbourne. Over the years, the Sisters have sought to maintain a balance between a ministry to those in need and a commitment to the Divine Office, personal prayer and a daily Eucharist. For many years, CHN was involved in institutions, such as children's homes and a Mission house. There were many and varied types of outreach. The Holy Name Girls' High School was established in Papua New Guinea, and the indigenous Community of the Visitation of Our Lady fostered there.

Today, Sisters are engaged in parish work in ordained and lay capacities, and in a variety of other ministries, including hospital chaplaincies, spiritual companionship and leading of Quiet Days and retreats. The offering of hospitality to people seeking spiritual refreshment or a place away from their normal strains and stresses has become an important part of the life and ministry. St Julian's Retreat Centre is now closed as we are building new accommodation for the sisters on that site. Our original Convent will become the new Retreat and Spirituality Centre which will open in 2017.

Other Australian Addresses

68 Pickett Street, Footscray, VIC 3011

2/7 & 8/7 James Street, Brighton, VIC 3186

Office Book

CHN adaptation of the Anglican Office Book.

Community Wares: Cards, marmalade and handicrafts are sold at the Community House.

SISTER CAROL CHN

(Mother Superior, assumed office 12 April 2011, re-elected March 2014)

Council members: SISTERS ANDREA, AVRILL, MARGOT & VALMAI

Sister Andrea	Sister Lyn	Sister Ruth
Sister Avrill	Sister Maree	Sister Sheila *(priest)*
Sister Elizabeth Gwen	Sister Margaret Anne *(priest) (in care)*	Sister Sheila Anne
Sister Felicity		Sister Shirley
Sister Hilary	Sister Margot *(priest)*	Sister Valmai
Sister Jean *(in care)*	Sister Pamela	
Sister Josephine Margaret	Sister Philippa *(in care)*	*Novices:* 1

Obituaries

1 Aug 2013	Sister Penelope, aged 92, professed 65 years
7 Oct 2013	Sister Francine, aged 90, professed 40 years
30 Nov 2014	Sister Betty, aged 85, professed 57 years

Oblates and Associates

The Order of **Oblates** is for women and men who desire to lead lives of prayer and dedication in close association with the Community. The Oblates have a personal Rule of Life based on the Evangelical Counsels of Poverty, Chastity and Obedience and renew their dedication annually.

The **Associates and Priest Associates** support and pray for the Community. Each of these Groups meet regularly at the Community's House for fellowship and spiritual input. Priest Associates offer the Eucharist with special intention for the Community and seek to promote the Religious Life.

An **Alongsider** shares in most aspects of the community's life and is allowed time to explore their spiritual life. The length and terms of stay are negotiated with the Mother Superior.

Guest and Retreat Facilities

Day groups of up to 25 people are welcome in the Prayer Group and Gathering Space. There is accommodation for six residential guests at the Community House and a Sister is available for help and guidance if requested. A self-contained hermitage in the grounds is available for private retreats. All guests are invited to join the sisters in worship.

Most convenient time for guests to telephone: 10am - 12.30 pm, 2pm - 5pm

Community Publication: An Associates Letter is published four times a year. Write to Sister Avrill, the Associates Sister, for a subscription, which is by donation. Oblates Letter. Community Newsletter available on the website.

Community History

Sister Sheila Smith Dunlop CHN, *Some Suitable Women*, Morning Star Publishing, Northcote, VIC, 2014.

Sister Elizabeth CHN, *Esther, Mother Foundress*, Melbourne, 1948.

Lynn Strahan, *Out of the Silence*, OUP, Melbourne, 1988.

Bishop Visitor: Most Revd Dr Philip Freier, Archbishop of Melbourne

Warden: Rt Revd Garry Weatherill, Bishop of Ballarat

Community of the Holy Name (UK Province)

CHN

Founded 1865

Convent of the Holy Name
Morley Road
Oakwood
Derby
DE21 4QZ
UK

Tel: 01332 671716
Fax: 01332 669712

Email: bursarsoffice @tiscali.co.uk

Website: www.chnderby.org

Bishop Visitor
Rt Revd John Inge, Bishop of Worcester

The Sisters combine the life of prayer with service to others in their evangelistic and pastoral outreach and by maintaining their houses as centres of prayer where they can be available to others. They run a small guest house in Derby. In our houses, and from the Convent in Derby, the Sisters are involved in parish work, hospital visiting, retreat-giving and work among the wider community, and with those who come for spiritual guidance.

The members of the Fellowship of the Holy Name are an extension of its life and witness in the world.

We encourage those who wish to live alongside for a period of time.

SISTER PAULINE MARGARET CHN
(Provincial Superior, assumed office 23 January 2013)
SISTER EDITH MARGARET CHN *(Assistant Superior)*

Sister Ruth
Sister Marjorie Jean
Sister Barbara
Sister Brenda
Sister Verena
Sister Jean Mary
Sister Lilias
Sister Theresa Margaret
Sister Mary Patricia
Sister Lisbeth
Sister Vivienne Joy
Sister Charity
Sister Elizabeth Clare
Sister Diana
Sister Carol
Sister Monica Jane
Sister Pippa
Sister Rosemary
Sister Irene
Sister Lynfa
Sister Elaine Mary
Sister Julie Elizabeth
Sister Catherine

Obituaries
4 Feb 2015 Sister Joy, aged 80, professed 57 years
16 Feb 2015 Sister Judith, aged 94, professed 64 years

Fellowship of the Holy Name
The Fellowship is comprised of ecumenically-minded Christians who feel called to share with the Community in their life of prayer and service.

Members have a personal Rule of Life, which they have drawn up in consultation with a particular Sister. This will include daily private prayer, regular prayer and worship with the local Christian community, as well as time and space for their own well-being and creativity. Each rule varies with the individual. A six-month probation living the rule is required before formal admission to the Fellowship. This usually takes place at the Convent in the context of the

Prime
7.45 am

Eucharist
8.00 am
(12.20 pm Tue & Thu)

Mattins
9.15 am
(8.45 am Tue & Thu)

Midday Office
12.45 pm
(12.05 pm Tue & Thu)

Vespers
5.00 pm

Compline
9.15 pm
(8.45 pm Sat)

Office Book
Daily Office CHN

Most convenient time to telephone:
10.00 am - 12 noon
2.00 pm - 5.00 pm
5.30 pm - 8.30 pm

Community Publication
Community magazine - contact the editor.
Set of four leaflets: Community of the Holy Name; Fellowship of the Holy Name; Living Alongside; Facilities.

Registered Charity:
No. 250256

Eucharist. There are regional meetings for members living in the same area, and the Community distributes newsletters throughout the year and encourages members to contribute articles for the Community magazine.

Other Addresses

St John's Rectory, St John's Road, Longsight, Manchester M13 0WU Tel: 01612 248596

64 Allexton Gardens, Welland Estate, Peterborough PE1 4UW Tel: 01733 352077

Community History

History of the Community of the Holy Name, 1865 to 1950, published by CHN, 1950.

Una C. Hannam, *Portrait of a Community*, printed by the Church Army Press, 1972. This was a heavily edited version of the original manuscript by the late Sister Constance CHN. A revised and updated version of the complete manuscript is now published as:
Sister Constance CHN, *What's in a Name?: Portrait of a Community*, CHN, 2015.

2015 Brochure - photographs and text celebrating 150 years of Community Life (with text mostly extracted from *Portrait of a Community*). Can be ordered from the Convent, £3 each.

Community Wares

Various cards.

Booklet of Stations of the Cross, from original paintings by Sister Theresa Margaret CHN, with biblical texts. Can be ordered from the Convent: £5.00 each, or for orders of ten or more £4.50 each.

Sister Pauline Margaret CHN, *Jesus Prayer,* £3.50. Can be ordered from the Convent or SLG Press.
Sister Verena CHN, *A Simplified Life*, Canterbury Press, Norwich. Available from the Convent £10.

Examples of icons can be viewed by request at the Convent. Commissions can be taken. Contact Sister Theresa Margaret CHN at the Convent.

Guest and Retreat Facilities

There are opportunities for individuals to make a private retreat at the guest house, and Sisters may be prepared to give help and guidance if requested. Six single rooms, one double - see our website. Individuals and groups can contact the Convent for day bookings (usually between 10am – 4 pm).

Community of the Holy Name (Lesotho Province)

CHN

Founded 1865 (in UK)
1962 (in Lesotho)

Convent of the Holy Name
PO Box 22
Ficksburg 9730
SOUTH AFRICA
Tel: 22400249

Website:
www.chnderby.org

Morning Prayer
6.30 am
(6.45 am Sun)

Terce
7.45 am (Sun only)

Eucharist
7.00 am (8.00 am Sun; 12 noon Wed)

Midday Office
12.15 pm (12.30 pm Sun, 11.45 am Wed)

Evening Prayer 5 pm

Compline 8.15 pm

Office Book
South African Prayer Book, supplemented by CHN Office Book

The Basotho Community of St Mary at the Cross was founded in Leribe, Lesotho, in 1923, under CSM&AA, Bloemfontein. In 1959, CHN Sisters were invited to take over this work and started at Leribe in 1962. They had invited the Sisters of S. Mary at the Cross to become members of CHN and the full amalgamation of the two communities was completed in 1964. As a multi-racial community, the witness against racism at a time when apartheid was in the ascendant in South Africa was an important strand of the Community's vocation. In succeeding years, the Sisters have continued the evangelistic and pastoral work which is also an important part of the CHN vocation. Sisters are involved in children's work, prison visiting, as well as other outreach in both Lesotho and South Africa. There is a church sewing room and wafer room. The Sisters in Leribe run a hostel for secondary school students. Some Sisters are 'Volunteers of Love' for families where there is HIV/AIDS. This work is enabled and strengthened by the daily round of prayer, both corporate and private, which is at the heart of the Community's Rule. A daily Eucharist at the centre of this life of prayer is the aim. There is a small guest house.

SISTER JULIA CHN
(Provincial Superior, assumed office April 2007)
SISTER MPOLOKENG CHN *(Assistant Superior)*

Sister Calista
Sister Alphonsina
Sister Hilda Tsepiso
Sister Lucia
Sister Angelina
Sister Mary Selina
Sister Josetta
Sister Gertrude
Sister Ryneth
Sister Lineo
Sister Exinia Tsoakae
Sister Lebohang
Sister Malineo
Sister Malefu

Novices: 1

Obituaries
2 Aug 2014 Sister Maria, aged 87, professed 56 years

Other houses: Please contact the main house.

Community Wares: Church sewing (including cassocks, albs, stoles); communion wafers; Mothers Union uniforms; mohair and woven goods from the Leribe Craft Centre and the disabled workshop, started by the Community.

Bishop Visitor: Rt Revd Adam Taaso

Community of the Holy Name (Zulu Province)

CHN

Founded 1865 (in UK)
1969 (in Zululand)

Convent of the Holy Name
Pt. Bag 806
Melmoth 3835
Zululand
SOUTH AFRICA
Tel: 3545 02892
Fax: 3545 07564

Email:
chnsisters @telkomsa.net

Website:
www.chnderby.org

Terce 6.30 am

Eucharist
6.30 am (Wed & Fri)
6.45 am (Tue & Thu)
4.30 pm (Mon)

Mattins 8.30 am

Midday Office
12.30 pm

Evening Prayer
4.00 pm (Mon & Wed)
5.00 pm (Tue & Thu)
4.30 pm (Fri)

Compline 7.45 pm

The Community of the Holy Name in Zululand was founded by three Zulu Sisters who began their Religious life with the Community in Leribe. All three Provinces of CHN have the same Rule of life, but there are differences of customary and constitutions to fit in with cultural differences. The daily life of the Community centres around the daily Office, and the Eucharist whenever the presence of a priest makes this possible.

The Sisters are involved extensively in mission, pastoral and evangelistic work. The Zulu Sisters have evangelistic gifts, which are used in parishes throughout the diocese at the invitation of parish priests. Several Sisters have trained as teachers or nurses. They work in schools or hospitals, where possible within reach of one of the Community houses. Their salaries, and the large vestment-making department at the Convent at Kwa Magwaza, help to keep the Community solvent. The sisters also facilitate the care of many orphans in their extended families.

MOTHER JABU CHN
(Provincial Superior, assumed office 2014)
SISTER SEBENZILE CHN *(Assistant Superior)*

Sister Claudia
Sister Olpha
Sister Nestar Gugu
Sister Nokuthula
Sister Sibongile
Sister Zodwa
Sister Mantombi
Sister Bonakele
Sister Nonhlahla
Sister Thulisiwe
Sister Thembelihle
Sister Benzile
Sister Samukelisiwe
Sister Thandazile
Sister Thandiwe
Sister Nondumiso
Sister Thokozile
Sister Duduzile
Sister Patricia
Sister Phindile
Sister Nqobile
Sister Sibekezelo
Sister Philisiwe
Sister Ntsoaki
Sister Nokubongwa
Sister Nomathemba
Sister Thandukwazi
Sister Zamandla
Sister Sindisiwe
Sister Bongile
Sister Maureen
Sister Neliswa
Sister Hlengiwe
Sister Nkosikhoma
Sister Thembekile
Sister Sizeka

Novices: 2

Office Book: Offices are mainly in Zulu, based on the South African Prayer Book & the CHN Office Book.

Community Wares
Vestments, cassocks, albs and other forms of dressmaking.

Other Houses
PO Box 175, Nongoma 3950, SOUTH AFRICA
St Benedict House, PO Box 27, Rosettenville 2130, SOUTH AFRICA

Bishop Visitor: Rt Revd Dino Gabriel, Bishop of Zululand

Community of the Holy Spirit

CHS

Founded 1952

454 Convent Ave
New York
NY 10031-3618
USA
Tel: 212 666 8249
Fax: 801 655 8249

Email: chssisters @chssisters.org

Website
www.chssisters.org

The daily schedule varies with the seasons.
Please call ahead for current schedule.
Monday is a Sabbath in each house of the Community, during which there is no corporate worship.

Each person is given an invitation to follow Christ. The Sisters of our monastic community respond to that invitation by an intentional living out of the vows of poverty, chastity, and obedience within the structure of a modified Augustinian Rule. Through the vow of poverty, we profess our trusting dependence upon God by embracing voluntary simplicity and responsible stewardship of creation. Through chastity, we profess the sanctity of all creation as the primary revelation of God. Through obedience, we profess our desire to be dependent on God's direction and to live and minister in ways that respect all creation, both now and for generations to come. Compassionate, respectful love is God's gift to life. Prayer and the worship of God are the lifeblood and heart of our Community and the source of inspiration for all that we undertake. Through our prayer, worship, and creative talents we encourage others to seek God. Through our ministries of hospitality, retreat work, spiritual direction, and education through simple, sustainable, spiritual living, we seek to grow in love and communion with all whose lives touch us and are touched by us. We also provide spiritual support for women and men who wish to be linked with our Community as Associates. By adopting a personal rule of life, they extend the Community's ministry through prayer, worship and service.

Other Address
The Melrose Convent - Bluestone Farm and Living Arts Center, 118 Federal Hill Road, Brewster, NY 10509-5307, USA
Tel: 845 363 1971 Fax: 845 746 2205
Email: Melroseconvent@chssisters.org

Office Book: CHS Office book

Sister Heléna Marie CHS, Sister Faith Margaret CHS,
Sister Catherine Grace CHS
(Community Council, assumed office June 2001)

Sister Élise
Sister Mary Christabel
Sister Mary Elizabeth
Sister Emmanuel
Sister Maria Felicitas
Sister Leslie
Sister Claire Joy
Sister Carol Bernice

Obituaries
3 Apr 2014 Sister Jerolynn Mary, aged 78, professed 48 years

Associates
From the Community's early days, Christian women and men have sought an active association with the Sisters, wishing to live out their baptismal commitments by means of a rule of life.

The Community provides four rules: Fellowship, St Augustine, Confraternity and Priest Associate. Each consists of prayer, reading, self-denial and stewardship. Each provides an opportunity for growth toward God and daily renewal of life in Christ. Each calls for a commitment to pray daily for the Sisters and all others in their life, worship and ministry, using the collect for Pentecost and the Lord's Prayer.

In consultation with the Sister for Associates, they may formulate their own rule if the ones provided cannot be fulfilled as they stand, or if they need to be expanded. As far as is possible Associates support the Community through gifts of time, talents and financial resources. There is an annual fee of $75, if possible.

Community Wares: [From Bluestone Farm]: Food items as available; crafts.

Community Publication: Periodic electronic newsletter. Please send email address to inquiries@chssisters.org.

Community History: The Revd Mother Ruth CHS, *"In Wisdom Thou Hast Made Them"*, Adams, Bannister, Cox, New York, 1986.

Guest and Retreat Facilities
The Longhouse at Melrose; seven rooms, total capacity eight. Closed irregularly; call in advance to make reservations.
Visit www.chssisters.org for further information.
Tel: 845 363 1972 ex 30 Email: BFLACreservations@chssisters.org

Most convenient time to telephone:
Generally, phones are staffed irregularly between 9.00 am and 5.00 pm EST Tuesday through Saturday, though you may leave a message at any time.

Bishops Visitor
Rt Revd Marc H. Andrus, Bishop of California
Rt Revd Allen K. Shin, suffragan Bishop of New York

Community of the Holy Trans-figuration

CHT

Founded 1982

St David's Bonda Mission
P Bag T 7904
Mutare
ZIMBABWE

The Community started in 1982 with 8 members who broke away from the Community of the Holy Name (Chita Che Zita Rinoyera). The Community is stationed at St David's Bonda Mission and it is an open community. We assist the Church in evangelistic work and other ministerial duties. Some members are employed by the diocese as priests and some as Evangelists. We run an orphanage with a maximum number of thirty young children. As of now, the age-group is going beyond this age range because of the HIV/AIDS pandemic. We are also a self-reliant community through land tilling and poultry. There is now another house at St Francis Mission, Shurugwi, in the diocese of Masvingo.

SISTER MILDAH CHT
(Mother, assumed office 2006)

Sister Merina
Sister Violet
Sister Dorothy
Sister Felicity
Evangelist Friar Henry

at Shurugwi:
Sister Gloria *(superior)*
Sister Winnie
Sister Lucy
Sister Gloria Mary
Rev Friar Fungayi Leonard

Postulants: 2

Obituaries: Sister Letwin

Community of Jesus' Compassion

CJC

Founded 1993

PO Box 153
New Hanover
3230
SOUTH AFRICA
Tel: 072 625 3039
(Mother's mobile)

Founded in the Diocese of Natal by a sister from the Community of the Holy Name in Zululand, CJC have been based in Newcastle and Ixopo. However, the sisters have now settled at New Hanover, which is half an hour's drive from the cathedral city of Pietermaritzburg. The main work of the sisters is evangelising in the local parish and children's ministry. The Sisters care for around thirty-five children, which is demanding, but good progress is being made.

On the 19th December 1998, the first professions within the community were received. The Community's formal recognition by the Church of the Province of South Africa followed in 2000 with the first life professions. In 2006, Sister Thandi became the first nun in the diocese to be ordained to the stipendiary ministry, and she now serves in a parish in Durban. Her priesting followed in June 2007.

Community Wares
Girdles, Prayer Book and Bible covers, vegetables.

Bishop Visitor: Rt Revd Rubin Phillip, Bishop of Natal

Morning Prayer, followed by Terce
5.30 am

Midday Prayer
12.30 pm

Evening Prayer
4.30 pm

Compline
8.15 pm

MOTHER LONDIWE CJC
(*Mother Superior, assumed office 8 January 2000*)
SISTER THANDI CJC (*Assistant Superior)*

Sister Yekisiwe
Sister Ntombi
Sister Zandile
Sister Nontokozo
Sister Thokozile
Sister Nqobile
Sister Nonhlanhla
Sister Mbali
Sister Thelma
Sister Ayanda
Sister Makhosazana
Sister Sibongile

Novices: 1 *Postulants:* 1

Office Book: Anglican Prayer Book 1989 of the CPSA Midday Office book & Celebrating Night Prayer

---

Community of Nazareth CN

Founded 1936

4-22-30 Mure
Mitaka
Tokyo 181-0002
JAPAN
Tel: 0422 48 4560
Fax: 0422 48 4601

Morning Prayer
6.25 am

Eucharist 7.00 am

Terce 8.15 am

Sext 12 noon

None after lunch

Evening Prayer
5.00 pm

Night Prayer 8.00 pm

Under the guidance of the Sisters of the Community of the Epiphany (England), the Community of Nazareth was born and has grown. The Community is dedicated to the Incarnate Lord Jesus Christ, especially in devotion to the hidden life which he lived in Nazareth.

In addition to the Holy Eucharist, which is the centre and focus of our community life, the Sisters recite a sixfold Divine Office. We run a Retreat house and make wafers.

We welcome enquirers and aspirants.

SISTER NOBU CN
(*Reverend Mother, assumed office 2008*)
SISTER MIYOSHI CN (*Assistant Mother)*

Sister Yachiyo
Sister Kayoko
Sister Chizuko
Sister Asako
Sister Setsuko

Juniors: 1
Postulants: 1

Obituaries
20 Jun 2013 Sister Junko, aged 85, professed 49 years

Associates: Clergy and laity may be associates.

Other Address
81 Shima Bukuro, Naka Gusuku Son, Naka Gami Gun, Okinawa Ken 901-2301, JAPAN

Community Wares: Wafers, vestments.

Guest and Retreat Facilities: There are some rooms for meditation and retreat, but not tourists. Please contact us to ask further details about staying.

Office Book: BCP of Nippon Seiko Kai Office Book

Bishop Visitor: Rt Revd Yoshimichi Ohata, Bp of Tokyo

Benedictine Community of Our Lady & Saint John

Alton Abbey

OSB

Founded 1884

Alton Abbey
Abbey Road
Beech, Alton
Hampshire
GU34 4AP
UK
Tel: 01420 562145
& 01460 563575
Email: abbot@ altonabbey.org.uk
or **guestmaster@ altonabbey.org.uk**

Morning Prayer
7.00 am

Conventual Mass
9.00 am (10 am Sun)

Midday Office
12.30 pm

Evening Prayer
4.45 pm

Night Prayer
8.30 pm (7.30 pm Sun)

The monks follow the Rule with its balance of prayer, work and study, supported by the vows of stability, conversion of life and obedience. A wide ministry of hospitality is offered, and visitors are welcome at the daily Mass and Divine Office. The purpose built monastery is built around two cloister garths; the Abbey Church dates from the beginning of the twentieth century. Set in extensive grounds, with contrast between areas that are cultivated and others that are a haven for wildlife, the Abbey is situated about four miles from Alton.

Rt Revd Dom Giles Hill OSB
(Abbot, assumed office September 2013)
Very Revd Dom Andrew Johnson OSB *(Prior)*

Revd Dom Nicholas Seymour OSB
Dom Anselm Shobrook OSB
Rt Revd Dom Timothy Bavin OSB
Brother John Towson OSB *(Guest Master)*
Brother Anthony Witherspoon OSB

Oblates
For details of the Oblates of St Benedict, please contact the Oblate Master.
For details of the Companions of Our Lady and Saint John, please contact the Master of the Companions.

Community Wares
Incense: contact Alton Abbey Supplies Ltd.
Tel: 01420 565977

Guest and Retreat Facilities
Guest house facilities for up to eighteen persons, for both group and individual retreats. There is a programme of retreats each year, available from the Guestmaster.
No smoking in the house.

Most convenient time to telephone: 4.00 pm - 4.30 pm.

Office Book: Alton Abbey Office Book

Website: www.altonabbey.org.uk

Bishop Visitor: awaiting appointment

Registered Charity: No. 229216

Community of the Resurrection

CR

Founded 1892

**House of the Resurrection
Mirfield
West Yorkshire
WF14 0BN
UK
Tel: 01924 494318
Fax: 01924 490489
Email:
community
@mirfield.org.uk**

Website: www.
mirfieldcommunity.
org.uk

Mattins
6.45 am (7.30 am Sun)

Midday Office
12.00 noon

Mass 12.15 pm
On festivals on week days, the time of Mass may change.

Evensong 6.00 pm

Compline 9.15 pm

Office Book
CR Office

Registered Charity
No. 232670

The Community consists of priests and laymen living a life of worship, work and study within the monastic life. They undertake a wide range of pastoral ministry including retreats, teaching and counselling.

GEORGE GUIVER CR
(assumed office 29 December 2002)
OSWIN GARTSIDE CR *(Prior)*

Roy France
Eric Simmons
Aidan Mayoss
Robert Mercer
Simon Holden
Crispin Harrison
Antony Grant
Nicolas Stebbing
John Gribben
Peter Allan
Philip Nichols
Thomas Seville
Steven Haws
Dennis Berk
Jacob Pallett

Obituaries
14 Feb 2014 Vincent Girling, aged 85, professed 56 years

Oblates, Companions & Associates
OBLATES, clergy and lay, are those who desire to make a special and permanent offering of themselves to God in association with the Community of the Resurrection.

COMPANIONS seek to live the baptismal vocation of all Christians through a commitment to each community to which they belong and also to the Community of the Resurrection; a commitment to Eucharistic worship, corporate and private prayer and the use of the sacrament of reconciliation; a commitment of time, talents and money. Those who wish to be Companions keep their commitments for at least a year before being admitted, and thereafter, with all Companions, renew their commitment each year. All Companions have a spiritual director or soul friend with whom their commitments are discussed and who undertakes to support them on their journey.

ASSOCIATES have a less demanding relationship with the Community for whatever reason, but do have an obligation of prayer and worship. For more information contact the Chaplain to the Companions at Mirfield.

Community History: Alan Wilkinson, *The Community of the Resurrection: A centenary history,* SCM Press, London, 1992.

CR: a brief history, Mirfield Pubs, 2014; £3.50 from Mirfield.

Bishop Visitor
Rt Revd Graham James, Bishop of Norwich

Community Publication: *CR Quarterly*. Write to the Editor. Many subscribe to this who are not Oblates, Companions or Associates. The minimum annual subscription is £15.00.

Community Wares: Postcards of the buildings, theological and spiritual books, leaflets on prayer, CDs of Community's music, clothes with logo: apply to Mirfield Publications at the House of the Resurrection. Purchases available online through the website.

Guest and Retreat Facilities: Retreats are listed on the website.

HOUSE OF THE RESURRECTION

Twenty-four single rooms, two double rooms, nine en-suite rooms, one small flat.

Most convenient time to telephone: 9.00 am - 12 noon, 2.00 pm - 6.00 pm

MIRFIELD CENTRE

The Centre offers a meeting place at the College for about fifty people. Small residential conferences are possible in the summer vacation. Day and evening events are arranged throughout the year to stimulate Christian life and witness.

The Mirfield Centre (College of the Resurrection), Mirfield, West Yorks WF14 0BW, UK Tel: 01924 481920 Fax: 01924 418921
Email: centre@mirfield.org.uk

COLLEGE OF THE RESURRECTION

The College, founded in 1902 and run by its own independent Council, trains men and women and also provides opportunities for others to study for degrees.

Principal: Fr Peter Allan CR

College of the Resurrection, Mirfield, West Yorkshire WF14 0BW, UK
Tel: 01924 481900 Email: registrar@mirfield.org.uk

Community of the Resurrection of Our Lord CR

Founded 1884

St Peter's, PO Box
Grahamstown 6140
SOUTH AFRICA
Tel & Fax:
046 622 4210

This Community was founded in 1884 by Bishop Allan Becher Webb and Cecile Isherwood to undertake pastoral and educational work in Grahamstown. These two types of work, and later Social Welfare work, have predominated throughout the Community's history. The regular life of monastic Offices and personal prayer and intercession has always been maintained in all houses, wherever situated. Grahamstown is now the only centre where the Community life continues. The Sisters are involved in various ministries: at the Cathedral and other churches as needed; in the Raphael Centre for people suffering from HIV/Aids etc; in visiting at Old Age Homes and the hospital; soup kitchens; and needlework/banners. In April 2012, the Community opened an orphanage, named Ikhay Lethu, in our old convent, with two sisters and a brother, aged 1-6. Since then we have received two more, the youngest two being 9 months and one year old. So the total of children is five: three girls and two boys.

Email:
motherzelma@geenet.co.za

MOTHER ZELMA CR *(priest)*
(Mother Superior, assumed office 24 November 2005)
SISTER KEKELETSO CR *(Assistant Superior)*
Sister Dorianne
Sister Carol *(priest)*
Sister Neheng

Morning Office
7.00 am

Eucharist
7.30 am

Midday Office
12.30 pm

Evening Office
5.30 pm

Compline 7.30 pm

Greater Silence: 9 pm

Office Book
Anglican Prayer Book 1989, CPSA; Traditional Midday Office & Compline

Community Wares
Cards, banners, girdles, stoles and altar linens etc, corporals and purificators.

Bishop Visitor
Rt Revd Eric Pike

Oblates and Associates

OBLATES OF THE RISEN CHRIST live under a Rule drawn up for each individual according to circumstances, on their observance of which they must report monthly to the Oblate Sister.

ASSOCIATES undertake a simple Rule, including regular prayer for the Community. Priest Associates undertake to give an address or preach on Religious Vocation at least once a year.

FRIENDS are interested in the Community and pray for it, and keep in touch with it.

There is a Fellowship Meeting twice a year, after Easter and near the Foundress's birthday on 14 November.

Also there is a Festival gathering of UK Associates at St Peter's Bourne, Whetstone, north London, on the Saturday nearest to St Peter's Day, 29 June, each year, at which two Sisters from South Africa are always present to preserve our links with the UK.

Community Publication: A Newsletter is sent out three times a year to all bishops and Religious communities of CPSA, and also to all the Oblates and Associates of the Community.

Guest and Retreat Facilities: Ten or more guests can be accommodated; though prior consultation is needed. The charge is negotiable. There is also a guest flatlet for two.

Community History and Books

A pictorial record of the Community's history, with commentary, was published in its centenary year, 1984. It was a collaborative work.

A Sister of the Community (compiler), *Mother Cecile in South Africa 1883-1906: Foundress of the Community of the Resurrection of Our Lord,* SPCK, London, 1930.

A Sister of the Community, *The Story of a Vocation: A Brief Memoir of Mother Florence, Second Superior of the Community of the Resurrection of Our Lord,* The Church Book Shop, Grahamstown, no date.

Guy Butler, *The Prophetic Nun*, Random House, 2000. (Life and art works, with colour illustrations, of Sisters Margaret and Pauline CR, and Sister Dorothy Raphael CSMV.) This is a coffee-table type book available in South Africa and the UK.

Community of the Sacred Name

CSN

Founded 1893

300 Tuam Street
Christchurch 8011
NEW ZEALAND
Tel: 03 366 8245
Email: comsacnm @xtra.co.nz

Morning Prayer 7.15 am

Mass 8.00 am (Thu & Fri)

Midday Office 12 noon

Vespers 5.15 pm

Compline 7.00 pm

Office Book
A New Zealand Prayer Book
He Karakia Mihinare o Aotearoa

Community Wares
Embroidery, cards, vestments.

Bishops Visitor
Rt Revd Victoria Matthews
Rt Revd Winston Halapua

The Community of the Sacred Name was founded in Christchurch in 1893 by Sister Edith (Deaconess). She was released from the Community of St Andrew in London to establish an indigenous community to respond to the needs of the colonial Church. A wide variety of teaching, childcare and parish work has been undertaken over the years. Today there are five houses. Since 1966, the Sisters have run a large children's home in Fiji and now also run St Mary's girls' hostel at Labasa, Vanua Levu. Three Sisters have returned to Christchurch and are currently living in the retreat house, which was part of the Barbadoes Street property. Four Sisters are based in Ashburton where we do ecclesiastical embroidery. Underpinning all the work is a life of worship.

MOTHER KELENI CSN
(Mother Superior, assumed office 9 November 2006)
SISTER KALOLAINE CSN *(Assistant)*

Sister Annette	Sister Mele	Sister Alena
Sister Brigid	Sister Litia	Sister Fehoko
Sister Lu'isa	Sister Judith	Sister Vutulongo
Sister Anne	Sister Miria	Sister Sandra

Oblates and Associates
The Community has Oblates, men and women called by God to live the contemplative life in the world.

We also have Companions, Associates, Friends of St Christopher's. For women or men, priests or lay people.

Community History
Ruth Fry, *The Community of the Sacred Name - a Centennial History,* 1993; copies available from Revd Mother.

Guest and Retreat Facilities
8 bedrooms for retreats or guests. Contact (03) 366 8245
Most convenient time to telephone: 9.15 am - 5.15 pm

Community Publication
Community *Newsletter*, published at Easter, Holy Name and Christmas. Write to the Reverend Mother.

Other addresses
53 Morris Road, RD2, Ashburton 7772, NEW ZEALAND Tel: 9030 307 1121

St Christopher's Home, PO Box 8232, Nakasi, Suva, FIJI Tel: 679 341 0458

St Mary's Hostel, PO Box 4121, Labasa, FIJI

PO Box 1824, Nuku'alofa, TONGA Tel: 27998

Community of the Sacred Passion

CSP

Founded 1911

Convent of the Sacred Passion
22 Buckingham Road
Shoreham-by-Sea
West Sussex
BN43 5UB
UK
Tel: 01273 453807
Email: communitysp@yahoo.co.uk

Morning Prayer 7.10 am

Prayer before noon 8.05 am

Mass 9.30 am (Mon, Thu, Fri)

Midday Office 12.10 pm

Evening Prayer 6.00 pm

Compline 7.30 pm

The Community was founded to serve Africa by a life of prayer and missionary work, bringing to Africans a knowledge of God's love. After the Church in Tanzania gained independence, and the Community of St Mary of Nazareth and Calvary (CMM), which they nurtured, became self-governing, CSP withdrew from Tanzania and now offers support from England. Much of the help is channelled through CMM to whom they offer encouragement, advice and financial support. The Sisters also collect money for some of the work that they founded, including the Polio Hostel at Kwa Mkono, caring for disabled children, and building work at the Nursing School at Muheza to cater for extra student nurses and modern equipment. At Shoreham, the Sisters offer hospitality for small day events and meetings. They are involved in guidance of individuals and have various contacts in the local community. The Sister in Clapham is involved with the World Community for Christian Meditation and has contacts with people of various faiths. Prayer remains the foundation of the life of the Community.

MOTHER PHILIPPA CSP
(Revd Mother, assumed office 30 August 1999)
SISTER JACQUELINE CSP *(Deputy Superior)*

Sister Dorothy	Sister Angela
Sister Gillian Mary	Sister Lucia
Sister Rhoda	

Oblates: Men and women who feel called to associate themselves with the aims of the community, by prayer and service, and by a life under a Rule. Their own Rule of Life will vary according to their particular circumstances. Oblates are helped and advised by the Oblates' Sister.

Associates: Men and women who share in the work of the community by prayer, almsgiving and service of some kind. They pray regularly for the community.

Priest Associates: Pray regularly for the community and offer Mass for it three times a year, of which one is Passion Sunday (the Sunday before Palm Sunday).

Friends: Pray regularly for the community and help it in any way they can. Although those who are enrolled as 'Associates' will continue in that category no more Associates will be enrolled but interested people will be welcomed as 'Friends'. Oblates and Priest Associates will continue to be accepted.

All those who are connected with the community are prayed for daily by the Sisters and remembered by name on their birthdays. They receive the four-monthly intercession paper, and newsletter.

Guest and Retreat Facilities

One room. Donations. Women only for overnight stay.

Most convenient time to telephone: 4 pm - 7.30 pm.

Community History

Sister Mary Stella CSP, *She Won't Say 'No': The History of the Community of the Sacred Passion*, 1984

Margaret Gooch, *Zanzibar to Shoreham in 100 years,* Paul Davies, Great Yarmouth, 2011 - obtainable from the Convent, £11, cheques payable to Community of the Sacred Passion.

Other Address:
725 Wandsworth Road
London SW8 3JF
UK

Bishop Visitor
Rt Revd Ian Brackley
Bishop of Dorking

Registered charity No:
800080

Community of St Andrew

CSA

Founded 1861

In the mid 19th century Elizabeth Ferard felt called to restore the diaconate of women. She was authorized by the Bishop of London, A. C. Tait, to begin an Institute to train women as Deaconesses which started on St Andrew's Day, 1861. The Bishop commissioned Elizabeth as the first Deaconess of the Church of England on 18 July 1862. The Bishop laid hands on the head of each person to be made Deaconess, give her his blessing and she would be admitted to the Community of the London Diocesan Deaconess Institution. From about 1887 the Community evolved into a Religious Community known as the Deaconess Community of St Andrew; thus the dual vocation of life commitment in community and ordained ministry in the Church. The fundamental ministry is the offering of prayer and worship, evangelism, pastoral work and hospitality, now mainly through retirement ministries. In 2011 we celebrated our 150th anniversary as a Community. Because the restoration of the Deaconess Order began with us, in 2012 we co-sponsored the celebration of the 150th anniversary of the Deaconess Order of the Church of England at Lambeth Palace.

Associates

Our Associates are part of our extended Community family. They may be men, women, clergy or lay, and follow a simple Rule of Life, which includes praying for the Sisters and their work. The Sisters pray for the Associates every day.

Office Book: Common Worship - Daily Prayer

Bishop Visitor*:* Rt Revd & Rt Hon Richard Chartres, Bishop of London

Correspondence address:
Revd Mother Lillian, CSA
St Mary's Convent & Nursing Home,
Burlington Lane,
Chiswick,
London W4 2QE

Tel: 020 8742 8434

Email:
lillianmorris959@btinternet.com

Registered Charity:
No 244321

REVD MOTHER LILLIAN CSA *(deacon)* Tel: 020 8742 0001
(Mother Superior, 1982-94, 2000-)
Revd Sister Donella *(deacon)* Tel: 020 8742 3172
Revd Sister Patricia *(deacon)* Tel: 020 8742 8434
all resident at: St Mary's Convent & Nursing Home, Burlington Lane, Chiswick, London W4 2QE

Sister Pamela *(deaconess)*
resident at: 17 War Memorial Place, Harpsden Way, Henley on Thames, Oxon RG9 1EP Tel: 01491 572224

Revd Dr Sister Teresa *(priest)*
resident at: St Andrew's House, 16 Tavistock Crescent, London W11 1AP
Tel: 020 7221 4604 Email: teresajoan@btinternet.com

Community History

Sister Joanna [Baldwin], Dss. CSA, "The Deaconess Community of St Andrew", *Journal of Ecclesiastical History*, Vol. XII, No.2, October 1961, 16pp.

Henrietta Blackmore, editor, *The Beginnings of Women's Ministry: The Revival of the Deaconess in the 19th-Century Church of England*, Boydell & Brewer, Woodbridge, 2007, ISBN 978-843-308-6.

Sister Teresa [Joan White], CSA, *The (Deaconess) Community of St Andrew, 1861-2011,* St Andrew's House, 2012, reprinted 2013, 225 pp. plus photos.

Sister Edna Mary [Skinner], Dss.CSA, *The Religious Life*, Penguin, Harmondsworth, 1968.

Community of St Clare

OSC

Founded 1950

St Mary's Convent
178 Wroslyn Road
Freeland, Witney
OX29 8AJ
UK
Tel: 01993 881225
Email: community @oscfreeland.co.uk

We follow a contemplative tradition that is eight hundred years old with a fresh and informal spirit. In the pattern of St Clare, hierarchy is tempered by mutuality and warm relations within the community. As the Second Order of the international Society of St Francis, we have brothers and sisters in the First and Third Orders, and we enjoy close, though informal, ties with the Roman Catholic Poor Clares.

Our worship and prayer throughout the day are interspersed with domestic tasks in the convent and guest house, and environmentally friendly work in the large garden and grounds where we raise fruit and vegetables to eat, and keep hens who give us eggs. We also engage in our industries (altar breads, printing, cards) which with the guest house help us to earn our living, and where possible to share with others. Responding to God's call in our daily lives within the enclosure, we also enjoy visitors, holidays and the use of books, newspapers and the internet for a wider view of daily life.

Women seriously interested in the contemplative life (with or without the intention of joining the community) are welcome to take part for up to a year in our life of Franciscan simplicity and joy.

SISTER DAMIEN DAVIES OSC
(Abbess, elected 13 May 2013)
SISTER PAULA FORDHAM OSC *(Assistant)*

Sister Alison Francis Hamilton	Sister Mary Margaret Broomfield
Sister Kathleen Marie Staggs	Sister Susan Elisabeth Leslie
Sister Mary Kathleen Kearns	*Novices:* 1

Website
www.oscfreeland.co.uk

Guest House
(for guests arriving)
The Old Parsonage
168 Wroslyn Road
Freeland, Witney
OX29 8AQ, UK
Tel: 01993 881227

Morning Prayer 7.30 am

Eucharist 8.30 am

Midday Prayer 12.30 pm

Evening Prayer 5.00 pm

Night Prayer 8.00 pm

Office Book
The Daily Office SSF

Community Wares: Printing, cards, crafts, altar breads.

Guest and Retreat Facilities
Men, women and children are welcome at the guest house. It is not a 'silent house' but people can make private retreats if they wish. 10 rooms (some double or twin-bedded). Donations, no fixed charge. Closed annually 16 Dec - 7 Jan.

Most convenient time to telephone:
For those wishing to stay at the Guest House – 6 pm - 7 pm Mon to Fri. For altar breads, printing, etc. 9.30 am - midday.

Community History: Petà Dunstan, *This Poor Sort,* DLT, London 1997, pp157-167

Bishop Protector
Rt Revd Stephen Cottrell, Bishop of Chelmsford

Community of St Francis

CSF

Founded 1905

As Franciscan sisters, an autonomous part of the Society of St Francis, our primary vocation is to live the gospel in the places to which we are called. The context is our life in community, under vows. Our wide range of backgrounds, abilities and gifts contributes to many ways of expressing the three elements of prayer, study and work. Prayer together and alone, with the Eucharist being central, is the heart of each house and each sister's life. Six sisters are priests; and three live the solitary life. Study nurtures our spiritual life and enables and enriches our ministries. Work encompasses practical domestic tasks and a wide range of ministries: currently these include hospitality, spiritual direction, hospice and theological college chaplaincy, administration, teaching computer skills, supporting people with various disabilities, parish work and missions, preaching, leading quiet days and retreats, writing, being a presence in poor urban areas, and work with deaf blind people. Some of this work is salaried, much is voluntary. Each new sister brings her unique gifts, thus enriching our shared life. Now in our second century, we are excited by the challenge of living the Franciscan life in today's world.

HELEN JULIAN CSF
(Minister General, assumed office February 2012)

EUROPEAN PROVINCE
SUE CSF
(Minister Provincial, assumed office February 2012)

Angela Helen
Beverley
Chris
Christine James
Elizabeth
Gina
Gwenfryd Mary
Hilary
Jannafer
Joyce
Judith Ann
Liz
Maureen
Nan
Patricia Clare

Sisters resident in Korea:
Frances
Jemma

Obituaries

21 Nov 2013	Jenny Tee, aged 58, professed 4 years
16 Dec 2013	Teresa, aged 84, professed 46 years, Minister General 1996-2002

Office Book: Daily Office SSF

Website: www.franciscans.org.uk

Bishop Protector
Rt Revd Stephen Cottrell, Bishop of Chelmsford

Companions & Third Order
Companions are individual Christians who wish to associate themselves with the Society through prayer, friendship and in seeking to live the spirit of the Gospel in the way of St Francis. For more information about becoming a Companion contact the Secretary for Companions, Hilfield Friary, Dorchester, Dorset DT2 7BE, UK.
For the Third Order SSF, *see separate entry.*

Community Publication
franciscan, three times a year. Subscription: £9.00 per year. Write to the Editor of *franciscan*, The Friary of St Francis, Hilfield, Dorset DT2 7BE, UK.

Minister General
Email: minister generalcsf@ franciscans.org.uk

UK Houses:

St Francis House
113 Gillott Road
Birmingham B16 0ET
Tel: 0121 454 8302
Email: birminghamcsf@ franciscans.org.uk

St Matthew's House
25 Kamloops Crescent
Leicester LE1 2HX
Tel: 0116 253 9158
Email: leicestercsf@ franciscans.org.uk

San Damiano
38 Drury Street
Metheringham
Lincs LN4 3EZ
Tel: 01526 321115
Email: metheringhamcsf@ franciscans.org.uk

The Vicarage
11 St Mary's Road
Plaistow
London E13 9AE
Tel: 020 8552 4019
Email: plaistowcsf @franciscans.org.uk

Registered Charity:
No. 286615

St Alphege Clergy House
Pocock Street
Southwark
London SE1 0BJ
Tel: 020 7928 8912
Email: southwarkcsf @franciscans.org.uk

Minister Provincial:
Email: ministercsf @franciscans.org.uk
Tel: 020 7928 7121

44-23, Suryu-gil,
Haepyeong-myeon,
Gumi-si
Gyeongsangbuk-do
730-872
REPUBLIC OF KOREA
Tel: (054) 451 2317
Email: csfkorea @gmail.com

St Francis House
3743 Cesar Chavez Street
San Francisco
CA 94110
USA
Tel: 415 824 0288

Email: csfsfo @aol.com

Website: www. communitystfrancis.org

Community History

Elizabeth CSF, *Corn of Wheat,* Becket Pubs, Oxford, 1981.
Helen Stanton, *For Peace and Good,* Canterbury Press, Norwich, *currently scheduled for 2015.*

Guest and Retreat Facilities

METHERINGHAM

In rural Lincolnshire on the edge of a peaceful village, the sisters welcome day visitors, either in the house or the comfortable hermitage in the garden. The house also has one room for a residential guest for retreat or quiet break. Two meeting rooms are available for groups of up to 8 and 24. The house is normally open to guests from Wednesday to Sunday. The sisters sometimes also welcome Working Guests who stay for a period sharing in the life and work.

SOUTHWARK

In central London the house welcomes day guests, and also has two rooms available for residential guests. Two meeting rooms accommodate groups of up to 8 and 20.

For more information please see the website, or contact the relevant house.

AMERICAN PROVINCE

The Sisters came to the United States in 1974, and for over thirty years we have engaged in many types of ministry, but with special concern for the poor, the marginalized, and the sick. We can be found in hospitals and nursing homes; among the homeless, immigrants, and people with AIDS; teaching student deacons and serving on diocesan commissions; providing spiritual direction and directing retreats in parishes. In all things we strive to be instruments of God's love.

PAMELA CLARE CSF
(Minister Provincial, assumed office June 2010)

Cecilia
Maggie
Jean
Ruth

Associates

Contact: Brother Derek SSF, Secretary for Associates, 2449 Sichel Street, Los Angeles, CA 90031-2315, USA.
Email: broderekssf@yahoo.com

Community Wares:

CSF Office Book, home retreat booklets, Franciscan prayer cards.

Community Publication
The Canticle. Contact St Francis House to subscribe - $5 for two years.

Community History
Pamela Clare CSF, 'The Early History of the First Order Brothers and Sisters of the Society of St Francis', *The Historiographer,* Vol L, No 4, (Fall 2012), The National Episcopal Historians and Archivists and The Historical Society of the Episcopal Church, Phoenx, AZ, USA.

Guest and Retreat Facilities: At the San Francisco house, there is a guest apartment, which has one bedroom (two beds) and a small kitchen. It has its own entrance. The suggested cost is $50 per night.

Most convenient time to telephone: 9.00 am - 5.00 pm, 7.45 pm - 9.00 pm.

Office Book: CSF Office Book

Bishop Protector: Rt Revd Nedi Rivera, Bishop of Eastern Oregon

---

Community of St John Baptist (UK)

CSJB

Founded 1852

Harriet Monsell House
Ripon College Cuddesdon
Oxfordshire
OX44 9EX
Tel: 01865 877100 (office)
01865 877102 (Community Room)

Email: csjbteam @csjb.co.uk

Registered Charity: No 236939

Founded by Harriet Monsell and Thomas Thelluson Carter to help women rejected by the rest of society, we are now a Community of women who seek to offer our gifts to God in various ways. These include parish and retreat work, spiritual direction, and ministry to the elderly. Two sisters are ordained to the priesthood and preside regularly at the Community and College Eucharists. One is part of the College Chaplaincy team and the other assists in local benefices. Sisters are also available to facilitate quiet days.

We have close links with the sisters of our affiliated community at Mendham, New Jersey, USA *(see separate entry);* and we also have links with the Justice and Peace Movement.

Daily life centres on the Eucharist and the Divine Office, and we live under the three vows of poverty, chastity and obedience. Following the *Rule of St Augustine*, we are encouraged to grow into 'an ever-deepening commitment of love for God and for each other as we strive to show forth the attractiveness of Christ to the world'.

In 2012, we moved to Ripon College, Cuddesdon, where we hope to contribute to the life of the community and the spiritual development of the students.

Website: www.csjb.org.uk

Community Publication
Associates' Letter, two or three times a year. Contact the magazine editor at csjbteam@csjb.org.uk for information.

Morning Prayer
7.30 am

Eucharist
8.00 am (during term)
9.30 am
(Sat and vacations)

Mid-day Office
12.30 pm

Evening Prayer
5.00 pm

Compline
8.30 pm

(all subject to variation in term time)

Office Book
Common Worship Daily Prayer,
with our own plainsong hymns and antiphons

Bishop Visitor
Bishop of Oxford

SISTER JANE OLIVE STENCIL CSJB
(Sister Co-ordinator, assumed office 3 February 2014)
Sister Monica Amy
Sister Elizabeth Jane Barrett
Sister Mary Stephen Britt
Sister Anne Proudley

Obituaries
11 Nov 2014 Sister Doreen Aldred,
aged 84, professed 54 years

Oblates & Associates
CSJB has women oblates. Men and women may become Associates or members of the Friends of Clewer - these answer to a call to prayer and service while remaining at home and work. This call includes a commitment to their own spiritual life development and to active church membership. Oblates, Associates and Friends support the Sisters by prayer and in other ways, and are likewise supported by the Community, and are part of the extended family of CSJB.

Community History
Books by Valerie Bonham, all published by CSJB:
A Joyous Service: The Clewer Sisters and their Work (1989) - revised edition 2012
A Place in Life: The House of Mercy 1849-1883 (1992)
The Sisters of the Raj: The Clewer Sisters in India (1997)

Guest and Retreat Facilities
Facilities vary according to the time of year and the needs of the student body. These should be booked through Ripon College Cuddesdon.
Most convenient time to telephone:
10 am-12.15 pm; 2.30 pm-4.30 pm, Mon to Sat.

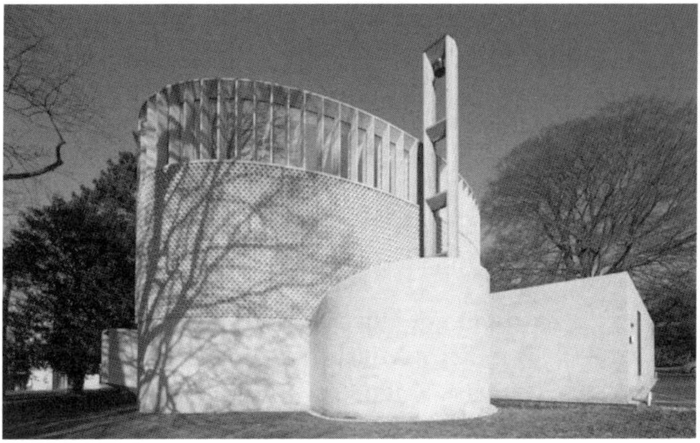

Community of St John Baptist
(USA)
CSJB

Founded 1852 (in UK)
1874 (in USA)

PO Box 240 -
82 W. Main Street
Mendham, NJ
07945
USA
Tel: 973 543 4641
Fax: 973 543 0327
Email:
csjb@csjb.org

Lauds
7.30 am

Eucharist
8.00 am

Terce
9.30 am

Noonday Office
12 noon

Vespers
5.45 pm

Compline
8.30 pm

Website
www.csjb.org

The Community of St John Baptist was founded in England in 1852. The spirit of the Community is to "prepare the way of the Lord and make straight in the desert a highway for our God." We follow the call of our patron through a life of worship, community, and service.

Our Community is made up of monastic women, who share life together under the traditional vows of poverty, chastity and obedience. Our life includes daily participation in the Eucharist and the Divine Office, prayer, and ministry to those in need. We also have married or single Oblates, who commit themselves to a Rule of life and service in the Church, and Associates, who make up the wider family of CSJB.

We live by an Augustinian Rule, which emphasizes community spirit. Those who live with us include Oblates and friends, as well as our pony, dog, and cat. Our Retreat House and guest wing are often full of persons seeking spiritual direction and sacred space. Our buildings are set in a beautiful wooded area. Our work includes spiritual direction, retreats, hospitality, youth ministry and ordained ministry (two sisters are priests). The Community participates in a mission in Africa, helps the homeless, and works in parishes.

SISTER ELEANOR FRANCIS CSJB
(Sister Superior, assumed office 14 December 2009)
SISTER BARBARA JEAN CSJB *(Novice Director)*

Sister Suzanne Elizabeth
Sister Laura Katharine
Sister Pamela
Sister Mary Lynne
Sister Margo Elizabeth
Sister Deborah Francis
Sister Linda Clare
Sister Victoria Michelle

Novices: 1

Oblates & Associates

Oblates make promises which are renewed annually. The Rule of Life includes prayer, study, service, spiritual direction, retreats. Associates keep a simple Rule. Membership is ecumenical.

Address of other house

St Mary's Mission House, 145 W. 46th Street, New York, NY 10036, USA. Tel: 212 869 5830

Office Book
Our own book based upon the Book of Common Prayer of the Episcopal Church of the USA

Community Publication
Community Notes, Michaelmas, Christmas, Easter Newsletters.

Most convenient time for guests to telephone:
between 10 am and 4.45 pm

Bishop Visitor
Rt Revd Prince Singh, Bishop of Rochester

Community History & Books

J. Simpson & E. Story, *Stars in His Crown*, Ploughshare Press, Sea Bright, NJ, 1976.

Books by Valerie Bonham, all published by CSJB:
A Joyous Service: The Clewer Sisters & their Work (2nd ed 2012)
A Place in Life: The House of Mercy 1849-1883 (1992)
The Sisters of the Raj: The Clewer Sisters in India (1997)
Living Stones: The CSJB in America (*expected publication* 2016)

P. Allan, M. Berry, D. Hiley, Pamela CSJB & E. Warrell, *An English Kyriale.*

Guest and Retreat Facilities

ST MARGUERITE'S RETREAT HOUSE

This has twenty-seven rooms. The address is the same as for the Convent but the telephone number is: 973 543 4582 There is one new room for a disabled person with disabled-access bathroom.

CONVENT GUEST WING

This has six rooms (for women only). The cost is $75.00 for an overnight stay with three meals. Closed Mon and Tue.

Community Wares

Tote bags, mugs, cards, jewelery, candles, ornaments, tapes, prayer beads.

Community of St John the Divine

CSJD

Founded 1848

Registered Charity
No. 210 254

Most people face times of transition when they are asked to let go of known securities and responded to new and challenging circumstances. As a small Community, we find ourselves in such a position, believing our stewardship of a large house is coming to an end and it is time to hand it on to others, who will have a Christian ministry

The five members of the Community have found a smaller house we hope to move to in Birmingham, so please pray for this time of waiting and preparation.

What is so important about this move? We hope to maintain a ministry welcoming people to the house for quiet days and spiritual accompaniment that will meet their need for quiet reflection. Another hope is that Sisters will have more time for reading, study, developing their own ministry and time for recreation.

All smaller Communities are facing similar situation: an opportunity for discovering how Religious life might be lived in a new way.

Sister Christine CSJD
& Sister Margaret Angela CSJD
(Leaders of the Community, assumed office April 2007)

Sister Elaine Sister Shirley
Sister Ivy

Obituaries
18 Jun 2014 Sister Teresa, aged 95, professed 65 years

Associates
Associates are men and women from all walks of life who desire to have a close link with the life and work of the Community. They make a simple Commitment to God, to the Community and to one another. Together with the Sisters, they form a network of love, prayer and service. (Guidelines available.)

Alongsiders
Alongsiders come to the Community for varying lengths of time, usually six months to one year. The aim is to provide an opportunity of sharing in the worship and life of the Community, and could be useful for a sabbatical, a time of spiritual renewal, study, to respond to a specific need, or to allow time and space to consider the way ahead. (Guidelines available.)

Community History
The brochure written for the 150th anniversary contains a short history.

Guest and Retreat Facilities
Quiet Days for individuals and groups. Facilities for residential individual private retreats. Openness to be used as a resource.

Most convenient time to telephone:
9.00 am, 2.30 pm, 6.00 pm

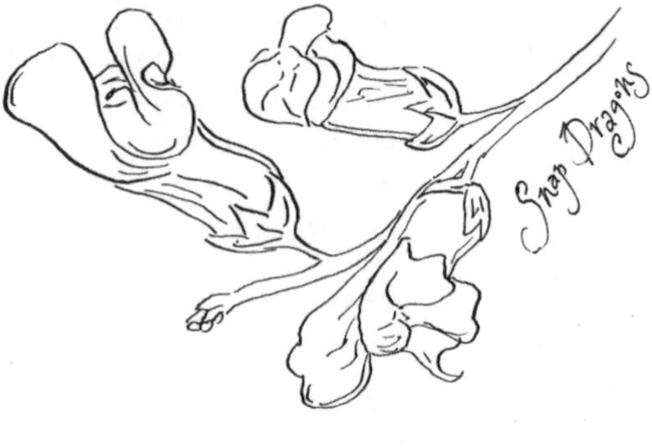

St John's House
652 Alum Rock Road
Birmingham
B8 3NS
UK

Tel: 0121 327 4174

Email: csjdivine@btconnect.com

Website
www.csjd.org.uk

Office Book
Theb Daily Office SSF (new revised edition 2010)

Community Wares:
Various hand-crafted cards for different occasions.

Community Publication
Annual report called *Making Connections*

Bishop Visitor
Rt Revd
David Urquhart,
Bishop of Birmingham

Community of St John the Evangelist

CSJE

Founded 1912

Founded in Dublin in 1912, CSJE was an attempt to establish Religious Life in the Church of Ireland, although it did not receive official recognition. The founder believed that a group of sisters living hidden lives of prayer and service would exercise a powerful influence. When he died in 1939, there were twenty-four professed sisters and six novices. From the 1930s, the Community had a branch house in Wales, which became the Mother House in 1967. In 1996, however, the Sisters returned to Dublin to the house originally taken over in 1959 from another small community. This present house was formerly a school and then a home for elderly ladies of the Church of Ireland. It is now a Registered Nursing and Residential Home under the care of the Community but run by lay people. The remaining Sisters of CSJE continue to live the Religious Life to the best of their ability and leave the future in the hands of God.

Sister Verity Anne CSJE
Sister Kathleen Brigid CSJE

St Mary's Home
Pembroke Park
Ballsbridge
Dublin 4
Irish Republic
Tel: 668 3550

Associates and Companions: Associates have a simple Rule, Companions a fuller and stricter Rule. Both groups are now much reduced in number.

Community History
A private booklet was produced for Associates in 1962.

Office Book: Hours of Prayer with the Revised Psalter.

Community of St Laurence

CSL

Founded 1874

The Community was founded in 1874. The Sisters cared for the 'Treasures' of the Church - those in need of love and care, including elderly ladies. In 2001 the Community moved to a new purpose-built convent in Southwell, adjacent to Sacrista Prebend Retreat House and the Cathedral. The Convent closed in 2012.

Sister Dorothea
Sister Margareta Mary

Associates
Associates pray regularly for the community, and include priests and lay people. We have over one hundred associates.

Registered Charity:
No. 220282

Bishop Visitor
Vacancy

Community of St Mary (Eastern Province)

CSM

An Anglican/ Episcopalian Order founded in 1865

St Mary's Convent
242 Cloister Way
Greenwich
NY 12834-7922
USA

Convent Phone:
518 692 3028
Farm Phone:
518 791 4142
Website:www.stmaryseast.org

Home of:
St Mary's Institute for Christian Studies
St Mary's on-the-Hill Cashmere
St Mary's Scriptorium

Matins 6.30 am (7.30 am Sat & Sun)

Mass 7.00 am (8.00 am Sat & Sun)

Terce 9.30 am

Sext 12 noon

Vespers 5.30 pm

Compline 7.30 pm

The Sisters of St Mary live a vowed life in community, centered on the daily Eucharist and a modified five-fold Divine Office. Each sister has time daily for private prayer and study. Our way of life is a modern expression of traditional monastic practice including silent meals in common, plainchant in English for much of our corporate worship, a distinctive habit, and a measure of enclosure.

Our ministry is an outward expression of our vowed life of poverty, chastity and obedience. The specific nature of our work has changed over the years since Mother Harriet and our first sisters were asked to take charge of the House of Mercy in New York City in 1865. Being "mindful of the needs of others," as our table blessing says, we have been led in many ways to care for the lost, forgotten and underprivileged. Today our work is primarily prayer, Benedictine hospitality, retreats, and Christian education, a micro-farm in Greenwich, NY, and care of orphans in Malawi. Sisters also go out from time to time to speak in parishes, lead quiet days and provide a praying community within the Diocese of Albany's Spiritual Life Center and the Diocese of Northern Malawi.

MOTHER MIRIAM CSM
(*Mother Superior, assumed office 31 August 1996*)
SISTER MARY JEAN CSM (*Assistant Superior*)

Sister Mary Angela
Sister Catherine Clare
Sister Mary Elizabeth
Sister Martha
Sister Monica
Sister Jane
Sister Silvia (*Junior*)

Novices: 2

Address of other house

Sisters of St Mary, St Mary's Convent, PO Box 20280, Luwinga, Mzuzu 2, MALAWI, South Central Africa

Community Publication: *St Mary's Messenger*, (print). Contact Subscription Editor, St Mary's Convent, Greenwich, NY 12834-7922. Cost to subscribers in the USA is $15, to those outside the USA $25.
ENews available at no cost via subscription to MotherMiriam@stmaryeast.org.

Guest and Retreat Facilities

Accommodations for seven in the Convent Guest wing and a further 50 accommodations on first-come, first-serve basis at adjacent Spiritual Life Center, in Greenwich, NY.

Most convenient time to telephone: 10 am - 7 pm ET.

Office Book
The Monastic Diurnal Revised, (CSM, New York, 1989): a modern English version of the *Monastic Diurnal* by Canon Winfred Douglas with supplemental texts based upon the American 1979 BCP. Copies are for sale.

Community Wares
Assorted illuminated greeting cards, cashmere yarn from the Sisters's micro-farm.

Bishop Visitor
Rt Revd William Love, Bishop of Albany

Associates
Associates of the Community of St Mary are Christian men and women, lay and clerical, who undertake a Rule of life and share in the support and fellowship of the Sisters, and of one another, whilst living dedicated and disciplined lives in the world. Any baptized, practicing Christian who feels called to share in the life and prayer of the Community of St Mary as part of our extended family is welcome to inquire about becoming an Associate. Each prospective Associate plans his or her own Rule with the advice of a Sister. An outline is provided covering one's routine participation in the Eucharist and the Divine Office, private prayer; abstinence and fasting, and charity and witness. Individual vocations and circumstances vary so widely in today's world that a 'one size fits all' Rule is no longer appropriate. The fellowship of Associates is the extended family of the Sisters and an active part of bringing the world to Christ. Contact the Mother Superior for more information.

Community History: Sister Mary Hilary CSM, *Ten Decades of Praise,* DeKoven, Racine, WI, 1965. (*out of print*).
Morgan Dix, *Harriet Starr Cannon,* Longman, NY, 1896.
Video: *The Hidden Life,* heritage videos, 2002 (58 minutes)

Community of St Mary

(Western Province)

CSM

Founded 1865

St John's -on-the-Lake
1840 N Prospect Avenue #504, Milwaukee WI 53202 USA
Tel: 414 239 7908

Email: srletitia504 @gmail.com

The Western Province of the Community of St Mary as set apart as a separate branch of the community in 1904. We share a common Rule, but have separate administration. Our basic orientation is toward a life of prayer, corporate and personal, reaching out to the Church and the world according to the leading of the Holy Spirit. We live singly or in small groups, each sister using her gifts for ministry as she feels led with the support of the whole group.

Sister Letitia Prentice CSM
(President, assumed office January 1992)
Sister Mary Grace Rom CSM

Obituaries
16 Jun 13 Sister Dorcas Baker, aged 71, professed 49 years
25 Jul 14 Sister Mary Paula Bush, aged 94, prof. 60 years

Associates
Associates (both men and women) are part of the community family. They follow a Rule of Life and assist the sisters as they are able.

Bishop Visitor
Rt Revd Steven A. Miller, Bishop of Milwaukee

Community of St Mary (Southern Province)

CSM

Founded 1865

1100 St Mary's Lane
Sewanee
TN 37375
USA
Tel: 931 598 0046
Fax: 931 598 9519
Email:
stmsis@att.net

Morning Prayer & Holy Eucharist
7.00 am
(8.00 am Holy Eucharist Sat & Sun)

Noonday Prayer
12 noon
(12.30 pm Sun)

Evening Prayer
5.00 pm

Compline 7.00 pm
(not Sat & Sun)

Office Book
BCP of ECUSA plus Plainsong Psalter, Book of Canticles

Bishop Visitor
Rt Revd John Bauerschmidt, Diocese of Tennesee

The Community of St Mary began in New York in 1865. It was the first women's monastic community founded in the United States, and now has three provinces. The Southern Province has its mother house in Sewanee, Tennessee, and a branch house in the Mountain Province, Philippines. The primary focus of our life together is prayer and worship. The sisters gather four times a day for corporate prayer. We nourish ourselves spiritually through meditation, spiritual reading, Bible study and retreats. The sisters take the three-fold vows of simplicity, chastity and obedience. We live in community and hold all things in common. We choose to live a simple life and endeavour to treat God's creation with care. Hospitality and mission are important components of our community's life.

SISTER MADELEINE MARY CSM
(Leader, assumed office 2013)

Sister Elizabeth Grace	Sister Margaret
Sister Mary Martha	Sister Mary Hope
Sister Mary Zita	Sister Ines *(Philippines)*

Obituaries

29 Aug 2014 Sister Lucy, aged 80, professed 57 years

Associates and Oblates

Associates are a fellowship of men and women who help CSM through friendship, prayer, support and by their dedicated lives in the world. Each associate writes his/her own rule of life, according to guidelines. We offer associates hospitality, retreats and spiritual companionship.

Oblates are a fellowship of men and women who pattern their lives on the monastic tradition of prayer and service. Oblates work closely with the sisters.

Other Address: St Mary the Virgin Church, St Mary's Convent, 2619 Sagada, Mountain Province, PHILIPPINES

Community wares: Photo cards, hand-painted note cards, rosaries (Anglican & Dominican).

Community publication: *The Messenger*

Community history: James Waring, *Saint Mary's, the Sewanee Sisters and their School,* Sewanee Trust, 2010

Guest and Retreat Facilities: St Dorothy's guest house. A one-bedroom unit with small kitchen and bath and a two-bedroom unit with kitchen and bath. All welcome. Contact CSM for the current fees.

Most convenient time to telephone

Mon-Sat, 9.30 am - 11.30 am, 2 pm - 5 pm

Community of St Mary the Virgin

CSMV

Founded 1848

St Mary's Convent
Wantage
Oxfordshire
OX12 9DJ
UK

OX12 9AU
(for those using sat nav)

Tel: 01235 763141
Email: guestwing @csmv.co.uk

Website:
www.csmv.co.uk

Lauds 7.00 am

Terce 8.15 am

Eucharist 10.00 am
(9.30 am Sun & feasts)

Sext 12.30 pm

Vespers 5.00 pm

Compline 8.15 pm

Office Book
CSMV publication

Registered Charity:
No 240513

As Sisters of CSMV, we are called to respond to our vocation in the spirit of Mary, Mother of Jesus: "Behold, I am the servant of the Lord. Let it be to me according to your word." Our common life is centred in the worship of God through the Eucharist, the Divine Office and in personal prayer. From this all else flows. For some, it will be expressed in ministry in neighbourhood and parish, in offering people a quiet place for reflection and in pastoral care for the elderly. For others it may be expressed in spiritual direction or in art work. A CSMV sister is making vestments with the All Saints Embroiderers who now meet at the Convent.

In February 2014, we closed our Smethwick house and are now focussing on ways of living together cooperatively in one place, at present at the Convent. This involves being open and welcoming to those who wish to stay on the Guest Wing and share something of our life. We have recognised that we need to move out of the Convent buildings in Wantage and are actively searching for a property more suited to our vision and circumstances. We hope to be engaging more directly with those living around us.

Sister Jean Frances CSMV
(Sister-in-charge, assumed office January 2013)
Sister Stella CSMV *(Deputy)*

Sister Barbara Noreen
Sister Catherine Naomi
Sister Honor Margaret
Sister Helen Philippa
Sister Valeria
Sister Phoebe Margaret
Sister Mary Jennifer
Sister Christine Ann
Sister Eileen
Sister Lorna
Sister Trudy
Sister Elizabeth Jane

Obituaries

19 Jun 2013 Sister Anna, aged 86, professed 31 years
20 Sep 2013 Sister Cecily Clare, aged 98, prof. 73 years
25 May 2014 Sister Christiana, aged 93, professed 64 years
5 Nov 2014 Sister Anne Julian, aged 88, prof. 59 years
5 May 2015 Sister Bridget Mary, aged 84, prof. 47 years

Oblates & Associates

Oblates

The Oblates of the Community respond to their vocation in the same spirit as Mary: "Here I am, the servant of the Lord. Let it be with me according to your word." Oblates may be married or single, women or men, ordained or lay. Most are Anglicans, but members of other denominations are also welcome. There is a common Rule, based on Scripture and the Rule of St Augustine, and each Oblate is encouraged to draw up a personal Rule of Life. There is a two-year period of mutual discernment by the Novice Oblate and the Oblate Council; the Promise made at Oblation with life intention is renewed annually. In addition to a close personal link with the Community, Oblates meet where possible in regional groups and gather annually for a day's summer meeting. A monthly letter and information is sent out as part of prayer and support for the Oblate Fellowship.

ASSOCIATES

Associates are those who wish to be received as 'friends' of the Community. Along with the Sisters, they too seek to live in the spirit of Mary's 'Fiat'. They live by a simple Rule of Life and undertake to pray regularly for the Community and for one another. The Associates' Link Sister acts as a bridge between the Associates and the Community, but she delegates the running of the Associates' fellowship to a Steering Group which keeps in touch with Associates by means of a quarterly newsletter, regular retreats and an annual Associates' Day held at the Convent.

Guest and Retreat Facilities

ST MARY'S CONVENT GUEST WING

The guest wing is a quiet place, enabling space and refreshment for all who come. Everyone is welcome at the Eucharist and Daily Office in St Mary Magdalene's Chapel. St Mary's Chapel is also available for private prayer and reflection. Facilities include sitting rooms, one with a library, a separate fiction library, dining room, informal quiet room, computer access and art room. There are attractive, secluded gardens and a water garden. For group retreats and group quiet days we offer a variety of rooms to accommodate most requirements. Conference facilities are also available. Those coming for individual quiet days are allocated a room, where they may rest. All other facilities are available to day guests and they are able to share in a meal in the guests' dining room if they so wish. The Community library may be available for reading on request. The Guest Wing is closed from after lunch on Sunday until Monday morning each week.

Rooms: Twenty bedrooms, including two twin rooms, one bedroom with sitting room, one small flat with en suite facilities, one ground-floor room with en suite shower for the less able. Full Board cost: £54.00 per person, per night.

Most convenient time to telephone

Contact the Guest Wing (01235 763141) 9.00 am - 7.00 pm, Mon to Sat. Answerphone outside these hours. Email: guestwing@csmv.co.uk

Community History

A Hundred Years of Blessing, SPCK, London, 1946.

Sister A. F. Norton, *A History of CSMV*, Parts I & II (1974 MA thesis) & Parts III & IV (1978 MPhil thesis), available for reading in the Convent library.

Community Wares: Books, cards, crosses and other church items.

Acting Bishop Visitor: Rt Revd Colin Fletcher, Bishop of Dorchester

Community of St Michael & All Angels

CSM&AA

Founded 1874

Serenitas Frailcare Centre
51 General Hertzog Avenue
Dan Pienaar
Bloemfontein 9301,
SOUTH AFRICA

Email: serenicare@ twiggefrailcare. co.za

The Community of St Michael and All Angels was founded by the second Bishop of Bloemfontein, Allan Becher Webb, for pioneer work in his vast diocese, which included the Orange Free State, Basutoland, Griqualand West and into the Transvaal. The sisters were active in mission, nursing and education. Sister Henrietta Stockdale became the founder of professional nursing in South Africa. The South African Synod of Bishops has placed her on the *CPSA Calendar* for yearly commemoration on 6 October. In 1874, the sisters established St Michael's School for Girls in Bloemfontein, which still exists today as one of the leading schools in South Africa. Today, one sister remains.

Sister Joan Marsh CSM&AA

Community Histories
Margaret Leith, *One the Faith,* 1971 & Mary Brewster, *One the Earnest Looking Forward,* 1991.
Booklets by Sister Mary Ruth CSM&AA: *Dust & Diamonds* (on work in Kimberley); *Cave, Cows & Contemplation* (on thirty years of work at Modderpoort Mission); *Ma'Mohau, Mother of Mercy* (on Sister Enid CSM&AA); *Medals for St Michael's* (CSM&AA in Anglo-Boer War); *Uphill all the Way* (on work in Basutoland/Lesotho)
Obtainable from St Michael's School, PO Box 12110, Brandway 9324, SOUTH AFRICA.

Bishop Visitor: Rt Revd Dintoe Letloenyane, Bishop of the Free State

Warden: Rt Revd T S Stanage, retired Bishop of Bloemfontein

Community of St Paul

CSP

Founded 1980

Maciene
MOZAMBIQUE

The Community was founded in 1980 in Maputo (Lebombo Province). The present house in Maciene was originally the branch house of the community and is where the sisters live today. They have been supported by CHN sisters from Zululand. The four sisters in life vows are all Portuguese-speaking.

Their present work includes a local ministry centred on the Cathedral, with hospitality offered through Bishop's House, support for the Sunday School and pastoral visiting.

Sister Cassilda
Sister Julieta
Sister Francina
Sister Persina

Community of St Peter

CSP

Founded 1861

St Peter's Convent
c/o St Columba's House
Maybury Hill
Woking, Surrey
GU22 8AB
UK
Tel: 01483 750739
(9.30am-5pm Mo-Th)
Fax: 01483 766208
Email:
reverendmother@ stpetersconvent. co.uk

Office Book: CCP

Community Publication:
Associates' newsletter at Petertide and Xmas; a letter sent by Reverend Mother, spring and autumn.

Community History
Elizabeth Cuthbert, *In St Peter's Shadow,* CSP, Woking, 1994

Registered Charity:
No. 240675

The Community was founded by Benjamin Lancaster, a Governor of St George's Hospital, Hyde Park, London. He wished his poorer patients to have convalescent care before returning to their homes. The Sisters also nursed cholera and TB patients, and opened orphanages and homes for children and the elderly. They were asked to go to Korea in 1892. They have close links with the Society of the Holy Cross in Korea, which was founded by the Community *(see separate entry)*. Since the closure of their Nursing/Care Home, new work is undertaken outside the Community in the way of continued care, using Sisters' abilities, talents and qualifications. The Sisters live in houses located where they can carry out their various works and ministry. They recite their fourfold daily Office either together in their houses or individually.

REVD MOTHER LUCY CLARE CSP
(Mother Superior, assumed office 29 June 2005)
(Fosbrooke House, Apartment 33, 8 Clifton Drive, Lytham, Lancashire, FY8 5RQ)

Sisters Margaret Paul, Rosamond & Georgina Ruth:
St Mary's Convent & Nursing Home, Burlington Lane, Chiswick, London W4 2QE

Sister Angela: 41 Sandy Lane, Woking, Surrey, GU22 8BA

Associates and Companions

The associates' fellowship meets at St Columba's at Petertide. The associates support the community in prayer and with practical help, as they are able. They have a simple rule and attend the Eucharist in their own Church. Companions have a stricter rule and say the Daily Office.

Guest and Retreat Facilities

Chaplain & Programme Developor: Revd Gillaine Holland
St Columba's House (Retreat & Conference Centre)
Maybury Hill, Woking, Surrey GU22 8AE, UK
Tel: 01483 713006 or 07069 067116 Fax: 01483 740441
Website: www.stcolumbashouse.org.uk

22 en-suite single bedrooms (2 with disabled facilities), 5 twin bedrooms (4 ensuite). Programme of individual and group retreats. Conference centre for residential and day use, completely refurbished in 2009 for retreatants, parish groups etc. Outstanding liturgical space with a pastoral, and liturgical programme.

Most convenient time to telephone: 9.30 am - 5.00 pm.

Bishop Visitor

Rt Revd David Walker, Bishop of Manchester

Community of St Peter, Horbury CSPH

Founded 1858

**St Peter's Convent
14 Spring End Road
Horbury
Wakefield
West Yorkshire
WF4 6DB
UK
Tel: 01924 272181**

**Email:
stpetersconvent
@virginmedia.com**

Lauds
7.30 am

Mass
8.00 am

Midday Office
12.00 noon

Vespers
6.00 pm

Compline
7.15 pm

The Community seeks to glorify God by a life of loving dedication to him, by worship and by serving him in others. A variety of pastoral work is undertaken including Quiet Days, spiritual direction and ministry to individuals in need. The spirit of the community is Benedictine and the recitation of the Divine Office central to the life.

TEAM LEADERSHIP *(assumed office 4 August 2014)*

Sister Gwynneth Mary
Sister Mary Clare *(priest)*
Sister Phyllis
Sister Jean Clare
Sister Robina
Sister Elizabeth

Sister Margaret Ann
2 Main Street, Bossall, York YO2 7NT, UK
Tel: 01904 468253

Oblates and Associates
The Community has both oblates and associates.

Guest and Retreat Facilities
There are no overnight facilities for guests.

Community Publication: Annual newsletter at Petertide

Bishop Visitor
Rt Revd Tony Robinson, Bishop of Wakefield

Community of the Servants of the Will of God

CSWG

Founded 1953

The Monastery of the Holy Trinity
Crawley Down
Crawley
West Sussex
RH10 4LH
UK

Tel: 01342 712074

Email:
(for guest bookings & enquiries)
brother.andrew@ cswg.org.uk

Vigils 5.00 am

Lauds 7.00 am

Terce 9.30 am

Sext 12.00 noon

Vespers 6.30 pm

Mass
7.00 pm Mon – Fri
11.00 am Sat & Sun

This monastery is set in woodland. The Community of men and women lives a contemplative life, uniting silence, work and prayer in a simple life style based on the *Rule of St Benedict*. The Community is especially concerned with uniting the traditions of East and West, and has developed the Liturgy, Divine Office and use of the Jesus Prayer accordingly.

FATHER COLIN CSWG
(Father Superior, assumed office 3 April 2008)
FATHER PETER CSWG *(Prior)*

Brother Martin
Sister Mary Angela *(at SSM Walsingham)*
Brother Christopher Mark
Brother John of the Cross
Brother Andrew

Postulants: 1

Associates
The associates keep a rule of life in the spirit of the monastery.

Community Publication
CSWG Journal: *Come to the Father*, issued Pentecost and All Saints. Write to the Monastery of the Holy Trinity.

Community History
Father Colin CSWG, *A History of the Community of the Servants of the Will of God,* 2002. Available from Crawley Down.

Guest and Retreat Facilities
Six individual guest rooms; meals in community refectory; Divine Office and Eucharist, all with modal chant; donations c.£20 per day.

Most convenient time to telephone: 9.30 am - 6.00 pm.

Community Wares
Mounted icon prints, Jesus Prayer ropes, candles and vigil lights, booklets on monastic and spiritual life.

Office Book
CSWG Divine Office and Liturgy

Bishop Visitor
Rt Revd John Hind

Community of the Sisters of the Church

CSC

Founded 1870

for the whole people of God

Worldwide Community Website: www. sistersofthechurch .org

ENGLAND
Registered Charity No. for CEA: 200240

CANADA
Registered Charity No. 130673262RR0001

AUSTRALIA
Tax Exempt - NPO

Founded by Emily Ayckbowm in 1870, the Community of the Sisters of the Church is an international body of lay and ordained women within the Anglican Communion. We are seeking to be faithful to the gospel values of Poverty, Chastity and Obedience, and to the traditions of Religious Life while exploring new ways of expressing them and of living community life and ministry today. By our worship, ministry and life in community, we desire to be channels of the reconciling love and acceptance of Christ, to acknowledge the dignity of every person, and to enable others to encounter the living God whom we seek.

The Community's patrons, St Michael and the Angels, point us to a life both of worship and active ministry, of mingled adoration and action. Our name, Sisters of the Church, reminds us that our particular dedication is to the mystery of the Church as the Body of Christ in the world.

The Eucharist and Divine Office (usually fourfold) are the heart of our Community life. Community houses provide different expressions of our life and ministry in inner city, suburban, coastal town and village setting.

LINDA MARY SHUTTLE CSC
(Mother Superior, assumed office July 2009)
Email: lindacsc@bigpond.com
29 Lika Drive, Kempsey, NSW 2440, AUSTRALIA

ENGLAND

SUSAN HIRD CSC
(UK Provincial, assumed office September 2008)
Email: susan@sistersofthechurch.org.uk
CATHERINE HEYBOURN CSC *(Assistant Provincial)*

Aileen Taylor	Rosina Taylor
Anita Cook	Ruth White
Annaliese Brogden	Sheila Julian Merryweather
Dorothea Roden	Sue McCarten
Hilda Mary Baumberg	Teresa Mary Wright
Jennifer Cook	Veronica Vasethe
Judith Gray	Vivien Atkinson
Mary Josephine Thomas	

Obituaries

24 Oct 2014 Ruth Morris, aged 90, professed 64 years
25 Dec 2014 Ann Mechtilde (Annie) Baldwin, aged 92, professed 64 years
16 Feb 2015 Scholastica Ferris, aged 103, prof. 78 years
8 Mar 2015 Marguerite Gillham, aged 96, prof. 66 years

Addresses in the UK

St Michael's Convent, 56 Ham Common, Richmond, Surrey TW10 7JH
Tel: 020 8940 8711 & 020 8948 2502
Email for general enquiries: info@sistersofthechurch.org.uk

82 Ashley Road, Bristol BS6 5NT Tel: 01179 413268
Email: bristol@sistersofthe church.org.uk

St Gabriel's, 27A Dial Hill Road, Clevedon, N. Somerset BS21 7HL
Tel: 01275 544471 Email: clevedon@sistersofthe church.org.uk

10 Furness Road, West Harrow, Middlesex HA2 0RL
Tel: 020 8423 3780 Email: westharrow@sistersofthe church.org.uk

112 St Andrew's Road North, St Anne's-on-Sea, Lancashire FY8 2JQ
Tel & Fax: 01253 728016

Canada

Arrived in Canada 1890. Established as a separate Province 1965.

Margaret Hayward CSC
(Provincial, assumed office 26 September 2009)
Email: margaretcsc@sympatico.ca

Heather Broadwell
Marguerite Mae Eamon
Michael Trott
Rita Dugger

Addresses in Canada

Sr Margaret Hayward CSC
(& the Community of the Sisters of the Church, c/o Sr Margaret)
Apt 1003 - 6 John St, Oakville, ON, L6K 3T1
Tel: 905 849 0225
General email: sistersofthechurch@sympatico.ca

Sr Michael Trott CSC, Apt 604 - 6 John St, Oakville, ON, L6K 3T1
Tel: 905 845 7186

Sr Marguerite Mae Eamon CSC, Unit 1110 - 1240 Marlborough Court, Oakville, ON, L6H 3K7 Tel: 905 842 5696

Sr Heather Broadwell CSC,
Unit 303 - 28 Duke St, Hamilton, ON, L8P 1X1 Tel: 289 396 6103

Australia

Arrived in Australia 1892. Established as a separate Province 1965.

Linda Mary Shuttle CSC
(Provincial, assumed office November 1999)
Email: lindacsc@bigpond.com

Audrey Floate
Elisa Helen Waterhouse
Fiona Cooper
Frances Murphy
Helen Jamieson
Rosamund Duncan

Addresses in Australia

Sisters of the Church, PO Box 1105, Glebe, NSW 2037
Email: cscaust@hotmail.com

Sisters of the Church, 29 Lika Drive, Kempsey, NSW 2440
Tel: 2 6562 2313 Fax: 2 6562 2314

Unit 15/75, St John's Road, Glebe, NSW 2037

PO Box 713, Melton, Victoria 3337 Tel: 3 9743 6028
Email: elisahelen.waterhouse@gmail.com

SOLOMON ISLANDS-PACIFIC

Arrived in Solomon Islands 1970. Established as a separate Province 2001.

KATHLEEN KAPEI CSC
(Provincial, assumed office 13 October 2013)
Email: kathleenkapei@gmail.com
EMILY MARY IKAI CSC *(Assistant Provincial)*
Email: emilymaryi@yahoo.com

Agnes Maeusia
Anneth Kagoa
Annie Meke
Beglyn Tiri
Betsy Samo
Beverlyn Aosi
Caroline Havideni
Clarine Tekeatu
Daisy Gaoka
Dexter Wilkins
Doreen Awaisi
Eleanor Ataki
Evelyn Yaiyo
Grace Papahu
Jennifer Clare
Jennifer Imua
Jessica Maru
Joan Yape
Joanna Suunorua
Kristy Arofa
Lillian Mary Manedika
Lucia Sadias
Margosa Funu
Marina Tuga
Mary Gharegha
Mary Gladys Nunga
Mary Kami
Mary Leingala
May Peleba
Patricia Kalali
Phyllis Sau
Priscilla Iolani
Rachel Teku
Rose Glenda Kimanitoro
Ruth Hope Sosoke
Vivian Marie Von Amevuvlian

Novices: 9
Postulants: 5

Obituaries

9 Apr 2014 Muriel Tisafa'a, aged 82, professed 21 years

Addresses in the Solomon Islands

Tetete ni Kolivuti, Box 510, Honiara

Patteson House, Box 510, Honiara Tel: 677 22413 & 677 27582

PO Box 7, Auki, Malaita Tel: 677 40423

St Gabriel's, c/o Hanuato'o Diocese, Kira Kira, Makira/Ulawa Province Fax: 677 50128 Mobile: 7553947

St Mary's, Luesalo, Diocese of Temotu, Santa Cruz
Mobile phone: 7440081

St Scholastica's House, PO Box 510, Honiara
Sisters of the Church, Henderson, PO Box 510, Honiara

Associates
Associates are men and women who seek to live the Gospel values of Simplicity, Chastity and Obedience within their own circumstances. Each creates his/her own Rule of Life and has a Link Sister or Link House. They are united in spirit with CSC in its life of worship and service, fostering a mutually enriching bond.

Community History
A Valiant Victorian: The Life and Times of Mother Emily Ayckbowm 1836-1900 of the Community of the Sisters of the Church, Mowbray, London, 1964.

Ann M Baldwin CSC, *Now is the Time: a brief survey of the life and times of the Community of the Sisters of the Church,* CSC, 2005.

Community Publication
Newsletter, twice a year.
Information can be obtained from any house in the community and by email.

Community Wares
Books by Sister Sheila Julian Merryweather: *Colourful Prayer*; *Colourful Advent; Colourful Lent.* All published by Kevin Mayhew, Buxhall, Stowmarket.
Some houses sell crafts and cards. Vestments are made in the Solomon Islands.

Guest and Retreat Facilities
Hospitality is offered in most houses. Ham Common and Tetete ni Kolivuti have more accommodation for residential guests as well as day facilities. Programmes are offered at Ham Common: please apply for details. Please contact individual houses for other information.

Office Book used by the Community
The Office varies in the different Provinces. Various combinations of the Community's own Office book, the New Zealand psalter, the UK *Common Worship* and the most recent prayer books of Australia, Canada and Melanesia are used.

Bishops Visitor

UK	Rt Revd Christopher Chessun, Bishop of Southwark
Australia	*awaiting appointment*
Canada	Rt Revd Michael Bird, Bishop of Niagara
Solomon Islands	Rt Revd Nathan Tome, Bishop of Guadalcanal

Address of Affiliated Community
Community of the Love of God (*Orthodox Syrian*)
Nazareth, Kadampanad South 691553, Pathanamthitta District, Kerala, INDIA
Tel: 473 4822146

Community of the Sisters of the Love of God

SLG

Founded 1906

Convent of the Incarnation
Fairacres
Parker Street
Oxford OX4 1TB
UK
Tel: 01865 721301
Fax: 01865 250798
Emails:
sisters@slg.org.uk
guests@slg.org.uk

Website:
www.slg.org.uk

Matins
6.00 am (6.15 am Sun & Solemnities)
Terce & Mass
9.05 am (no Mass Sat, ecept on major feasts)
Sext 12.15 pm
None
2.05 pm (3.05 pm Sun)
Vespers 5.30 pm
Compline 8.05 pm (7.35 pm in Winter)

Sat: unless a major feast, Office said privately until Vespers at 5.30 pm

A contemplative community with a strong monastic tradition founded in 1906, which seeks to witness to the priority of God and to respond to the love of God - God's love for us and our love for God. We believe that we are called to live a substantial degree of withdrawal, in order to give ourselves to the work of prayer which, beginning and ending in the praise and worship of God, is essential for the peace and well-being of the world. Through offering our lives to God within the Community, and through prayer and daily life together, we seek to deepen our relationship with Jesus Christ and one another. The Community has always drawn upon the spirituality of Carmel; life and prayer in silence and solitude is an important dimension in our vocation. The Community also draws from other traditions and the Divine Office and Eucharist are central to our life.

SISTER CLARE-LOUISE SLG
(Revd Mother, elected 27 May 2015)
SISTER AVIS MARY SLG *(Prioress)*

Sister Mary Margaret
Sister Benedicta
Sister Isabel
Sister Adrian
Sister Anne
Sister Jane Frances
Sister Mary Kathleen
Sister Barbara June
Sister Susan
Sister Edmée
Sister Christine
Sister Rosemary
Sister Helen Columba
Sister Catherine
Sister Julie
Sister Shirley Clare
Sister Alison
Sister Tessa
Sister Margaret Theresa
Sister Raphael
Sister Stephanie Thérèse
Sister Freda
Sister Judith *(Novice Guardian)*
Sister Eve
Sister Elizabeth
Sister Helen

Obituaries

6 Dec 2013 Sister Mary Magdalene, aged 101, professed 67 years
16 Mar 2014 Sister Edwina, aged 95, professed 46 years

Oblates and associates

The Community includes Oblate Sisters, who are called to the contemplative life in the world rather than within the monastic enclosure. There are three other groups of associates: Priest Associates, Companions, and the Fellowship of the Love of God. Information about all these may be obtained from the Revd Mother at Fairacres.

Community Publication: *Fairacres Chronicle.*
Published twice a year by SLG Press (see under Community Wares).

Community Wares
SLG Press publishes the *Fairacres Chronicle* and a range of books and pamphlets on prayer and spirituality. Contact details:
The Editor, SLG Press, Convent of the Incarnation, Fairacres, Parker Street, Oxford OX4 1TB, UK
Tel: 01865 241874 Fax: 01865 241889
Best to telephone: Mon-Fri 10.00 am - 2.45 pm. A message can be left if there is no-one currently in the office.
Email: General matters: editor@slgpress.co.uk
Orders only: orders@slgpress.co.uk Website: www.slgpress.co.uk

Guest and Retreat Facilities
There is limited accommodation for private retreats, for both men and women, at Fairacres. Please write to or email the Guest Sister to make a booking.
Email: guests@slg.org.uk Tel (for guest sister): 01865 258152 (with voicemail)

Most convenient time to telephone:
10.30 am - 12 noon; 3.30 pm - 4.30 pm; 6.00 pm - 7.00 pm
Sunday and Friday afternoons, and Saturdays, are ordinarily covered by an answer phone, but messages are cleared after Vespers.

Office Book: SLG Office

Bishop Visitor: Rt Revd Michael Lewis, Bishop of Cyprus & the Gulf

Registered Charity: No. 261722
SLG Charitable Trust Ltd: registered in England 990049

Community of the Sisters of Melanesia

CSM

Founded 1980

KNT/Headquarter
Verana'aso
PO Box 19
Honiara
SOLOMON ISLANDS

First Office, Mattins & Mass 5.45 am

Morning Office 7.45 am

Mid-day Office & Intercession 11.55 am

Afternoon Office 1.30 pm

Evensong & Meditation 5.30 pm

Compline 8.45 pm

Office Book
CSM Office Book (adapted from MBH Office book)

The community of the Sisters of Melanesia is a sisterhood of women in Melanesia. It was founded by Nester Tiboe and three young women of Melanesia on 17 November 1980. Nester believed that a Religious community of women in Melanesia was needed for the work of evangelism and mission, similar to the work of the Melanesian Brotherhood, founded by Brother Ini Kopuria.

On 17 November 1980, the four young women made their promises of Poverty, Celibacy, and Obedience to serve in the community. The ceremony took place at St Hilda's Day at Bunana Island and officiated by the Most Reverend Norman Kitchener Palmer, the second Archbishop of the Province of Melanesia.

The community aims to offer young women in Melanesia an opportunity of training for ministry and mission, so that they may serve Christ in the church and society where they live. To provide pastoral care for women and teenage children and uphold the Christian principles of family life. To be in partnership with the Melanesian Brotherhood and other Religious communities by proclaiming the Gospel of Jesus Christ in urban and rural areas in the islands. To give God the honour and glory, and to extend His Kingdom in the world.

Professed. c. 50, Noviciate c. 40

Addresses of other houses in the Solomon Islands
Joe Wate Household, Longa Bay, Waihi Parish, Southern Region, Malaita
Marau Missionary Household, Guadalcanal
NAT Household, Mbokoniseu, Vutu, Ghaobata Parish, East Honiara, Guadalcanal
Sir Ellison L. Pogo Household, Honiara

Community Wares
Vestments, altar linen, weaving and crafts.

Associates: The supporters of the Community of the Sisters of Melanesia are called Associates, a group established in 1990. It is an organization for men and women, young and old, and has over one thousand members, including many young boys and girls. All promise to uphold the Sisters in prayer, and they are a great support in many ways. The Associates of the Community of the Sisters of Melanesia are in the Solomon Islands, Australia and Canada.

Bishop Visitor
Most Revd David Vunagi, Archbishop of Melanesia

Community of the Transfiguratio n

CT

Founded 1898

495 Albion Avenue
Cincinnati
Ohio 45246
USA
Tel: 513 771 5291
Fax: 513 771 0839
Email:
ctsisters@aol.com

Website www.ctsisters.org

Lauds
7.00 am (Sun 6.45am)

Morning Prayer
7.20am (Sun 7.05am)

Holy Eucharist
7.30 am

Noon Office
12.35 pm
(Sat Intercessions 12.25pm)

Evensong
5.00 pm

Compline
8.00 pm (Sun 7.30pm)

Office Book
CT Office Book

The Community of the Transfiguration, founded in 1898 by Eva Lee Matthews, is a Religious community of women dedicated to the mystery of the Transfiguration. Our life is one of prayer and service, reflecting the spirit of Mary and Martha, shown forth in spiritual, educational and social ministries. The Mother House of the community is located in Cincinnati, Ohio, where our ministries include a retreat and spirituality center, a school and a recreation center. The community also offers a retreat ministry on the West Coast; and in the Dominican Republic, the Sisters minister to malnourished children and their families through medical clinics and a school. The Sisters live their life under the vows of poverty, chastity and obedience. The motto of the community is Benignitas, Simplicitas and Hilaritas - Kindness, Simplicity and Joy.

SISTER TERESA MARIE CT
(Mother Superior, assumed office 24 June 2008)
SISTER MARCIA FRANCIS CT *(Assistant Superior)*

Sister Joan Michael
Sister Monica Mary
Sister Hilary Mary
Sister Priscilla Jean
Sister Mary Elizabeth
Sister Ann Margaret
Sister Jacqueline Marie
Sister Johanna Laura
Sister Jean Gabriel
Sister Rachel Margaret
Sister Nadine Elizabeth
Sister Eleanor Grace
Sister Hope Mary
Sister Diana Dorothea
Sister Lynn Julian
Sister Marian Therese

Obituaries

10 Apr 2014 Sister Althea Augustine, aged 89, professed 59 years
6 Jun 2014 Sister Mary Evelyne, aged 93, professed 53 years
27 Dec 2014 Sister Alice Lorraine, aged 87, professed 54 years, Mother Superior 1993-97

Associates & Oblates

The Community has Associates and Oblates.

Guest and Retreat Facilities

Transfiguration Spirituality Center: 40 beds
Various guest houses and rooms: 16 beds.

Bishop Visitor: Rt Revd Christopher Epting

Other addresses

Transfiguration Spirituality Center, 469 Albion Avenue, Cincinnati, Ohio 45246, USA Website: tscretreats.org

Bethany School, 555 Albion Avenue, Cincinnati, Ohio 45246, USA
Website: www.bethanyschool.org

Sisters of the Transfiguration, 1633 "D" Street, Eureka, California 95501, USA

St Monica's Recreation Center, 10022 Chester Road, Cincinnati, Ohio 45215, USA

Dominican Republic Ministry:
Sister Jean Gabriel CT, DMG # 13174 *or*
Sister Priscilla Jean CT, DMG # 19105
Agape Flights, 100 Airport Avenue, Venice, Florida 34285, USA

Community Publication: *The Quarterly*

Community history and books

Mrs Harlan Cleveland, *Mother Eva Mary CT: The story of a foundation,* Morehouse, Milwaukee, WI, 1929.

Sibyl Harton, *Windfall of Light: a study of the Vocation of Mother Eva Mary CT*, Roessler, Cincinnati, OH, 1968.

Sister Monica Mary Heyes CT, *Women of Devotion*, Orange Frazer Press, Cincinnati, OH, 2014.

Congrégation des Compagnons de Saint Benoît (Congregation of the Companions of Saint Benedict)

CCSB

Founded 2007

The Congregation of the Companions of St Benedict is an Anglican Religious order comprising priests, lay brothers and sisters faithful to Anglican doctrine and morals.

Its main branch is situated at St Scholastica's Priory, Yaoundé, Cameroon. A women's branch could be joined to it to form a spiritual family according to the norms of the Anglican Church.

The Congregation, Benedictine in its spirituality, has a double aim: the worship of God according to the *Book of Common Prayer* (ECUSA); and the care of abandoned children to ensure their educational, professional and familial integration.

Its members lead a semi-contemplative life based on the three vows of poverty, chastity and obedience. Concerning its commitment to social justice, the Congregation intends to found in the near future a reception centre to house at least 50 children.

Bishop Visitor: Mgr Thomas Dibo Elango,
Bishop of the Anglican Diocese of Cameroon

Prieuré Sainte Scholastique
BP 20629, Yaoundé, CAMEROON

Email: sanctibenedictifratres@rocketmail.com

Matins 6.00 am
Holy Mass 7.00 am
Angelus & Rosary 2pm
Vespers 7.00 pm
Exposition 8.00 pm
Compline 9.00 pm

BROTHER EMMANUEL OBA'A CCSB
(Prior-General, assumed office 11 July 2007)
REVD BROTHER FRANÇOIS MBOZO'O CCSB *(Sub-prior)*

Brother Benoît Essaga Ndjana
Brother Calvin Bayiga
Brother Jean Flore Zeh
Brother Jean Zoa
Brother Magloire Bessala
Brother Max Ngamao
Brother Robert Meva'a

Novices: 3
Postulants: 5

Fikambanan'ny Mpanompovavin I Jesoa Kristy

(Society of the Servants of Jesus Christ)

FMJK

Founded 1985

The FMJK sisters were founded by Canon Hall Speers in 1985. They live in the village of Tsinjohasina, on the high plateau above the rice fields, situated some fifteen kilometres from Antananarivo, the capital of Madagascar. The sisters work in the village dispensary and are active in visiting, Christian teaching and pastoral work in the villages around. They are an independent community but have been nurtured by a connection with CSMV, Wantage, in the UK.

Convent Hasina, BP 28
Ambohidratrimo 105
Antananarivo 101
MADAGASCAR

Bishop Visitor
Most Revd Ranarivello Samoelajaona, Archbishop of the Indian Ocean

SISTER JACQUELINE FMJK
(Masera Tonia, assumed office 5 June 2002)
SISTER CHAPITRE FMJK *(Prioress)*

Sister Ernestine
Sister Georgette
Sister Isabelle
Sister Odette
Sister Voahangy
Sister Vololona
Sister Fanja

Novices: 1
Postulants: 1

Community Wares: Crafts and embroidery.

Office Book: FMJK Office and Prayer Book

Other house:
Antaralava, Soamanandray, BP 28, Ambohidratrimo 105, Antananarivo 101, MADAGASCAR

Little Brothers of Francis

LBF

Founded 1987

Franciscan Hermitage
"Eremophilia"
PO Box 162
Tabulam
NSW 2469
AUSTRALIA

Website: www.franciscanhermitage.org

Brothers have times of Solitude in their hermitage, which vary from a day to weeks or months, where they have their own personal rhythm of prayer and manual work.

Office Book
LBF Office book, developed to provide for our needs as a Franciscan Hermitage

Bishop Protector
Rt Revd
Godfrey Fryar

We are a community of Brothers who desire to deepen our relationship with God through prayer, manual work, community, and times of being alone in our hermitages. We follow the Rule written by Saint Francis for Hermitages in which three or four brothers live in each fraternity. As others join us we envisage a federation of fraternities with three or four brothers in each. There are several sources of inspiration for the Little Brothers of Francis. They are:

The Gospels
The four Gospels (Matthew, Mark, Luke and John) are central to our spirituality, and the main source material for our meditation and prayer life.

St Francis
Francis would recall Christ's words and life through persistent meditation on the Gospels, for his deep desire was to love Christ and live a Christ-centred life. He was a man of prayer and mystic who sought places of solitude, and hermitages played a central role in his life. Significant events, like the initiation of the Christmas Crib tradition, happened at the hermitage at Greccio, and, of course, he received the stigmata while he was at the hermitage at Mount La Verna.

Though the early brothers embraced a mixed life of prayer and ministry, Francis wanted places of seclusion - hermitages, for the primacy of prayer, in which three or four brothers lived, and for which he wrote a rule.

St Francis's Rule for Hermitages
In his brief rule for life within the hermitage, Francis avoided a detailed document and set out the principles that are important. Liturgy of the Hours is the focus, and sets the rhythm of the daily prayer. Each hermitage was to have at the most four Brothers, which meant they would be both 'little' and 'fraternal'. Within this framework, Brothers could withdraw for periods of solitude. The hermitages were not to be places or centres of ministry.

Desert Fathers
The stories and sayings of the Desert Fathers contain a profound wisdom for any who are serious about the inner spiritual journey. This is why they have held such prominence in monastic circles in both East and West down through the centuries, and why they are a priority source for us.

The Land
A strong connectedness to a spiritual and physical

Vigil Office
followed by
Lectio Divina
(private)
2.00 am or 4.00 am

Meditation
6.00 am

Angelus and Mattins
7.00 am

Terce
9.00 am

Angelus and Sext
12 noon

None (private)
3.00 pm

Vespers
6.00 pm

Compline
8.00 pm

home has always been a part of our charism, not unlike St Francis' love for his 'Portiuncula' or Little Portion. In shaping and building our hermitage over the years our environment has shaped and formed us. Droughts, bushfires, floods and bountiful years have brought us into a real and living relationship with the land in this place.

Brother Howard LBF
Brother Wayne LBF
Brother Geoffrey Adam LBF

Friends
Friends are individuals, or self-organized groups, who value the contemplative life as lived by the Brothers and support them in various ways.
Contact person for Australia:
Father Dennis Claughton Email: parish@ang.org.au
Contact person for New Zealand:
Ian Lothian Email: ianlothian@xtra.com.nz

Community Publication: The *Bush Telegraph.*
Contact the Brothers for a subscription, which is by donation.

Community Wares: Hand-carved holding crosses, jam, marmalade, cards and honey.

Guest and Retreat Facilities: There is a guest hermitage for one person. A fee of $60 per night is negotiable.

The Melanesian Brotherhood

MBH

Founded 1925

Email: mbhches @solomon.com.sb

SOLOMON ISLANDS REGION
The Motherhouse of the Melanesian Brotherhood
Tabalia
PO Box 1479
Honiara
SOLOMON ISLANDS
TEL: +677 26355
FAX: +677 23079

PAPUA NEW GUINEA REGION
Dobuduru Regional Headquarters
Haruro
PO Box 29
Popondetta
Oro Province
PAPUA NEW GUINEA

SOUTHERN REGION
Tumsisiro Regional Headquarters
PO Box 05
Lolowai, Ambae
VANUATU

The Melanesian Brotherhood was founded by Ini Kopuria, a native Solomon Islander from Guadalcanal, in 1925. Its main purpose was evangelistic, to take and live the Gospel in the most remote islands and villages throughout the Solomon Islands, among people who had not heard the message of Christ. The Brotherhood's method is to live as brothers to the people, respecting their traditions and customs: planting, harvesting, fishing, house building, eating and sharing with the people in all these things. Kopuria believed that Solomon Islanders should be converted in a Melanesian way.

Today, the work of the Brotherhood has broadened to include work and mission among both Christians and non-Christians. The Melanesian Brotherhood now has three Regions in the Pacific: Solomon Islands (includes Brothers in the Philippines and Vancouver); Papua New Guinea; and Southern (Vanuatu, New Caledonia & the Diocese of Polynesia). There is a Region for Companions and any Brothers in Europe.

Following an ethnic conflict in the Solomon Islands 1998-2003, the Melanesian Brotherhood have been increasingly called upon as peace makers and reconcilers, work for which they were awarded the United Nations Pacific Peace Prize in 2004.

The Brotherhood has also led missions in New Zealand, Australia, Philippines and UK; their missionary approach includes music, dance and a powerful use of drama. There was a further mission in the UK in 2013 conducted with members of four Anglican Religious communities in Melanesia, entitled the Simply Living Mission. The Brothers and Sisters visited seven dioceses in England.

The Brotherhood aims to live the Gospel in a direct and simple way following Christ's example of prayer, mission and service. The Brothers take the vows of poverty, chastity and obedience, but these are not life vows but for a period of three years, which can be renewed. They train for four years as novices and normally make their vows as Brothers at the Feast of St Simon and St Jude. Most of the Brothers are laymen but a few are ordained.

THE MOST REVD DAVID VUNAGI,
ARCHBISHOP OF MELANESIA *(Father of the Brotherhood)*

(Head Brother, election pending 24 October 2015)

Timetable of the Main House

First Office and Mattins
5.50 am
(6.20 am Sun & holidays)

Holy Communion
6.15 am
(7.15 am Sun & holidays)

Morning Office
8.00 am

Midday Office
12 noon
(Angelus on Sun & holidays)

Afternoon Office
1.30 pm
(not Sun & holidays)

Evensong 5.30 pm
(6.00 pm Sun & holidays)

Last Office 9.00 pm

Office Book
Offices and Prayers of the Melanesian Brotherhood 1996 (not for public sale)

Website:
www.orders.anglican.org/mbh

SOLOMON ISLANDS REGION
THE MOST REVD DAVID VUNAGI,
ARCHBISHOP OF MELANESIA *(Regional Father)*
BROTHER EZEKIEL TEMA MBH *(Regional Head Brother)*
Mr Alphonse Garimae *(Brotherhood Secretary)*
Brother Eddie Labaki MBH *(Regional Secretary)*
Brother Nathan Kusa MBH *(Companions Chief Secretary)*
Revd Jeffrey Akoai MBH *(Mission Coordinator)*
Brother Nelson Bako MBH *(Chief Tutor)*

SOUTHERN REGION
THE RT REVD JAMES LIGO,
BISHOP OF VANUATU & NEW CALEDONIA
(Regional Father)
BROTHER NATHANIEL TAGOA MBH
(Regional Head Brother)
To be appointed (Regional Secretary)
To be appointed (Regional Companions Secretary)

PAPUA NEW GUINEA REGION
THE MOST REVD CLYDE MERVIN IGARA,
ARCHBISHOP OF PNG
(Regional Father)
BROTHER JOHNSON INGAMAVU MBH
(Regional Head Brother)
Brother Kelliot Betu MBH *(Regional Secretary)*
To be appointed (Regional Companions Secretary)

EUROPE REGION *(for Companions)*
THE RT REVD DR ROWAN WILLIAMS, LORD WILLIAMS OF OYSTERMOUTH, *former Archbishop of Canterbury*
(Regional Father)

Professed Brothers: 282
(Solomon Islands: 148; PNG: 80: Southern Region: 49: Palawan: 4; Canada: 1)
Novices: 171
(Solomon Islands: 102; PNG: 12: Southern Region: 53; Palawan: 4)

Obituaries

30 Oct 2014 Brother Thomas Dakatia MBH, years of service 2004-2014

6 Nov 2014 Brother Jackson Lodo *novice* MBH, years of service 2011-2014

SOLOMON ISLANDS REGION

The Solomon Islands Region is divided into Sections according to each Diocese. Each Section has its own Section Father.

CENTRAL MELANESIA DIOCESAN SECTION

Section Father: The Most Revd David Vunagi, Archbishop of Melanesia
Address for all SI houses in this Section:

PO Box 1479, Honiara, Guadacanal, SOLOMON ISLANDS

BROTHER MICHAEL BOSAWAI MBH *(Section Elder Brother)*
BROTHER HARRY RAYNALD MBH *(Elder Brother)*
Central Headquarters, Tabalia
BROTHER GABRIEL GWALI MBH *(Brother in charge)*
St Barnabas Cathedral Working Household, Honiara Tel: 24609 Fax: 23079
BROTHER THOMAS HUBRA MBH *(Brother in charge)*
Bishopsdale Working Household, Honiara Tel: 27695 Fax: 23079
BROTHER SCARLET SIAMA MBH *(Brother in charge)*
Chester Rest House Tel: 26355 Fax: 23079 Email: mbhches@solomon.sb.com
BROTHER ANDREW VAKA MBH *(Brother in charge)*
Working Household, Bellona Island

PALAWAN MISSION DISTRICT, PHILIPPINES

BROTHER SIMON PETER MBH *(Brother in charge)*
Iglesia Philipina Independiente (I.F.I.), De los Reyos Road 2, 5300 Puerto Princesa City, 5300 Palawan, PHILIPPINES

CENTRAL SOLOMONS DIOCESAN SECTION

Section Father: The Rt Revd Ben Seka, Bishop of Central Solomons
BROTHER SAMSON LABE MBH *(Section Elder Brother)*
BROTHER BELSHAZAR MEIPA MBH *(Elder Brother)*

Thomas Peo Section Headquarters,
c/o Central Solomons Diocesan Office, PO Box 52, Tulagi, Central Province

BROTHER BERNARD WALAKUKU MBH *(Brother in charge)*
Nathaniel Sado Working Household, Savo Island
BROTHER WINSTON HEKE MBH *(Brother in charge)*
Lango Working Household, Small Ngella Island

GUADALCANAL DIOCESE SECTION

Section Father: The Rt Revd Nathan Tome, Bishop of Guadalcanal
Address for other houses in this section:

c/o Central Headquarters, Tabalia, PO Box 1479, Honiara

BROTHER JOHN MEWIR MBH *(Elder Brother)*
Ini Kopuria Household, Kolina, Guadalcanal
BROTHER BELSHAZZA PAERE MBH *(Elder Brother)*
Olimauri Household, Mbambanakira, Guadalcanal
BROTHER JOHN MANE MBH *(Elder Brother)*
Calvary Household, Surapau, Guadalcanal
BROTHER PAUL TANAKA MBH *(Brother in charge)*
Selwyn Rapu Working Household, Guadalcanal

MALAITA DIOCESAN SECTION

Section Father: The Rt Revd Samuel Sahu, Bishop of Malaita
Assistant Section Father: The Rt Revd Alfred Hou, Assistant Bishop of Malaita
Address for houses in this Section:
c/o Malaita Diocesan Office, PO Box 7, Auki, Malaita Province

BROTHER ROBERT BEREOKA MBH *(Elder Brother)*
BROTHER REVIDENCE PUA MBH *(Elder Brother)*
Airahu Section Headquarters
BROTHER JACK ALICK MBH *(Brother in charge)*
Kokom Working Household, Auki
BROTHER JOHN MANWARING MBH *(Elder Brother)*
Apalolo Household, South Malaita

YSABEL DIOCESAN SECTION

Section Father: The Rt Revd Richard Naramana, Bishop of Ysabel
Address for houses in this section:
c/o Ysabel Diocesan Office, PO Box 6, Buala, Isabel Province

BROTHER SELWYN MANO MBH *(Section Elder Brother)*
BROTHER JEFFERY HAGAMARIA MBH *(Elder Brother)*
Welchman Section Headquarters, Sosoilo
BROTHER BEN ARIEL MBH *(Elder Brother)*
Poropeta Household, Kia
BROTHER NICHOLAS HOU MBH *(Brother in charge)*
Alfred Hill Working Household, Jejevo
BROTHER EDMOND GEREA MBH *(Brother in charge)*
John Pihavaka Household, Gizo
BROTHER CARLBET MOANA MBH *(Elder Brother)*
Noro Working Household, New Georgia Island

HANUATO'O DIOCESAN SECTION

Section Father: The Rt Revd Alfred Karibongi, Bishop of Hanuato'o
Address for houses in this section:
c/o Hanuato'o Diocesan Office, Kirakira, Makira Province

BROTHER STEVEN ODO MBH *(Section Elder Brother)*
BROTHER CLEMENT BUBE MBH *(Elder Brother)*
Fox Section Headquarters, Poronaohe, Makira
BROTHER BARNABAS MAMATA MBH *(Elder Brother)*
Simon Sigai Household, Makira
BROTHER JAMES TATAHI MBH *(Brother in charge)*
Mumunioa Working Household, Makira
BROTHER DON SMITH MBH *(Brother in charge)*
John Hubert Waene Working Household, Makira

TEMOTU DIOCESAN SECTION

Section Father: The Rt Revd George Takeli, Bishop of Temotu
Address for houses in this section:
c/o Temotu Diocesan Office, Lata, Temotu Province

BROTHER NICKSON VAHI MBH *(Section Elder Brother)*
BROTHER LAZARUS VAVHA MBH *(Elder Brother)*
Makio Section Headquarters, Santa Cruz Island
BROTHER PAUL HAPU MBH *(Brother in charge)*
Utupua Working Household, Utupua
BROTHER DAVID WAGIRO MBH *(Brother in charge)*
Lata Working Household, Santa Cruz Island

SOUTHERN REGION

VANUATU SECTION

Section Father: The Rt Revd James Ligo, Bishop of Vanuatu & New Caledonia
Tumsisiro Regional Headquarters, Ambae
Saratabulu Household, West Ambae
Hinge Household, Lorevilko, East Santo
Suriau Household, Big Bay, Santo Bush
Caulton Weris Working Household
Patterson Household, Port Vila

BANKS & TORRES SECTION

Section Father: The Rt Revd Patteson Alfred Worek, Bishop of Banks & Torres
Lency Section Headquarters, Vanua Lava Island
Towia Working Household

PAPUA NEW GUINEA REGION

POPONDOTA SECTION

Section Father: The Rt Revd Lindsley Ihove, Bishop of Popondetta
Dobuduru Regional Headquarters, Popondetta
Gorari Household; Nedewari Household; Domara Household

PORT MORESBY SECTION

Section Father: The Rt Revd Peter Ramsden, Bishop of Port Moresby
ATS Section Headquarters, Oro Village
Pivo Household; Moro Guina

DOGURA SECTION

Section Father: The Rt Revd Tennyson Bogar, Bishop of Dogura

Sirisiri Section Headquarters
Pumani Household; Podagha Project Household; Tabai Isu Working Household

AIPO RONGO SECTION

Section Father: The Rt Revd Nathan Ingen, Bishop of Aipo Rongo
Aiome Section Headquarters
Kumburub Household; Kuiyama Household; Saniap Working Household

NEW GUINEA ISLANDS SECTION

Section Father: The Rt Revd Allan Migi, Bishop of New Guinea Islands
Hosea Sakira Section Headquarters
Aseke Household; Saksak Household

Companions

The Melanesian Brotherhood is supported both in prayer, in their work and materially by the Companions of the Melanesian Brotherhood (C.O.M.B.). They have their own Handbook with both Pacific and Europe versions.

For more information about becoming a Companion, please contact:
Mrs Barbara Molyneux, 11 Milton Crescent, Heswall, Merseyside, CH60 5SS, UK
Tel: (0)151 342 6327 Email: bjmolyneux@hotmail.com

or Companions Chief Secretary, PO Box 1479, Honiara, Solomon Islands
or at the same address: Mr Alphonse Garimae, Secretary to the Brotherhood,
Tel: +677 26377 (8 am - 4 pm) Email: agarimae@yahoo.com

Alongside Companions, the Brotherhood also has associates whose ministry is more closely associated with the community, except that they do not take the threefold vow. They work voluntarily without wages just like the brothers.

Community Publications

Companions' Newsletter for the Europe Region (once a year)
- contact Mrs Barbara Molyneux, address under 'Companions' below.

Community History and other books

Brian Macdonald-Milne, *The True Way of Service: The Pacific Story of the Melanesian Brotherhood, 1925-2000,* Christians Aware, Leicester, 2003.

Richard Carter, *In Search of the Lost: the death and life of seven peacemakers of the Melanesian Brotherhood*, Canterbury Press, Norwich, 2006.

Charles Montgomery, *The Shark God: Encounters with myth and magic in the South Pacific,* Fourth Estate/Harper Collins, London, 2006.

Guest and Retreat Facilities

The Community offers hospitality ministry through Chester Rest House in Honiara, Solomon Islands. Two Brothers are mandated to welcome guests and offer a Christian welcome to any person who may want accommodation in their Rest House. This Rest House was funded by Chester Diocese in UK. It is an alcohol-free environment and every guest is ensured to be safe and enjoy the environment. It has 8 twin-bedded rooms, self-catering at £30 per room per night, and 8 self-contained single rooms, self-catering at £75 per room per night. A conference room to accommodate 10-15 people is also available at £10 per day, self-catering. Contacts for advance bookings can be made through email: mbhches@solomon.com.sb or telephone +677 26355.

All the Brotherhood's Headquarters and Section Headquarters can provide simple accommodation for visitors. Retreats can be made by prior arrangement with the relevant Chaplain at Central, Regional or Section headquarters. Tabalia Headquarters has a guest house with eight twin-bedded rooms, self-catering, no cost but a contribution is much appreciated. Meetings, workshops and Retreats can be made by prior arrangement with the Section Elder Brother/Elder Brother at Tabalia.

Women are not allowed to enter the Brotherhood square (St Simon & Jude), which usually is outside the chapel of every Brotherhood station (not in Honiara). Women are not allowed to enter Brothers' dormitories.

Order of the Holy Cross

OHC

Founded 1884

Holy Cross Monastery
PO Box 99
(1615 Rt. 9W)
West Park
NY 12493
USA
Tel: 845 384 6660
Fax: 845 384 6031

Email: **ohcsuperior@gmail.com**

Website: www.holycrossmonastery.com

Mattins 7.00 am

Holy Eucharist 9.00 am

Midday Prayer 12 noon

Vespers 5.00 pm

Compline 8.10 pm

Mondays are observed as a sabbath day on which there are no scheduled liturgies.

The Order of the Holy Cross is a Benedictine monastic community open to both lay and ordained. The principles governing the Order's life are those of *The Rule of St Benedict* and *The Rule of the Order of the Holy Cross*, written by its founder James Otis Sargent Huntington.

The liturgical life of each house centers around the corporate praying of the Divine Office and the celebration of the Holy Eucharist. Members are also expected to spend time in private prayer and meditation.

The work of the Order is varied, depending on the nature of the household and the gifts and talents of its members. Houses range from traditional monastic centers with active retreat ministries to an urban house from which brothers go forth to minister. Four brothers live independently as Monks Not In Residence.

Members are engaged in preaching, teaching, counselling, retreat conducting, spiritual direction, parish and diocesan support work, evangelism, hospice care, and ministry with the homeless. The South African community administers educational and scholarship programs for local children and operates a primary school.

Other Addresses

Mount Calvary Monastery and Retreat House, PO Box 1296, Santa Barbara, CA 93102, USA
Tel: 805 682 4117
Website: www.mount-calvary.org

Holy Cross Priory, 204 High Park Avenue, Toronto, Ontario M6P 2S6, CANADA
Tel: 416 767 9081 **Fax: 416 767 4692**
Website: www.ohc-canada.org

Mariya uMama weThemba Monastery, PO Box 6013, Grahamstown 6141, SOUTH AFRICA
Tel: 46 622 8111 **Fax: 46 622 6424**
Website: www.umaria.co.za

Community Publications

The following are three times a year (cost by donation):
Mundi Medicina (West Park, NY);
Uxolo (Grahamstown, South Africa);
Mount Calvary Monastery (Santa Barbara, CA);
Holy Cross Priory (Toronto, Ontario)

Office Book

A Monastic Breviary (OHC) or Lauds and Vespers (Camaldolese Monks OSB).

ROBERT LEO SEVENSKY OHC
(*Superior, assumed office 2008*)
SCOTT WESLEY BORDEN OHC (*Assistant Superior*)

Thomas Schultz
Christian George Swayne
Laurence Harms
Samuel DeMerell
Rafael Campbell-Dixon
Bede Thomas Mudge
Ronald Haynes
Brian Youngward
Roy Parker
Adrian Gill
David Bryan Hoopes
Adam McCoy
Carl Sword
William Brown
Timothy Jolley
James Robert Hagler
Robert Michale Pierson
Leonard Abbah
Reginald-Martin Crenshaw
Richard Paul Vaggione
Lary Pearce
John Forbis
Bernard Jean Delcourt
James Randall Greve
Daniel Ludik
Robert Magliula
James Michael Dowd
Roger Stewart
José Folgueira
Peter James Rostron

Novices: 3

Obituaries

27 Sep 2014	Nicholas Radlemiller, age 74, professed 41 years
6 May 2015	Andrew Colquhoun, aged 77, professed 23 years

Associates: The Associates of Holy Cross are men and women of many different Christian traditions affliated to the Order through a Rule of Life and annual retreats and reports.

Guest and Retreat Facilities
WEST PARK: 39 rooms at US$75 per night ($95 weekends). Accommodations for couples and individuals. Closed Mondays.
SANTA BARBARA: 24 beds at US$90 per night ($100 weekends). Closed Mondays.
GRAHAMSTOWN: 19 rooms (doubles and singles). Apply to Guestmaster for rates. Closed Mondays.
TORONTO: 2 single rooms. Canadian $40 per night.

Community History: Adam Dunbar McCoy OHC, *Holy Cross: A Century of Anglican Monasticism,* Morehouse-Barlow, Wilton, CT, 1987.

Community Wares: Incense and Publications (West Park).

Bishop Visitor: Rt Revd Andrew M. L. Dietsche

Order of the Holy Paraclete

OHP

Founded 1915

St Hilda's Priory
Sneaton Castle,
Whitby
North Yorkshire
YO21 3QN
UK
Tel: 01947 602079
Fax: 01947 820854
Email:
ohppriorywhitby@btinternet.com

Website:
www.ohpwhitby.org

Morning Prayer
7.30 am

Eucharist
7.45 am (Mon, Wed, Fri & Sat)
9.30 am (Sun)
12.30 pm (Thu)

Midday Office
12.40 pm
12.15 pm (Thu)
12 noon (Sat)

Vespers 6.00 pm
(4.30 pm Sun)

Compline 7.45 pm

No services in chapel on Tuesdays

Founded as an educational order, the sisters have diversified their work in UK to include hospitality, retreats and spiritual direction, hospital chaplaincy, inner city involvement, preaching and mission, and development work overseas.

The Mother House is at St. Hilda's Priory, Whitby. Some sisters work in the adjacent Sneaton Castle Centre, which caters for a wide variety of day and residential groups. Other UK houses are in York, Dormanstown (near Redcar), Bishopsthorpe and Sleights (near Whitby).

The Order has had a long-standing commitment to Africa since 1926. Most of the work begun by the sisters has been handed over to local people who continue to run the projects. The Order has two houses in Ghana. In Jachie, Sister Aba runs an eye clinic while Sister Alberta makes tie-dye and batik. In Sunyani, Sister Mavis and Sister Benedicta Anne make communion hosts, have a shop and are beginning a small vocational school teaching computer and crafts to girls who were unable to complete their education. Both houses still foster vocations to the Religious life.

Central to the Order's life in all its houses are the Divine Office and Eucharist, and a strong emphasis on corporate activity.

Houses in the UK

St Oswald's Pastoral Centre, Woodlands Drive, Sleights, Whitby, N Yorks YO21 1RY
Tel: 01947 810496 Email: ohpstos@globalnet.co

1A Minster Court, York YO7 2JJ
Tel: 01904 557276
Email: sistersohp@googlemail.com

3 Acaster Lane, Bishopsthorpe, York, N Yorks YO23 2SA Tel: 01904 777294
Email: ohpbishopsthorpe@archbishopofyork.org

All Saints House, South Avenue, Dormanstown, TS10 5LL Tel: 01642 486424
Email: sisteranita@btinternet.com

Houses in Africa

Resurrection House, PO Box 596, Sunyani, Brone Ahafo, GHANA Tel: 233 243 706840
Email: nyamebekyere2010@yahoo.com or ohpjac@yahoo.com

Jachie, Convent of the Holy Spirit, PO Box AH 9375, Ahinsan, Kumasi Ashanti, GHANA
Tel: 233 242 203432 Email: Adedzewa@gmail.com

SISTER DOROTHY STELLA OHP
(Prioress, assumed office 15 July 2005)
SISTER HEATHER FRANCIS OHP *(Sub-Prioress)*

Sister Ursula
Sister Barbara Maude
Sister Olive
Sister Janet
Sister Alison
Sister Michelle
Sister Muriel
Sister Anita
Sister Hilary Joy
Sister Grace
Sister Janette
Sister Janet Elizabeth
Sister Betty
Sister Benedicta
Sister Caroline
Sister Margaret Elizabeth
Sister Marion Eva
Sister Erika
Sister Maureen Ruth
Sister Margaret Anne
Sister Jocelyn
Sister Carole
Sister Mavis
Sister Linda
Sister Aba
Sister Pam
Sister Helen
Sister Karan
Sister Alberta
Sister Helena
Sister Louisa Ann

Novices: 1

Obituaries

31 Aug 2014	Sister Marjorie, aged 93, professed 63 years
19 Dec 2014	Sister Mary Nina, aged 97, professed 55 years
22 Feb 2015	Sister Patricia, aged 89, professed 50 years
18 Mar 2015	Sister Nancye, aged 97, professed 51 years

Tertiaries and Associates

THE OHP TERTIARY ORDER is a fellowship of women and men, united under a common discipline, based on the OHP Rule, and supporting one another in their discipleship. Tertiaries are ordinary Christians seeking to offer their lives in the service of Christ, helping the Church and showing love in action. They value their links with each other and with the Sisters of the Order, at Whitby and elsewhere, and when possible they meet together for mutual support in prayer, discussion and ministry. The Tertiary Order is open to communicant members of any Trinitarian Church.

THE OHP ASSOCIATES are friends of the Order who desire to keep in touch with its life and work while serving God in their various spheres. Many have made initial contact with the Sisters through a visit or parish mission, or via another Associate. All are welcome, married or single, clergy or lay, regardless of religious affiliation.

THE FRIENDS OF OHP is a group open to men and women, of any religious affiliation or none, with an interest in OHP. The annual subscription of £10 includes a copy of the OHP newsletter and an invitation to an annual meeting.

Community Publication: *OHP Newsletter*, twice a year. Write to The Publications Secretary at St Hilda's Priory. Annual subscription: £4.50 for the UK, £5.50 for the rest of Europe and £7.00 for the rest of the world.

Community Wares

Cards and craft items. St Hilda's Priory has a shop selling books, cards, church supplies and religious artefacts.
Email: sneatonshop@btinternet.com

Community History

A Foundation Member, *Fulfilled in Joy,* Hodder & Stoughton, London, 1964.
Rosalin Barker, *The Whitby Sisters,* OHP, Whitby, 2001.

Guest and Retreat Facilities

St Hilda's Priory: six rooms (four single; one double; one twin) available in the Priory or nearby houses. Individuals or small groups are welcome for personal quiet or retreat, day or residential. If requested in advance, some guidance can be provided. There is no programme of retreats at the Priory. Contact the Guest Sister with enquiries and bookings.

Sneaton Castle Centre: seventy-one rooms (one hundred and twenty beds). The Centre has conference, lecture and seminar rooms with full audio-visual equipment, and recreational facilities. There are two spacious dining rooms and an excellent range of menus. Guests are welcome to join the community for worship or to arrange their own services in the Chapel.

Contact the Bookings Secretary, Sneaton Castle Centre, Whitby YO21 3QN.
Tel: 01947 600051 See also the website: www.sneatoncastle.co.uk

St Oswald's Pastoral Centre: 13 rooms (16 beds). 3 self-catering units.

Most convenient time to telephone:: 9 am - 5 pm, Mon-Fri; 10 am - 12 noon Sat

Office Book: OHP Office

Registered Charity: No. 271117

Bishop Visitor: Most Revd John Sentamu, Archbishop of York

Order of Julian of Norwich OJN

Founded 1985

2812 Summit Ave
Waukesha
WI 53188-2781
USA

Tel: 262 549 0452

Email: ojn@orderofjulian.org

The Order of Julian of Norwich is a contemplative order of the Episcopal Church. The monks and nuns live together under the vows of poverty, chastity, obedience, and prayer 'in the spirit of our Blessed Mother St Julian'. Life in community is grounded in the Eucharist and fourfold Daily Office, and includes study, work, and times of solitude and recreation. Then practice of enclosure allows the solitude and liberty to live as deeply as possible into the life of prayer and friendship with God. Serving God in one another, in guests, and before God's altar, the monks and nuns are committed to prayer, intercession, and conversion of heart, centered on relationship with Jesus Christ and growing up into Christ through life in common.

As the three windows of Julian's anchorhold opened, one to the altar, one to the room of the lay sisters, and one to the public lane, so the life of the Order looks to the worship of God, to the support and fellowship of the wider community of the Order and to the service of the Church and the world. For further information on the Order or its affiliates, please address the Guardian.

REVD MOTHER HILARY CRUPI OJN
(*Guardian, assumed office 30 April 2010*)
SISTER THERESE POLI OJN *(Warden)*

Revd Father John-Julian Swanson
Sister Cornelia Barry
Brother Barnabas Leben

Website:
www.orderofjulian.org

Silent Prayer/ Morning Prayer
3.45 am

Mass
7.30 am

Midday Office
11.30 am

Silent Prayer/ Evensong
4.00 pm

Compline
7.00 pm

Office Book
The BCP of ECUSA with enrichments

Community Publication
Julian's Window quarterly. Subscription free. Contact Sister Cornelia OJN

Bishop Visitor
Rt Revd
Wendell N. Gibbs, Jr., Bishop of Michigan

Associates and Oblates

ASSOCIATES AND OBLATES of the Order are those who respond to the Holy Spirit's invitation to draw nearer to Jesus under the patronage of St Julian of Norwich, called to the contemplative life in the world. Their rules of life, adaptations of the monastic Rule, unite their lives of prayer to that of the monastery and commit them to a regular practice of silent prayer, worship and study, in the context of their own particular vocations. In varying degree, they bring this contemplative practice into their parishes and communities by their transformation of their lives through the deepening of their relationship with Christ.

ASSOCIATES are committed to a simple form of the rule adaptable to many different walks of life.

OBLATES, after a period of discernment and formation, profess vows requiring regular discipline and reflection in the Christian commitment, with a rule of life closely modelled on that of the Order's monastics. A vow of celibacy is possible for Oblates within the Order.

Guest and Retreat Facilities

Two guest rooms for individual silent retreat. There is no charge.

Community History and other books

Teunisje Velthuizen, ObJN, *One-ed into God: The first decade of the Order of St Julian of Norwich,* The Julian Press, 1996.

Gregory Fruehwirth OJN, *Words for Silence,* Paraclete Press, Orleans, MA, 2008.

John Julian Swanson OJN, *The Complete Julian,* Paraclete Press, Orleans, MA, 2009.

Community Wares

Original icons, mounted icon prints and icon cards; prayer benches; and soap are all made by the community for their support. The Shop specializes in books about Julian of Norwich and contemplative and monastic spirituality.
Email: jshop@orderofjulian.org

Order of St Anne at Bethany

OSA

Founded 1910

25 Hillside Avenue
Arlington
MA 02476-5818
USA

Tel: 781 643 0921
Fax: 781 648 4547

Email: bethany convent@aol.com

Morning Prayer
7.00 am

Eucharist
8.00 am (Tue-Fri)
7.30 am (Sun)

Midday prayers
12 noon

Evensong 5.00 pm

Compline 7.30 pm

Office Book
SSJE Office Book

We are a small multi-cultural community of women committed to witnessing to the truth that, as Christians, it is here and now that we demonstrate to the Church and the world that the Religious Life lived in community is relevant, interesting, fulfilling and needed in our world and our times. We strive to recognize and value the diversity of persons and gifts. We believe that God has a vision for each one of us and that opportunities to serve the Church and the world are abundant. For this to become real, we know that our spirits and hearts must be enlarged to fit the dimensions of our Church in today's world and the great vision that God has prepared for our Order. We are especially grateful for our continuing ministry within the Diocese of Massachusetts.

The Rule of the Order of St Anne says our houses may be small, but our hearts are larger than houses. Our community has always been 'people-oriented' and we derive a sense of joy and satisfaction in offering hospitality at our Convent, at the Bethany House of Prayer and in our beautiful chapel. Always constant in our lives are our personal prayer and our corporate worship, our vows of Poverty, Celibacy and Obedience, our commitment to spiritual growth and development of mind and talents, and our fellowship with one another and other Religious communities, as friends and sisters.

SISTER ANA CLARA OSA
(Superior, assumed office 1992)

Sister Olga	Sister Maria Agnes
Sister Felicitas	Sister Maria Teresa

Associates
We have an associate program and continue to receive men and women into this part of our life.

Community Wares: Communion altar bread.

Community History
Sister Johanna OSA (editor), *A Theme for Four Voices,* privately printed, Arlington, Mass., 1985

Revd Charles C Hefling & Sister Ana Clara OSA, *Catch the Vision: celebrating a century of the Order of St Anne,* Order of St Anne-Bethany, Arlington, Mass., 2010

Bishop Visitor: Rt Revd Alan M. Gates,
Bishop of Massachusetts

Guest and Retreat Facilities
The Bethany House of Prayer, 181 Appleton Street, on the grounds of the Convent and Chapel, sponsors, coordinates and offers a variety of programs and events including Quiet Days, Special Liturgies, contemplative prayer, spiritual direction, day-retreats, hospitality and workshops. For more information call 781 648 2433.

Order of St Anne

Chicago

OSA

Founded 1910

1125 North LaSalle Blvd
Chicago
Illinois 60610
USA

Tel: 312 642 3638

Email: stannechicago @hotmail.com

Website: www. sistersofstannechicago .org

Matins 6.40 am
Eucharist 7.00 am
(Church of the Ascension)
Terce 8.30 am
Sext 12 noon
Vespers 5.00 pm
Compline 7.00 pm

Office Book: Monastic Diurnal revised

The Order of St. Anne was founded in 1910 by Father Frederick Cecil Powell of the Society of St. John the Evangelist in Arlington Heights, Mass. The Sisters live a modified Benedictine Rule, dedicated to a life of prayer and good works beneficial to all people including children. The Sisters of St. Anne came to Chicago in 1921 invited by then rector of the Church of the Ascension, the Revd Stoskopf, to do parish work and other needed services in the Diocese of Chicago. The Chicago convent is autonomous, although Sisters live as part of the church of the Ascension.

According to our Rule "the Order of St. Anne cannot be designated as professing exclusively the contemplative, the mixed or active spirit" since all three may be found within the Order. The principal of the Order is the life of God within it and whatsoever He may say to us – whether to sit at His feet only or feed His lambs - which we must do. While our works are important, it must be kept in mind that God calls us to a life of prayer. The Sisters are involved in parish work, especially at the Church of the Ascension doing whatever is needed. The sisters also work with the homeless, alcoholics, addicts and other emotionally and mentally disturbed people. The sisters work as teachers, counsellors and hospital chaplains. A future plan is for a recovery home for addicts, alcoholics and emotionally disturbed women.

SISTER JUDITH MARIE OSA
(Superior, assumed office 2007)
Sister Barbara Louise OSA
Resident Companion: Ms Dorothy Murray

Associates
We have an associate program for men and women.

Community Publication: PROEIS

Guest and Retreat Facilities
Two guest rooms in Convent (women only). No charge, donations accepted. Individual retreats; spiritual direction and counselling available.

Bishop Visitor: Rt Revd Jeffrey Lee, Bishop of Chicago

Order of St Benedict

St Mark's Abbey, Camperdown

OSB

Founded 1975

Benedictine Abbey
PO Box 111
Camperdown
Victoria 3260
AUSTRALIA

Tel: 3 5593 2348
Fax: 3 5593 2887
Email: benabbey@ dodo.com.au

Website: www. anglicanbenedictine .org.au

Vigils 4.30 am

Lauds 6.30 am

Terce & Conventual Mass 8.15 am

Sext 11.45 am

None 2.10 pm

Vespers 5.00 pm

Compline 7.30 pm

Office Book
Camperdown breviary

Abbot Visitor
Rt Revd Dom Bruno Marin OSB

The community was founded in the parish of St Mark, Fitzroy, in the archdiocese of Melbourne on 8 November 1975. In 1980, after working in this inner city parish for five years, and after adopting the *Rule of Saint Benedict*, they moved to the country town of Camperdown in the Western District of Victoria. Here the community lives a contemplative monastic life with the emphasis on the balanced life of prayer and work that forms the Benedictine ethos. In 1993, the Chapter decided to admit women and to endeavour to establish a mixed community of monks and nuns. The community supports itself through the operation of a printery, icon reproduction, manufacture of incense, crafts and a small guest house. In 2005, the Chapter petitioned the Subiaco Cassinese Congregation of the Benedictine Confederation for aggregation to the Congregation. After a period of probation, this was granted on the Feast of SS Peter and Paul 2007. The fruits of our association are already being shown forth.

Dom Placid Lawson — *Novices:* 1
Sister Raphael Stone

Obituaries

28 Aug 2014 Rt Revd Dom Michael King, aged 72, professed 28 years, Abbot 2002-2014
3 Oct 2014 Sister Mary Philip Bloore, aged 87, professed 48 years

Oblates

Oblates of St Mark's Abbey are both lay and ordained Christians who live the spirit of the *Rule of St Benedict* according to their individual circumstance in the world. After a period of probation, a commitment is made which brings the Oblate into a spiritual and practical affiliation with our monastic community.

Guest and Retreat Facilities

Small guest house (St Joseph's), which can accommodate 4 (6 with 2 twin rooms) people, open to men and women, for private retreats. Guests eat main meal (midday) with the community, prepare own breakfast and evening meal in the guesthouse with provisions provided. Guests are welcome to attend the services in the church from Lauds daily. Minimum donation of $70 per person per night requested.

Community Publication: Yearly newsletter in December - free download from website or $6 per hard copy.

Community Wares: Printing, icons, cards, incense, devotional items.

Diocesan Bishop: Rt Revd Garry Weatherill

Order of St Benedict Community of St Mary at the Cross,

Edgware

OSB

Founded 1866

Edgware Abbey
94A Priory Field Drive, Edgware
Middlesex
HA8 9PU
UK

Tel: 020 8958 7868

Email: info@edgwareabbey.org.uk *or* **nuns.osb.edgware@btconnect.com**

Website: www.edgwareabbey.org.uk

Vigils (private)
Lauds 8.00 am
Midday Office 11.55 am (not Sun)
Vespers 5.30 pm
Compline 8.00 pm

Mass weekdays:
7.45 am or 11.00 am
11 am (Sun/feast days)

Living under *The Rule of Benedict* and dedicated to St Mary at the Cross, the vocation of this community is to stand with Christ's Mother beside those who suffer; its heart in prayer, the Divine Office & the Eucharist are central to its life. Beginning in Shoreditch, Mother Monnica Skinner and Revd Henry Nihill worked together, drawn to the desperate poverty and sickness around them. Awareness of the needs, especially of 'incurable children', led to the building of a hospital, marking the beginning of the community's life work. Developing to meet the needs of each generation, this ministry continues today in the provision of Henry Nihill House, a 30-bed care home with nursing for disabled and elderly frail persons, in the beautiful grounds of Edgware Abbey.

Edgware Abbey is a haven of peace which enfolds many visitors. All are offered Benedictine hospitality with space for rest and renewal. The small comfortable Guest Wing provides short stay retreat accommodation and space for parish Away Days and meetings. All guests are welcome to participate in the Community's offering of the Divine Office and Eucharist. Edgware Abbey is easily accessible from the M1, A1, tube and rail.

RT REVD DAME MARY THÉRÈSE ZELENT OSB
(Abbess, elected 30 March 1993)
Dame (Mary Eanfleda) Barbara Johnson

Oblates: Our Oblates are part of our extended Community family: living outside the cloister; following the spirit of the *Holy Rule of St Benedict*; bonded with the Community in prayer and commitment to service.

Community Publication: *Abbey Newsletter*, published yearly. There is no charge but donations are welcome. Obtainable from the Convent.

Guest and Retreat Facilities
The Guest Wing: 3 comfortable bedrooms for B & B retreat accommodation; guest reception area with kitchenette; space for small day groups & clergy groups, parish quiet day groups etc.; use of chapel and garden; small parking area.

Bishop Visitor: Rt Revd Peter Wheatley

Office Book: Divine Office with own form of Compline.

Registered Charity: No. 209261

Order of St Benedict

Malling Abbey

OSB

Founded 1891

St Mary's Abbey
52 Swan Street
West Malling, Kent
ME19 6JX
UK
Tel: 01732 843309
Fax: 01732 849016

Website: www.mallingabbey.org

Vigils 4.30 am (5.00 am Sun)

Lauds 6.50 am (8.10 am Sun)

Eucharist 7.30 am (9.00 am Sun)

Terce 8.45 am

Sext 12.00 noon

None 3.00 pm

Vespers 4.45 pm (5.00 pm Sun)

Compline 7.30 pm

Office Book
Malling Abbey Office

We are Benedictine nuns: our vocation is to seek and serve God in the context of the common life within the enclosure of the Abbey grounds. The priority and sufficiency of God are the bedrock of our spirituality. The rhythm of our day is shaped by the Eucharist and seven-fold Office and our times for personal prayer and lectio divina.

Silence and simplicity, prayer and hospitality express our core values. We welcome opportunities to share our monastic heritage, to encourage ecumenical and interfaith understanding and to practise the responsible stewardship of God's creation.

Currently we are working with the Diocese of Rochester to establish a Centre for Retreats and Spirituality at the Abbey. Our contribution to this venture of faith is to undergird the Centre with prayer. The essentials of our life will remain as our role in the Centre evolves. We shall continue the Benedictine tradition of hospitality in our own separate guest wing. For more details of our daily life and work, or to arrange a visit, please see our website.

Mother Mary David Best OSB
(Abbess, elected 16 September 2008)
Sister Mary Stephen Packwood OSB *(Prioress)*
Sister Macrina Banner
Sister Mary Mark Brooksbank
Sister Mary John Marshall
Sister Ruth Blackmore
Sister Mary Cuthbert Archer
Sister Mary Gundulf Wood
Sister Bartimaeus Ives
Sister Mary Michael Wilson
Sister Miriam Noke
Sister Mary Owen DeSimone
Sister Margaret Joy Harris
Sister Anne Clarke

Novices: 1

Obituaries
30 Mar 2015 Sister Felicity Spencer, aged 92 years, professed 45 years (CSA 1970, Malling from 1983)

Bishop Visitor: Rt Revd Laurie Green

Community Wares
Cards and booklets, created and painted by the sisters, are on sale at the Abbey.

Oblates

Oblates are men and women who feel called by God to follow the Benedictine way in their lives outside the cloister. After a two-and-a-half-year period of training and discernment they make a promise of the conversion of their life during the Eucharist and are then welcomed into the oblate family. Their commitment is expressed in a personal Benedictine rule of life, which balances their personal prayer, worship and *lectio divina* with their responsibility to family and work.

Community History

Sisters Mary David & Miriam (editors), *Living Stones: The Story of Malling Abbey*, privately published, Malling Abbey, 2005.

Guest and Retreat Facilities

In the Abbey guest wing, we can welcome 4 self-catering guests in single occupancy ensuite rooms. We can also offer hospitality to a few day guests or small groups. Our guests come to share in the worship and God-centred quiet, and to have the space and time for spiritual reflection and refreshment. There is no charge, though donations are welcome (bookings@mallingabbey.org).

Most convenient time to telephone:
9.30 am - 11.00 am

Order of St Benedict Mucknell Abbey OSB

Founded 1941

Mucknell Abbey
Mucknell Farm Lane
Stoulton
Worcestershire
WR7 4RB
Tel: 01905 345900
Email: abbot@mucknellabbey.org.uk

Website
www.mucknellabbey.org.uk

Office of Readings 6.00 am

Lauds 7.00 am

Terce 8.45 am

Eucharist Noon (11 am Sun & solemnities)

None 2.15 pm

Vespers 5.30 pm

Compline 8.30 pm (8.00 pm in winter)

The contemplative community of monks and nuns sold their former monastery in Burford in 2008 and bought a farm near Worcester and transformed it into a monastery incorporating as many 'sustainable' features as possible. Having moved into their new home in November 2010, the Community is seeking to maintain an atmosphere of stillness and silence in which the Community and its guests are enabled to be open and receptive to the presence of God. The recitation of the Divine Office and the celebration of the Eucharist constitute the principal work of the Community. The ministry of hospitality, the development of the surrounding 40 acres of land (which comprises a large kitchen garden, orchard, newly-planted woodland and hay meadows), the production of incense for a world-wide market, and various income-generating crafts provide a variety of manual work for members of the Community and those guests who wish to share in it. The monastery seeks to celebrate the wonder and richness of Creation and to model a responsible stewardship. The Community's concern has always been to pray for Christian Unity, and it now rejoices in having a Methodist presbyter in its number. Dialogue with people of other faiths and those seeking a spiritual way, either within or outside an established religious tradition, is a priority.

Rt Revd Brother Stuart Burns OSB
(Abbot, elected 14 October 1996)
Brother Philip Dulson OSB *(Prior)*

Sister Mary Bernard Taylor
Brother Thomas Quin
Brother Anthony Hare
Sister Mary Kenchington
Brother Ian Mead
Sister Sally Paley
Brother Luke Fox
Sister Alison Fry

Novices: 2
Alongsiders: 4

Friends: There is a Friends' Association.
Contact: *friends@mucknellabbey.org.uk*

Community Wares
Incense: *incense@mucknellabbey.org.uk*
Hand-written icons, using traditional materials, and block mounted icon prints: *icons@mucknellabbey.org.uk*
Chinese brush painted cards: *cards@mucknellabbey.org.uk*
Rosaries and hand-carved Holding Crosses: *craftsales@mucknell.org.uk*

Office Book: Mucknell Abbey Office

Bishop Visitor: Rt Revd John Inge, Bishop of Worcester

Community publications
There are up-dates on the Community's website.
The Rule of St Benedict – inclusive translation by Abbot Stuart.

Guest and Retreat Facilities
Six guest rooms and one room for an individual having a quiet day. No groups.

Most convenient time to telephone: 9.30 am-11.30 am; 2.30 pm-3.45 pm.
Email enquiries are preferred: *bookings@mucknellabbey.org.uk*

Registered Charity: No. 221617

Order of St Benedict

Servants of Christ Priory

OSB

Founded 1968

Contact details temporarily unknown

A community united in love for God and one another following the Benedictine balance of prayer, study and work reflects the life of the monks. Both the remaining members of the community are now in care accommodation.

THE VERY REVD CORNELIS J. DE RIJK OSB
(Prior, assumed office November 1985)
The Revd Lewis H. Long

Oblates
Oblates follow a rule of life consistent with the *Rule of St Benedict* adapted to their lifestyle.

Office Book: The BCP of ECUSA

Bishop Visitor
Rt Revd Kirk Stevan Smith, Bishop of Arizona

Order of St Benedict Salisbury OSB

Founded 1914

St Benedict's Priory
19A The Close
Salisbury SP1 2EB
UK
Tel: 01722 335868
Email:
salisbury.priory@gmail.com

Vigils 5.30 am

Morning Worship & Eucharist
at Cathedral 7.30 am
(Eucharist
10.30 am Sun;
10 am at Priory Thu)

Lauds (at Priory)
8.00 am Sun & Thu

Terce 10.00 am

Midday Prayer
12.45 pm
(at Sarum College)
12.15pm Sat & Sun
(at Priory)

Evensong
at Cathedral
(times vary)

Compline 8.30 pm

The monastery aims to provide an environment within which the traditional monastic balance between worship, study and work may be maintained with a characteristic Benedictine stress upon corporate worship and community life. To this end, outside commitments are kept to a minimum.

Very Revd Dom Simon Jarratt OSB
(Conventual Prior, elected 13 December 2005)
(Rt Revd) Dom Kenneth Newing OSB *(Sub-Prior)*
Dom Francis Hutchison
Dom Bruce De Walt

Oblates
An extended confraternity of oblates, numbering over 250 men and women, married and single, seek to live according to a rule of life inspired by Benedictine principles. From the start, the community has believed in the importance of prayer for Christian unity and the fostering of ecumenism. Details can be obtained from the Oblate Master.

Community History
Petà Dunstan, *The Labour of Obedience,* Canterbury Press, Norwich, 2009

Community Publications
Books:
Augustine Morris, *Oblates: Life with Saint Benedict* £4.25.
Simon Bailey, *A Tactful God: Gregory Dix,* £12.99.

Guest and Retreat Facilities
The Community is currently extending the Priory to provide better facilities for day visitors. There are no facilities for residential guests, although Sarum College next door is open for bed & breakfast.

Most convenient time to telephone
9.00 am - 9.50 am; 10.30 am - 12.15 pm; 3.00 pm - 4.45 pm
Tel: 01722 335868

Office Book: Own Office books at the Priory.

Bishop Visitor
Rt Revd Dominic Walker OGS

Registered Charity
Pershore Nashdom & Elmore Trust - No. 220012

St Gregory's Abbey Three Rivers OSB

Founded 1939

St Gregory's Abbey
56500 Abbey Road
Three Rivers
Michigan
49093-9595
USA
Tel: 269 244 5893
Fax: 269 244 8712
Email: abbot@ saintgregorys threerivers.org

Website
www.saintgregorys threerivers.org

Matins 4.00 am (5.30 am Sun & solemnities, with Lauds)

Lauds 6.00 am

Terce & Mass 8.15 am (8.30 am Sun & solemnities)

Sext 11.30 am (12 noon Sun & solemnities, with None)

None 2.00 pm

Vespers 5.00 pm

Compline 7.45 pm

St Gregory's Abbey is the home of a community of men living under the *Rule of St Benedict* within the Episcopal Church. The center of the monastery's life is the Abbey Church, where God is worshipped in the daily round of Eucharist, Divine Office, and private prayer. Also offered to God are the monks' daily manual work, study and correspondence, ministry to guests, and occasional outside engagements.

RIGHT REVD ANDREW MARR OSB
(*Abbot, elected 2 March 1989*)
VERY REVD AELRED GLIDDEN OSB (*Prior*)

Father Benedict Reid*
Father Jude Bell
Father William Forest
Brother Martin Dally
Brother Abraham Newsom

**resident elsewhere*

Community Publications and History

Abbey Newsletter, published four times a year. Free.

Singing God's Praises, published 1998. It includes articles from community newsletters over the past sixty years and also includes a history of St Gregory's. Copies can be bought from the Abbey, price $20 a copy, postpaid.

Come Let Us Adore: St Gregory's 1999-2011, a successor to the above. Published by iUniverse and available from online bookstores such as Amazon.

Andrew Marr OSB, *Tools for Peace: the spiritual craft of St Benedict and René Girard*, available from online bookstores.

Community Wares: The Abbey calendar.

Guest and Retreat Facilities

Both men and women are welcome as guests. There is no charge, but $40 per day is 'fair value for services rendered' that is not tax-deductible. For further information and arrangements, contact the guest master by mail, telephone or e-mail at *guestmaster@saintgregorysthreerivers.org*

Associates

We have a Confraternity which offers an official connection to the Abbey and is open to anyone who wishes to join for the purpose of incorporating Benedictine principles into their lives. For further information and an application form, please write the Father Abbot.

Office Book: The community uses home-made books based on the Roman Thesaurus for the Benedictine Office.

Bishop Visitor: Rt Revd Arthur Williams, suffragan Bishop of Ohio (retired)

Order of St Helena

OSH

Founded 1945

**Convent of St Helena
414 Savannah Barony Drive
North Augusta
SC 29841
USA**

Email: **sisters@osh.org**

Website
www.osh.org

Matins 7.30 am

Eucharist 8.00 am

Diurnum and intercessions 12 noon

Vespers 5.00 pm

Compline 7.00 pm

Bishop Visitor
Rt Revd
Neil Alexander,
Bishop of Atlanta

Registered Charity No: US Government 501 (c)(3)

The Order of St Helena witnesses to a contemporary version of traditional monasticism, taking a threefold vow of Poverty, Celibate Chastity and Obedience. Our life in community is shaped by the daily Eucharist and fourfold Office, plus hours of personal prayer and study, and from this radiates a wide range of ministries.

As an Order, we are not restricted to any single area of work but witness and respond to the Gospel, with individual sisters engaging in different ministries as they feel called by God and affirmed by the community. Our work is thus wonderfully varied: sisters work in parishes as priests or as pastoral assistants; they lead retreats, quiet days and conferences; work with the national Church and various organizations; offer spiritual direction; are psychotherapists; teach; serve in hospital chaplaincies and community service programs. Four sisters are ordained priests. The Order is led by a three-member Leadership Council:

SISTER MARY LOIS MILLER OSH *(Administrator)*
REVD SISTER CAROL ANDREW OSH *(Pastoral)*
REVD DR ELLEN FRANCIS POISSON OSH
(Vocations/Formation)

Sister Ruth Juchter	Sister June Thomas
Sister Ellen Stephen	Sister Ann Prentice
Sister Barbara Lee	Sister Linda Elston
Sister Benedicta	Sister Faith Anthony
Revd Sister Rosina Ampah	Sister Miriam Elizabeth

Obituaries

28 Sep 2014 Sister Cintra Pemberton, aged 78, professed 34 years

3 Oct 2014 Sister Elsie Reid, aged 90, professed 33 years

Associates

ASSOCIATES - open to all women and men. Write to the Secretary for Associates at the Augusta Convent.

Guest and Retreat Facilities: Guest house, 8 single rooms.

Community Publication : OSH newsletter: subscribe on OSH website for subscription (paper or electronic); no charge.

Community Wares and Books

Hand-made rosaries: write to Sister Mary Lois for Dominican rosaries and to Sr Linda for Anglican rosaries.
Icon reproductions: www.ellenfrancisicons.org
Greeting cards by Sister Faith Anthony, see OSH website.
Sister Cintra Pemberton OSH, *Soulfaring: Celtic pilgrimage then and now,* SPCK & Morehouse, 1999.

Doug Shadel and Sister Ellen Stephen OSH, *Vessel of Peace: The voyage toward spiritual freedom*, Three Tree Press, 1999.
Sister Ellen Stephen, OSH, *The Poet's Eye: collected poetry,* Academica Press, 2012.
Sister Ellen Stephen, OSH, *Some Antics,* Order of Saint Helena, 2012.
Sister Rosina Ampah, *The Beautiful Cloth: stories and proverbs of Ghana,* Yellow Moon Press, 2010.
Sister Ellen Stephen OSH, *Together and Apart: a memoir of the Religious Life*, Morehouse, Harrisburg, PA, 2008.

Office Book: *The Saint Helena Breviary, Monastic Edition*, which includes all the music in plainchant notation, is now published. It follows closely the BCP of the Episcopal Church of the USA. The focus is on inclusive language and expanded imagery for God, following principles set forth by the Standing Commission for Liturgy and Music of the Episcopal Church, USA. The *Saint Helena Psalter*, extracted from the Breviary, was published in November 2004, *The Saint Helena Breviary, Personal edition*, in July 2006, both by Church Publishing Co., Inc.
Saint Helena Breviary, Monastic Edition: available on CD (in PDF format) for a $25 donation (www.osh.org/ contributions.html)

Sisterhood of the Holy Nativity

SHN

Founded 1882

W14164 Plante Dr.
Ripon
WI 54971
USA
Tel: 920 748 1479
Email: abizac50 @hotmail.com

Matins 7.30 am
Eucharist 8.00 am
Noonday Prayer 12 noon
Vespers 5.30 pm (6.30 pm Sun)
Compline 8.00 pm

Ours is a mixed life, which means that we combine an apostolic ministry with a contemplative lifestyle. The Rule of the Sisterhood of the Holy Nativity follows the model of the Rule of St Augustine of Hippo. As such, we strive to make the love of God the motive of all our actions. The 'charisms', which undergird our life, are Charity, Humility, Prayer, and Missionary Zeal. Our work involves us with children's ministries such as Sunday School, Summer Camp and Vacation Bible School, as well as ministry to those we meet in everyday life.

SISTER ABIGAIL SHN
(Revd Mother, assumed office 2012)

Sister Margaretta	Sister Kathleen Marie
Sister Columba	Sister Charis

Associates: These are men and women who connect themselves to the prayer life and ministry of the community, and keep a Rule of Life.

Community Publication
We put out a newsletter occasionally. There is no charge. Anyone interested may contact us at the address above or by email.

Office Book: *The Monastic Breviary*, published by the Order of the Holy Cross.

Bishop Visitor
Rt Revd Mathew Gunter, Bishop of Fond du Lac

Sisterhood of St John the Divine

SSJD

Founded 1884

St John's Convent
233 Cummer Ave
Toronto
Ontario M2M 2E8
CANADA
Tel: 416 226 2201
ext. 301
Fax: 416 222 4442
Emails:
convent@ssjd.ca
guesthouse@ssjd.ca
Website www.ssjd.ca

Morning Prayer
8.30 am

Holy Eucharist
12 noon (8.00 am Sun)

Mid-day Office
12.15 pm (when Eucharist not at noon)

Evening Prayer
5.00 pm

Compline 8.10 pm
(Tue, Wed, Thu & Fri)

Office Book
Book of Alternative Services 1985; SSJD Daily Office Binder with inclusive language psalter.

The Sisterhood of St John the Divine is a monastic community of women within the Anglican Church of Canada. Founded in Toronto, we are a prayer- and gospel-centred monastic community, bound together by the call to live out our baptismal covenant through the vows of poverty, chastity and obedience. These vows anchor us in Jesus' life and the transforming experience of the Gospel. Nurtured by our founding vision of prayer, community and service, we are open and responsive to the needs of the Church and the world, continually seeking the guidance of the Holy Spirit in our life and ministries.

St John's Convent nurtures and supports the life of the whole Sisterhood. Our guest house welcomes individuals and groups who share in the community's prayer and liturgy; offers regularly scheduled retreats and quiet days, spiritual direction, and discernment programs for those seeking guidance in their life and work; and provides Sisters to preach, teach, speak, lead retreats and quiet days. Our programs help people build bridges between secular culture, the Church, and the monastic tradition. The Sisterhood witnesses to the power of Christ's reconciling and forgiving love through the gospel imperatives of prayer, spiritual guidance, justice, peace, care for creation, hospitality, ministering to those in need, and promoting unity, healing, and wholeness.

The Sisters advocate for a vision of health care at the St. John's Rehab site of Sunnybrook Hospital which expresses SSJD's values in a multi-faith, multi-cultural setting. The Sisters provide spiritual and pastoral support for patients, staff and volunteers.

Other address

ST JOHN'S HOUSE, 3937 St Peters Rd, Victoria, British Columbia V8P 2J9
Tel: 250 920 7787 Fax: 250 920 7709
E-mail: bchouse@ssjd.ca

A community of Sisters committed to being a praying presence in the Diocese of British Columbia. Prayer, intentional community, hospitality, and mission are at the heart of our life in the Diocese and beyond.

Community Wares

A variety of cards made by Sisters or Associates. Good selection of books on spiritual growth for sale at the Convent (not by mail) and a few CDs. Anglican rosaries made by the Sisters, some knitted items and prayer shawls.

Bishop Visitor: Most Revd Colin Johnson

Sister Elizabeth Rolfe-Thomas SSJD
(Reverend Mother, assumed office 6 May 2015)

Sister Wilma Grazier
Sister Beryl Stone
Sister Doreen McGuff *(Sub-Prioress)*
Sister Patricia Forler
Sister Jocelyn Mortimore
Sister Margaret Ruth Steele
Sister Sarah Jean Thompson
Sister Anitra Hansen
Sister Jessica Kennedy
Sister Constance Joanna Gefvert *(priest)*
Sister Elizabeth Ann Eckert
Sister Brenda Jenner
Sister Anne Norman
Sister Helen Claire Gunter
Sister Sue Elwyn
Sister Louise Manson
Sister Dorothy Handrigan
Sister Debra Johnston
Sister Susanne Prue

Novices: 1

Obituaries

4 Oct 2013	Sister Jean Marston, aged 76, professed 45 years
28 Feb 2014	Sister Merle Milligan, aged 94, professed 45 years
20 Jul 2014	Sister Margaret Mary Watson, aged 82, professed 29 years

Associates, Oblates and Alongsiders

Our approximately nine hundred **Associates** are women and men who follow a Rule of Life and share in the ministry of the Sisterhood. The Sisterhood of St John the Divine owes its founding to the vision and dedication of the clergy and lay people who became the first Associates of SSJD. A year of discernment is required before being admitted as an Associate to see if the Associate Rule helps the person in what she/he is seeking; and to provide the opportunity to develop a relationship with the Sisters and to deepen the understanding and practice of prayer. The Associate Rule provides a framework for the journey of faith. There are three basic commitments: belonging to a parish; the practice of prayer, retreat, study of scripture, and spiritual reading; and the relationship with SSJD. Write to the Associate Director nearest you for further information.

The **Oblates** of the Community are women who wish to make a promise of prayer and service in partnership with the Sisterhood. Each Oblate develops her own Rule of Life in partnership with the Oblate Director, her spiritual director, and a support group. A year of discernment is also required, as well as an annual residency program. Write to The Reverend Mother at the Convent in Toronto for more information.

An **Alongsider** is a woman who lives "at the edge" of the community of the Sisterhood of St. John the Divine, moving back and forth between the monastery and the world outside. She lives outside the cloister in the convent's guest house but participates in many of the community activities (including common prayer in chapel and recreation) and shares in household tasks. Alongside the Sisters, she is committed to a daily practice of personal prayer, spiritual reading and reflection on sacred Scripture.

Community History and Books

Sister Eleonora SSJD, *A Memoir of the Life and Work of Hannah Grier Coome, Mother-Foundress of SSJD, Toronto, Canada,* OUP, London, 1933 (out of print).

The Sisterhood of St John the Divine 1884-1984, published 1931 as *A Brief History;* 4th revision 1984, (out of print).

Sister Constance Joanna SSJD, *From Creation to Resurrection: A Spiritual Journey,* Anglican Book Centre, Toronto, 1990.

Sister Constance SSJD, *Other Little Ships: The memoirs of Sister Constance SSJD,* Patmos Press, Toronto, 1997.

Sister Thelma-Anne McLeod SSJD, *In Age Reborn, By Grace Sustained,* Path Books, Toronto, 2007.

Dr Gerald D Hart, *St John's Rehab Hospital, 1885-2010, the Road to Recovery,*York Region Printing, Autora, ON, 2010

Jane Christmas & Sister Constance Joanna SSJD (editors), *A Journey Just Begun: The Story of an Anglican Sisterhood,* Dundurn, 2015.

Community Publication: *The Eagle* (newsletter). Contact the Convent Secretary. Published three times a year. $10.00 suggested annual donation.

Guest and Retreat Facilities: Guest House has 37 rooms (42 people) used for rest, quiet time and retreats. Contact the Guest Sister at the Convent for details about private accommodation, scheduled retreats, quiet days and other programs.

The Sisters in Victoria also lead quiet days and retreats and have room for one guest. Please contact St John's House, BC, for detailed information.

Sisterhood of St Mary

SSM

Founded 1929

St Andrew's Mission
PO Haluaghat
Mymensingh
BANGLADESH

Prayer 6.30 am

Meditation 8.00 am

Prayers
9.00 am, 11.30 am,
3.00 pm, 6.00 pm

Compline 8.00 pm

The community is located on the northern border of Bangladesh at the foot of the Garo hills in India. The community was formed in Barisal at the Sisterhood of the Epiphany, and was sent here to work among the indigenous tribal people, side by side with St Andrew's Mission. Membership of the Sisterhood has always been entirely indigenous. The first sisters were Bengalis. The present sisters are the fruit of their work - Garo and Bengali. They take the vows of Poverty, Purity and Obedience and live a very simple life. They lead a life of prayer and formation of girls. They also look after the Church and do pastoral work among women and children in the Parish.

SISTER MIRA MANKHIN SSM
(Sister Superior, assumed office 2002)
Sister Anita Raksam
Sister Bregita Doffo
Sister Mala Chicham

Community Wares: Some handicrafts and vestments for church use and sale.

Office Book: Church of Bangladesh BCP & own book for lesser Offices.

Bishop Visitor: Most Revd Paul Sarker,
Bishop of Dhaka

Sisters of Charity

SC

Founded 1869

83 Fore Street
Plympton
Plymouth
PL7 1NB
UK
Tel: 01752 336112
Email:
plymptonsisters@gmail.com

Morning Prayer 8.00 am

Vespers 5.00 pm

Compline 7.00 pm

Office Book
Common Worship

A Community following the Rule of St Vincent de Paul and so committed to the service of those in need. The Sisters are involved in parish work and the Community also has a nursing home in Plympton.

MOTHER ELIZABETH MARY SC
(Revd Mother, assumed office 21 April 2003)
SISTER CLARE SC *(priest) (Assistant)*

Sister Theresa
Sister Angela Mary
Sister Mary Joseph
Sister Gabriel Margaret
Sister Mary Patrick

Oblates and Associate Members

The Community has a group of Oblates and Associate Members, formed as a mutual supportive link. We ask them to add to their existing rule the daily use of the Vincentian Prayer. Oblates are also asked to use the Holy Paraclete hymn and one of the Daily Offices, thereby joining in spirit in the Divine Office of the Community. Oblates are encouraged to make an annual retreat. Associate Members support us by their prayers and annual subscription.

Other address

Saint Vincent's Nursing Home, Fore St, Plympton, Plymouth , PL7 1NE **Tel: 01752 336205**

Guest and Retreat Facilities

We welcome individuals for Quiet Days.

Most convenient time to telephone: 6.00 pm - 8.00 pm

Bishop Visitor: Rt Revd Martin Shaw

Registered Charity: No. X33170

Sisters of the Incarnation

SI

Founded 1981

The sisters live under vows of poverty, chastity and obedience in a simple life style, and seek to maintain a balance between prayer, community life and work for each member and to worship and serve within the church. They combine the monastic and apostolic aspects of the Religious Life. The monastic aspects include prayer, domestic work at home, community life and hospitality. The sisters are engaged in parish ministry.

The community was founded in the diocese of Adelaide in 1981 as a contemporary expression of the Religious Life for women in the Anglican Church. In 1988, the two original sisters made their Profession of Life Intention win the Sisters of the Incarnation, before the Archbishop of

The House of the Incarnation
6 Sherbourne Terrace
Dover Gardens
SA 5048
AUSTRALIA
Tel: 08 8296 2166
Email: sisincar @bigpond.com

Office Book
A Prayer Book for Australia (1995 edition): MP, EP and Compline Midday Prayer is from another source.

Adelaide, the Visitor of the community. One member was ordained to the diaconate in 1990 and the priesthood in 1992. The governing body of the community is its chapter of professed sisters, which elects the Guardian, and appoints an Episcopal Visitor and a Community Advisor.

REVD SISTER JULIANA SI
(*Guardian, assumed office 2013*)
Sister Patricia

Friends
The community has a group of Friends who share special celebrations and significant events, many of whom have supported the community from the beginning, while others become Friends as we touch their lives. There is no formal structure.

Bishop Visitor: Rt Revd Dr K Rayner

Sisters of Jesus Way

Founded 1979

Website:
www.redacre.org.uk

Redacre
24 Abbey Road
West Kirby
Wirral
CH48 7EP
UK
Tel: 0151 6258775

Email:
sistersofjesusway @redacre.org.uk

Two Wesley deaconesses founded the Sisters of Jesus Way. There have been many strands that have been instrumental in the formation of the community but primarily these have been the Gospels, the Charismatic Renewal, the teaching and example of the Pietists of the 17th and early 18th centuries as practised in some German communities and the lives of saints from many denominations.

Our calling is to love the Lord Jesus with a first love, to trust the heavenly Father as his dear children for all our needs both spiritual and material and to allow the Holy Spirit to guide and lead us. Prayer, either using the framework of a simple liturgy or informal, is central to all that we do. We make life promises of simplicity, fidelity and chastity. Our work for the Lord varies as the Holy Spirit opens or closes doors. We welcome guests, trusting that as the Lord Jesus lives with us, they will meet with him and experience his grace. Music, some of which has been composed by the sisters, is very much part of our life. We work together, learning from the Lord to live together as a family in love, forgiveness and harmony.

Morning Prayer
8.00 am

Intercessory prayer
(community only)
12.25 pm

Evening Prayer
7.00 pm

Registered Charity
No 509284

SISTER MARIE
(Little Sister, assumed office 1991)
SISTER SYLVIA *(Companion Sister)*

Sister Hazel
Sister Florence
Sister Beatrice
Sister Susan
Sister Louise
Novices: 1

Brother of the Way: Brother Elliot

Alongsiders: 1

Associates

The Followers of the Lamb are a small group of women following a simple Rule of Life and committed to assisting the Sisters.

Guest and Retreat Facilities

7 single rooms, 3 twin rooms. Several rooms for day visitors and small groups.

Most convenient time to telephone:

9.40am-12.40pm; 2.15pm-5.45pm; 7.20pm-8.45pm

Community Publication: Twice-yearly teaching and newsletter. Contact Sr Louise.

Community History

Written by the Sisters of Jesus Way and available from the Community:
To Love You Only: The Story of Lynda & a Community, Church in the Market Place Publications, 2013. A further book is in preparation.

Community Wares

CD: *Come Lord Jesus* (music composed, sung & played by the Community).
A further CD is in preparation.

Office Book: The Community uses its own liturgy.

Bishop Guardian: Rt Revd Dr Peter Forster, Bishop of Chester

Society of the Holy Cross

SHC

Founded 1925

15 Road 21
Seijong Daero
Jung-ku
Seoul 100-120
KOREA
Tel: 2 735 7832
or 2 735 3478
Fax: 2 736 5028
Email:
holycross1925
@daum.net

Website
www.sister.or.kr

Morning Prayer
6.15 am

Holy Eucharist
6.45 am

Midday Prayer
12.30 pm
(12 noon Sun & great feast days)

Evening Prayer
5.00 pm

Compline 8.00 pm

Office Book
Revised Common Prayer for MP & EP and Compline; & SHC material for Midday Office

The community was founded on the feast day of the Exaltation of the Holy Cross in 1925 by the Rt Revd Mark Trollope, the third English bishop of the Anglican Church in Korea, admitting Postulant Phoebe Lee and blessing a small traditional Korean-style house in the present site of Seoul. The Community of St Peter, a Nursing Order in Woking, Surrey, England, sent eighteen Sisters as missionaries to Korea between 1892 and 1950, who nourished this young community for a few decades. Sister Mary Clare CSP, who was the first Mother Superior of this community, was persecuted by the North Korean communists and died during the 'Death March' in the Korean War in 1950. This martyrdom especially has been a strong influence and encouragement for the growth of the community. Our spirituality is based on a modified form of the Augustinian Rule harmonized with the Benedictine one. Bishop Mark Trollope, the first Visitor, and Sister Mary Clare CSP compiled the Divine Office Book and the Constitution and Rule of the Community. The activities that are being continuously practised even now include pastoral care in parishes, running homes for the elderly and those with learning difficulties, conducting Quiet Days, and offering people spiritual direction.

We run spiritual prayer meetings and workshops weekly in March-June 2015 to celebrate our 90th anniversary for those who want to improve their faithful life. We lead Ignatian Contemplation Prayer, Lexio Divina, Centering Prayer, Rosary, Way of the Cross, Silence Prayer and Meditanz (Meditation in Dancing). We also have a programme of 'A day in Religious life' and weekend Retreats for individuals and in groups.

SISTER ALMA SHC
(Reverend Mother, assumed office 1 Jan 2010, re-elected 2013)
SISTER HELEN ELIZABETH SHC *(priest) (Assistant Superior)*

Sister Monica
Sister Phoebe Anne
Sister Edith
Sister Cecilia
Sister Maria Helen
Sister Etheldreda
Sister Catherine *(priest)*
Sister Maria Clara
Sister Pauline
Sister Angela
Sister Theresa
Sister Grace
Sister Helen Juliana
Sister Lucy Edward
Sister Martha
Sister Prisca *(Novice Guardian)*

Friends and Associates

FRIENDS are mostly Anglicans who desire to have a close

link with the community. They follow a simple Rule of Life, which includes praying for the Sisters and their work. Friends also form a network of prayer, fellowship and mutual support within Christ's ministry of wholeness and reconciliation. About one hundred members gather together for the annual meeting in May in the Motherhouse. The committee members meet bi-monthly at the convent in Seoul.
ASSOCIATES: forty-two friends have been trained for admission and vow-taking for full membership between 2005 and 2011.

Other Addresses

St Anne's Nursing Home for Elderly People,
79 Jundeungsa Road, Onsuri, Kilsang, Kangwha, Inch'on, 417-841
South Korea Tel: 32 937 1935 Fax: 32 937 0696
Email: anna1981@kornet.net Website: www.oldanna.or.kr

St Bona House for Intellectually Handicapped People,
123-9 Keumgo Neam Road, Kadok, Chongwon, Chungbuk 363-853, South Korea Tel: 43 297 8348 Fax: 43 298 3156
Email: sralma@naver.com Website: www.bona.or.kr

Community Publication: *Holy Cross Newsletter*, published occasionally, in Korean. Sister Catherine SHC, *Holy Vocation* (booklet for the SHC 75th anniversary, 2000)

Community History
Jae Joung Lee, *Society of the Holy Cross 1925-1995*, Seoul, 1995 (in Korean).
Sisters Maria Helen & Catherine, *The SHC: the First 80 Years*, 2005
Sister Helen Elizabeth (ed), *Fragrance of the Holy Cross,* 2010 (story of Sister Mary Clare in Korean)

Guest and Retreat Facilities: The Community organizes Retreats and Quiet Days monthly for Associates and groups and individuals.

Community Wares: Vestments and latar lines. Wafers and wine for Holy Eucharist for all the parishes in Korea.

Bishop Visitor: Most Revd Paul Kim, Bishop of Seoul, Presiding Bishop of Korea

Society of the Precious Blood (UK)

SPB

Founded 1905

Burnham Abbey
Lake End Road
Taplow,
Maidenhead
Berkshire SL6 OPW
UK
Tel & Fax:
01628 604080
Emails:
General:
burnhamabbey@btinternet.com
Prayer requests:
intercessions@burnhamabbey.org
Hospitality:
hospitality@burnhamabbey.org

Website: www.burnhamabbey.org

Lauds 7.30 am
Eucharist 9.30 am
Angelus & Sext 12.00 noon
Vespers 5.30 pm
Compline 8.30 pm

Office Book
SPB Office Book

Registered Charity
No. 900512

We are a contemplative community whose particular work within the whole body of Christ is worship, thanksgiving and intercession. Within these ancient Abbey walls, which date back to 1266, we continue to live the Augustinian monastic tradition of prayer, silence, fellowship and solitude. The Eucharist is the centre of our life, where we find ourselves most deeply united with Christ, one another and all for whom we pray. The work of prayer is continued in the Divine Office, in the Watch before the Blessed Sacrament and in our whole life of work, reading, creating, and learning to live together. This life of prayer finds an outward expression in welcoming guests, who come seeking an opportunity for quiet and reflection in which to deepen their own spiritual lives, or to explore the possibility of a religious vocation.

Sister Victoria Mary SPB
(Reverend Mother, assumed office 6 August 2011)

Sister Margaret Mary	Sister Mary Philip
Sister Mary Bernard	Sister Mary Benedict
Sister Dorothy Mary	Sister Miriam Mary
Sister Jane Mary	Sister Grace Mary
Sister Mary Laurence	

Companions and Oblates: Oblates are men and women who feel drawn by God to express the spirit of the Society, united with the Sisters in their life of worship, thanksgiving and intercession. They live out their dedication in their own situation and make a yearly Promise.

Men and women who desire to share in the prayer and work of the Society but cannot make as full a commitment to saying the Office may be admitted as Companions.

Community History
Sister Felicity Mary SPB, *Mother Millicent Mary,* 1968.
Booklets and leaflets on the history and life of the Abbey.

Community Wares: We have a small shop for cards.

Community Publications: *Newsletter,* yearly at Christmas. *Companions/Oblates Letter,* quarterly.

Guest and Retreat Facilities: Small guest wing with 3 single en suite rooms for individual (unconducted) retreats. Rooms available for Quiet Days or groups of up to 20.

Most convenient time to telephone: 10.30 am - 11.45 am; 3.30 pm - 4.30 pm; 7.00 pm - 8.00 pm

Bishop Visitor: Rt Revd Stephen Cottrell,
Bishop of Chelmsford

Society of the Precious Blood (southern Africa)

SPB

Founded 1905

St Monica's House of Prayer
46 Green Street
West End
Kimberley, 8301
SOUTH AFRICA

Tel: 00275 38 331161

Email: sisterelainespb@gmail.com

Morning Prayer 7.00 am

Eucharist 8.30 am (Thu & Fri)

Midday Office 12 noon

Evening Prayer 5.00 pm

Compline 8.00 pm

Office Book
Daily Prayer & An Anglican Prayer Book 1989, CPSA

Five Sisters of the Society of the Precious Blood at Burnham Abbey went to Masite in Lesotho in 1957 to join with a community of African women, with the intention of forming a multi-cultural contemplative community dedicated to intercession. In 1966, this community at Masite became autonomous, although still maintaining strong ties of friendship with Burnham Abbey. In 1980, a House of Prayer was established in Kimberley in South Africa, which developed a more active branch of the Society. Sadly, due to diminishing numbers, health issues and finance, the Lesotho Priory was closed on 1 March 2014 and the sisters there dispersed. The Kimberley house continues its ministry.

SISTER ELAINE MARY SPB
(Prioress, assumed office 24 September 1997) *(at Kimberley)*

Sister Theresia Mary
Sister Lucia Mary
(both in Lesotho)

Sister Diana Mary *(in UK)*
Sister Camilla Mary
(at Kimberley)

Obituaries
7 Mar 2014 Sister Josephine Mary, aged 88, professed 64 years

Oblates and Companions
The Community has thirteen oblates (in Lesotho, South Africa, Zambia, New Zealand and the UK), and eighty-six Companions and Associates (in Lesotho, South Africa and the UK). All renew their promises annually. Oblates are sent prayer material regularly. Companions and Associates receive quarterly letters and attend occasional quiet days.

Community Publication
Annual *Newsletter;* apply to the Prioress. No charge.

Community History and books
Sister Theresia Mary SPB, *Father Patrick Maekane MBK*, CPSA, 1987.
Evelyn Cresswell (Oblate SPB), *Keeping the Hours,* Cluster Pubs, Pietermaritzburg, 2007.

Guest and Retreat Facilities
Single room cottage.

Bishops Visitor
Rt Revd Adam Taaso, Bishop of Lesotho
Rt. Revd Oswald P.P. Swartz, Bishop of Kimberley and Kuruman

Society of the Sacred Advent

SSA

Founded 1892

Sisters House
18 Petrie Street
Ascot
QLD 4007
AUSTRALIA
Tel: 07 3262 5511
Fax: 07 3862 3296
Email:
eunice@stmargarets.qld.edu.au

Quiet time 6.00 am

Morning Prayer
6.30 am
(7.00 am Sun & Mon)

Eucharist 7.00 am
(7.30 am Sun)

Midday Prayer
12 noon

Evensong 5.00 pm

Compline 7.30 pm
(8.00 pm Wed & Sat)

Bishop Visitor
Rt Revd Godfrey Fryar, (retired bishop)

The Society of the Sacred Advent exists for the glory of God and for the service of His Church in preparation for the second coming of our Lord and Saviour Jesus Christ.

Members devote themselves to God in community under vows of poverty, chastity and obedience. Our life is a round of worship, prayer, silence and work. Our Patron Saint is John the Baptist who, by his life and death, pointed the way to Jesus. We would hope also to point the way to Jesus in our own time, to a world which has largely lost touch with spiritual realities and is caught up in despair, loneliness and fear.

As part of our ministry, Sisters may be called to give addresses, conduct Retreats or Quiet Days, or to make themselves available for spiritual direction and parish work. The aim of the Community is to grow in the mind of Christ so as to manifest Him to others. The Society has two Schools, St Margaret's and St Aidan's.

SISTER EUNICE SSA
(Revd Mother, assumed office 21 March 2007)

Sister June Ruth	Sister Beverley
Sister Sandra	Sister Gillian

Fellowship and Company

THE COMPANY/FELLOWSHIP OF THE SACRED ADVENT began in 1987. This group of men and women, clergy and lay, bound together in love for Jesus Christ and His Church in the spirit of St John the Baptist, seeks to proclaim the Advent challenge: 'Prepare the Way of the Lord.' Members have a Rule of Life and renew their promises annually.

Members of the Company/Fellowship are part of our extended Community family. The Sisters arrange Retreats and Quiet Days and support them with their prayers, help, or spiritual guidance, as required.

Other address

Society of the Sacred Advent, 261 Anduramba Road, Crows Nest, Queensland 4355, AUSTRALIA

Community History

Elizabeth Moores, *One Hundred Years of Ministry,* published for SSA, 1992.

Ray Geise, *Educating Girls since 1895,* Victory Press, Bribie Island, QLD, 2012.

Community Wares: Cards and crafts.

Community Publication
There is a Newsletter, twice yearly. For a subscription, write to Sister Sandra SSA. The cost is A$5 per year.

Guest and Retreat Facilities
No restrictions
Brisbane – day groups or quiet days only: no longer available overnight.
Crows Nest – day groups or quiet days; and cottage for retreats with three bedrooms.

Office Book
A Prayer Book for Australia; *The Daily Office SSF* is used for Midday Prayer.

Society of the Sacred Cross

SSC

Founded 1914 (Chichester); to Wales in 1923

Tymawr Convent
Lydart
Monmouth
Gwent
NP25 4RN
UK

Tel: 01600 860244

Email:
tymawrconvent @btinternet.com

Website
www. tymawrconvent.org

The community, part of the Anglican Church in Wales, lives a monastic, contemplative life of prayer based on silence, solitude and learning to live together, under vows of poverty, chastity and obedience, with a modern rule, Cistercian in spirit. At the heart of our corporate life is the Eucharist with the daily Office and other times of shared prayer spanning the day. All services are open to the public and we are often joined by members of the neighbourhood in addition to our visitors. Our common life includes study, recreation and work in the house and extensive grounds. It is possible for women and men, married or single, to experience our life of prayer by living alongside the community for periods longer than the usual guest stay. Hospitality is an important part of our life at Tymawr and guests are most welcome. We also organise and sponsor occasional lectures and programmes of study for those who wish to find or develop the life of the spirit in their own circumstances. The community is dedicated to the crucified and risen Lord as the focus of its life and the source of the power to live it.

Community Wares
Colour photographs cards of Tymawr available at 70p each (including envelope).

Community Publication: *Tymawr Newsletter*, yearly at Advent. Write to the above address.

Companions, Oblates and Associates
There are 7 Companions; 43 Oblates, living in their own homes, each having a personal Rule sustaining their life of prayer; 112 Associates, women and men, who have a simple commitment.

Morning Prayer
7.15 am

Terce 8.45 am

Eucharist
12.00 noon

Evening Prayer
5.15 pm

Silent Corporate Prayer
7.45 pm

Compline 8.15 pm

Office Book
Celebrating Common Prayer, with additional SSC material.

Bishop Visitor
Rt Revd
Dominic Walker OGS

Registered Charity:
No. 1135334

SISTER GILLIAN MARY SSC
(Revd Mother, assumed office 2010)
SISTER VERONICA ANN SSC *(Assistant)*
Sister Lorna Francis*
Sister Heylin Columba*
Sister Rosalind Mary
Sister Elizabeth
Sister Danielle
Novices: 2

* *Living the contemplative life away from Tymawr*

Guest and Retreat Facilities
The community offers facilities for individual guests and small groups. There are five rooms (one twin) in the guest wing of the main house for full board. Michaelgarth, the self-catering guest house, offers facilities for individuals and groups (five singles and two twin), and also for day groups. Individuals may have private retreats with guidance from a member of the community. The community occasionally organises retreats and study days. Pilgrimages around the grounds, on a variety of themes, can be arranged. Please write with a stamped addressed envelope for details.

Most convenient time to telephone: 6.45 pm – 8.00 pm only, except Mondays, Fridays and Sundays.

Community History
A Continuous Miracle: the history of the Society of the Sacred Cross. Copies can be obtained from Tymawr Convent.

Society of the Sacred Mission

SSM

Founded 1893

Office Book
Celebrating Common Prayer

Bishops Visitor
Rt Revd
Stephen Conway,
Bishop of Ely
(PROVINCE OF EUROPE)

Rt Revd
Garry Weatherill,
Bishop of Ballarat
(SOUTHERN PROVINCE)

Most Revd
Thabo Makgoba,
Archbishop of Cape Town
(SOUTHERN AFRICAN PROVINCE)

Founded in 1893 by Father Herbert Kelly, the Society is a means of uniting the devotion of ordinary people, using it in the service of the Church. Members of the Society share a common life of prayer and fellowship in a variety of educational, pastoral and community activities in England, Australia, Japan, Lesotho, and South Africa.

PROVINCE OF EUROPE
JONATHAN EWER SSM
(*Provincial, assumed office February 2014*)

Frank Green
Ralph Martin
Andrew Muramatsu
Edmund Wheat
Robert Stretton
Mary Hartwell
Margaret Moakes
Anthony Purvis

Associates:
Paul Golightly
Elizabeth Baker
Robin Baker
Marcus Armstrong
Joan Golightly
Karen Walker
Kevin Stephenson

Associates and Companions (applicable to all provinces)

ASSOCIATES: are men and women who share the life and work of a priory of the Society.

COMPANIONS: are men and women who support the aims of the Society without being closely related to any of its work. They consecrate their lives in loving response to a vocation to deepen their understanding of God's will, and to persevere more devotedly in commitments already made: baptism, marriage or ordination.

Addresses

Provincial & Administrator:

The Well, Newport Road, Willen MK15 9AA, UK
Tel: 01908 241974 Email: ssmlondon@yahoo.co.uk

St Antony's Priory, Claypath, Durham DH1 1QT, UK Tel: 0191 384 3747
Email: info@stantonyspriory.co.uk

1 Linford Lane, Milton Keynes, Bucks MK15 9DL, UK Tel: 01908 663749

Community History

Herbert H Kelly SSM, *An Idea in the Working,* SSM Press, Kelham, 1908.

Alistair Mason, *SSM: History of the Society of the Sacred Mission,* Canterbury Press, Norwich, 1993.

Ralph Martin SSM, *Towards a New Day: a monk's story,* Darton, Longman & Todd, London, 2015.

Community Publication: *SSM News* (newsletter of the Province of Europe) The Secretary, SSM Newsletter, The Well, Newport Road, Willen MK15 9AA, UK

AUSTRALIAN PROVINCE

CHRISTOPHER MYERS SSM

(Provincial, assumed office November 2009)

David Wells	*lay members:*	Iris Trengrove
Dunstan McKee	Geoff Pridham	Sue Ballett
Colin Griffiths	Lynne Rokkas	Cate Pennington
Margaret Dewey	John Lewis	Andrew Easton
Steven de Kleer	Des Benfield	Ryan Bennett
Gregory Stephens	Joyce Bleby Lewis	

Obituaries

24 Jan 2015 Laurence Eyers, aged 102, professed 64 years

Address

St John's Priory, 14 St John's Street, Adelaide, SOUTH AUSTRALIA 5000
Tel: 8 8223 2671 Email: ssm.s.province@esc.net.au

Community Publication:

Sacred Mission (newsletter of the Southern Province):
The Editor, St John's Priory, 14 St John's Street, Adelaide, SOUTH AUSTRALIA 5000

SOUTHERN AFRICAN PROVINCE

(re-founded September 2004)

TANKI MOFANA SSM

(Provincial, assumed office January 2013)

Michael Lapsley	Moiloa Mokheseng	*Novices*: 3
William Nkomo	Mosuoe Rakuoane	Karabo Thulo
Mosia Sello		Tefo Rachaka
Moeketsi Khommonngoe		Mabokoane Mabote

Addresses

SSM Priory, PO Box 1579, Maseru 100, LESOTHO
Tel: 22315979 Fax: 22310161
Email: ssmmaseru@tlmail.co.ls

33 Elgin Road, Sybrand Park, Cape Town, SOUTH AFRICA, 7708
Tel: 21 696 4866
Email: michael.lapsley@attglobal.net

Community Publication

Michael Lapsley SSM, *Redeeming the Past: my journey from Freedom Fighter to Healer,* Orbis, 2012.

Society of St Francis

SSF

Founded 1919 (USA)
1921 (UK)

Minister General
Email: clark.berg@s-s-f.org

Minister Provincial (European Province)
Email: ministerssf@franciscans.org.uk

European Province Website: www.franciscans.org.uk

Office Book
The Daily Office SSF
(revised edition 2010)

Bishop Protector
Rt Revd
Stephen Cottrell,
Bishop of Chelmsford

Community History
Petà Dunstan
This Poor Sort
DLT, London, 1997
£19.95 + £2 p&p

European Province SSF
Registered Charity:
No. 236464

The Society of St Francis has diverse origins in a number of Franciscan groups which drew together during the 1930s to found one Franciscan Society. SSF in its widest definition includes First Order Brothers, First Order Sisters (CSF), Second Order Sisters (OSC) and a Third Order (TSSF). The First Order shares a common life of prayer, fraternity and a commitment to issues of justice, peace and the integrity of creation. In its larger houses, this includes accommodation for short-term guests; in the city houses, the Brothers are engaged in a variety of ministries, chaplaincies and care for the poor and marginalised. They are also available for retreat work, counselling and sharing in the task of mission in parishes and schools. They also work in Europe and have houses in the Americas, Australasia, the Pacific, and Korea.

CLARK BERGE SSF
(Minister General, assumed office 1 November 2007)

EUROPEAN PROVINCE

BENEDICT SSF
(Minister Provincial, assumed office June 2012)
PHILIP BARTHOLOMEW SSF *(Assistant Minister)*

Amos
Angelo
Anselm
Austin
Benjamin
Christian
Christopher Martin
Cristian Michael
Damian
David
David Jardine
Donald
Edmund
Eric Michael
Giles
Hugh
Jason Robert
John
Joseph Emmanuel
Julian
Kentigern John
Kevin
Malcolm
Martin John
Micael Christopher
Nicholas Alan
Peter
Raymond Christian
Reginald
Robert
Samuel
Thomas Anthony
Vincent

Novices: 3

Obituaries

19 May 2014	Martin, aged 89, professed 62 years
11 Sep 2014	Raphael, aged 78, professed 40 years

Companions: Companions are individual Christians who wish to associate themselves with the Society through prayer, friendship and in seeking to live the spirit of the Gospel in the way of St Francis. For more information about becoming a Companion contact: The Secretary for Companions at Hilfield Friary.
Third Order: see separate entry.

Addresses All email addresses are @franciscans.org.uk

The Friary, Alnmouth, Alnwick, Northumberland NE66 3NJ
Tel: 01665 830213 Fax: 01665 830580 Email: alnmouthssf

Westcott House, Jesus Lane, Cambridge CB5 8BP
Tel: 01223 562766 Email: cambridgessf

St Matthias' Vicarage, 45 Mafeking Road, Canning Town, London E16 4NS Tel: 020 7511 7848 Email:canningtownssf

The Master's Lodge, 58 St Peter's Street, Canterbury, Kent CT1 2BE
Tel: 01227 479364 Email: canterburyssf

St Mary-at-the-Cross, Glasshampton, Shrawley, Worcestershire WR6 6TQ Tel: 01299 896345 Fax: 01299 896083 Email: glasshamptonssf

The Friary, Hilfield, Dorchester, Dorset DT2 7BE
Tel: 01300 341345 Fax: 01300 341293 Email: hilfieldssf

25 Karnac Road, Leeds LS8 5BL Tel: 0113 226 0647 Email: leedsssf

House of the Divine Compassion, 42 Balaam St, Plaistow, London E13 8AQ Tel: 020 7476 5189 Email: plaistowssf

85 Crofton Road, Plaistow, London E13 8QT
Tel: 020 7474 5863 Email: donaldssf

St Anthony's Friary, St Anthony's Vicarage, Enslin Gardens, Newcastle upon Tyne, NE6 3SRT Tel: 0191 276 0117 Email: newcastlessf

Anglican Chaplaincy, Via San Gabriele dell'Adollarata 12, 06081 Assisi (Pg), ITALY Bookings: passf@franciscans.org,uk

Community Wares: Hilfield Friary shop has on sale 'Freeland' cards, SSF publications and books of Franciscan spirituality and theology, as well as traidcraft goods. Alnmouth and Glasshampton also have small shops selling cards.

Guest and Retreat Facilities

HILFIELD: 8 bedrooms (2 twin-bedded) for men and women and 2 self-catering houses of 6 bedrooms each for the use of families and groups. Individually-guided retreats are available on request. There are facilities for day guests and for groups of up to 40. The brothers living at Hilfield are now joined by lay men and women, including families, who together comprise the Hilfield Friary Community, an intentional Franciscan community focussing on peace, justice and the integrity of creation. The Hilfield Peace and Environment Programme is an annual programme of courses & events which shares Franciscan insights on the care of creation and reconciliation *(www.hilfieldfriary.org.uk)*. The Friary is normally closed Sun pm - Tue am.

ALNMOUTH: The Friary has 12 rooms (including 1 twin-bedded) for men or women guests. Conducted retreats are held each year and individually-guided retreats are available on request. The recently-innovated chalet is available for families and groups

Community Publications
franciscan, three times a year - annual subscription is £8.00. Write to the Subscriptions Secretary at Hilfield Friary.
Books available from Hilfield Friary book shop include:
The Daily Office SSF, £10 + £2 p&p.

in particular need referred by churches and social services. The Friary is closed for 24 hours from Sunday afternoon.

GLASSHAMPTON: This has a more contemplative ethos. The guest accommodation, available to both men and women, comprises five rooms. Groups can visit for the day, but may not exceed fifteen people. The friary is closed from noon on Mondays for 24 hours and at Christmas time.

Brother Benedict receives the profession of a brother in the SSF European province

San Damiano
573 Dolores Street
San Francisco
CA 94110, USA
Tel: 415 861 1372
Fax: 415 861 7952
Email: judehillssf@aol.com

St Francis Friary
2449 Sichel Street
Los Angeles
CA 90031, USA
Tel: 323 222 7495

PROVINCE OF THE AMERICAS

The Province of the Americas of SSF was founded as the Order of St Francis in 1919 by Father Claude Crookston, who took the name Father Joseph. Under his leadership the community developed, based first in Wisconsin and then on Long Island, New York. The Order originally combined a monastic spirituality with a commitment to missions and evangelizing. In 1967, the OSF friars amalgamated with SSF in the UK and became the American Province of SSF.

Our lives are structured around our times together of formal prayer and the Eucharist, which give our lives a focus. Brothers engage in a wide variety of ministries: community organizing, missions, work in parishes and institutions, counselling and spiritual direction, study, the arts, serving the sick and infirm and people with AIDS, the homeless, workers in the sex industry, political work for the rights of people who are rejected by society. We come from a wide variety of backgrounds and cultural traditions. Living with each other can be difficult, but we work hard to find common ground and to communicate honestly with each other. God takes our imperfections and, in the mystery of Christ's body, makes us whole.

Minister Provincial
Tel: 415 861 7951
Fax: 415 861 7952
Email: judehillssf @aol.com

Website
www.s-s-f.org

Office Book
SSF Office Book

Bishop Protector
Rt Revd Jon Bruno, Bishop of Los Angeles

JUDE SSF
(Minister Provincial, assumed office May 2005)

Ambrose-Christobal	Ivanildo
Antonio Sato	Leo-Anthony
Clark Berge *(Minister General)*	Robert Hugh
Derek	*Novices:* 1
Desmond Alban	*Postulants:* 2
Dunstan	

Guest and Retreat Facilities
None at present. San Damiano sometimes has one small guest room available.

Community Publication
Clark Berge SSF, *The Vows Book: Anglican Teaching on the Vows of Obedience, Poverty and Chastity,*
Vest Pocket Publications, Mt Sinai, NY, 2014

THE PROVINCE OF THE DIVINE COMPASSION

The Hermitage
PO Box 46
Stroud
NSW 2425
AUSTRALIA
Tel: 2 4994 5372
Fax: 2 4994 5527
Email: ssfstrd@ bigpond.com

The Friary
PO Box 6134
Buranda
Brisbane
QLD 4102
AUSTRALIA
Tel: 7 3391 3915
Fax: 7 3391 3916

Website: www. franciscan.org.au

SSF friars went from England to Papua New Guinea in the late 1950s and the first Australian house was established in 1964. The first New Zealand house followed in 1970. In 1981, the Pacific Province was divided into two: Australia/New Zealand and the Pacific Islands. The latter was divided again in 2008 into Papua New Guinea and the Solomon Islands. In 1993 the first Koreans joined to form the Korean Franciscan Brotherhood, initially linked by covenant with SSF. They were received as members of SSF in 2010. Reflecting the geographic diversity of the province the name was changed to Province of the Divine Compassion in 2011.

CHRISTOPHER JOHN SSF
(Minister Provincial, assumed office 2012)

Alfred BoonKong	Daniel	Nathan-James
Brian	Donald Campbell	Noel-Thomas
Bruce-Paul	James Andrew	Raphael Suh
Cyril	Lawrence	Stephen
Damian Kenneth	Lionel	William

Friary of the Divine Compassion
PO Box 13-117
Hillcrest
Hamilton 3251
Aotearoa New Zealand
Tel: 7 856 6701
Email: friary @franciscan.org.nz

Website: www. franciscan.org.nz

The Friary
156 Balsan-Ri
Nam-Myeon
Chuncheon 200-922
Republic of Korea
Tel: 33 263 4662
Fax: 33 263 4048
Email: kfb1993@kornet.net

Website: www.francis.or.kr

Guest and Retreat Facilities

There is limited accommodation for short stay guests in the Brisbane, Stroud, Hamilton and Korea houses. In all cases, payment is by donation. Additionally, in Korea larger numbers can be accommodated at the nearby Diocesan Retreat House managed by the Brothers.

At Stroud, the old monastery of the Community of St Clare is also available for accommodation.

Contact: Friends of the Old Monastery,
oldmonasterystroud@gmail.com

Community Publication

New Zealand: *Franciscan Angles (4 per year)*
Australia: *Franciscan Angles, (3 per year)*
Korea: *newsletter* in Korean (quarterly)
All are available on the relevant websites or by email. To subscribe to printed copies, please contact the Hamilton, Brisbane or Korea address as appropriate. In all cases, subscription is by donation.

Community Wares

Holding Crosses (Stroud & Korea)
Candles (Korea)

Office Book: The Daily Office SSF

Bishops Protector

Rt Revd John Stead, Bishop of Willochra *(Protector General)*
Rt Revd Jim White, Assistant Bishop of Auckland *(Deputy Protector for New Zealand)*
Most Revd Paul Kim, Bishop of Seoul *(Deputy Protector for Korea)*

Papua New Guinea Province

Oswald Dumbari SSF
(Minister Provincial, assumed office July 2012)

Anthony Kambua
Charles Iada
Clement Vulum
Collin Velei
Dominic Ombed
Jerry Ross
Laurence Hauje
Lindsay Ijiba
Nathaniel Gari
Reuben Arthur
Wallace Yovero
Willbert Bebena
Worrick Marako

Novices: 1

Bishop Protector

Most Revd Clyde Mervin Igara, Archbishop of Papua New Guinea

Addresses in PNG

Saint Mary of the Angels Friary, Haruro, PO Box 78, Popondetta 241, Oro Province Tel: 329 7060
Email (Provincial Secretary): br.worrickssf@gmail.com

Saint Francis Friary, Koki, PO Box 1103, Port Moresby, NCD
Tel & fax: 320 1499 Email: ssfpng@daltron.com.pg

Martyrs' House, PO Box 35, Popondetta, Oro Province
Tel & fax: 3297 491

Philip Beawa Friary, Ukaka, PO Box 22, Alotau, Milne Bay Province

Province of the Solomon Islands

Samson Siho SSF
(Minister, assumed office 2015)

Amos Helo	Ellison Sero	Judah Kea	Selwyn Tione
Athanasius Faifu	Francis Ngofia	Joseph Lent Fugui	Stephen Hovu
Andrew Laukiara	Gilford Taetalau	Luke Manitara	Steven Siosi Amau
Andrew Manu	Harry Belafalu	Martin Tawea	Thomas Peleba
Benjamin Tabugau	Hilton Togara	Matthew Sikoboki	William Malama
Clifton Henry	Hubert Tavoto	Moffat Behulu	
Commins Romano	John Kogudi	Patrick Paoni	*Novices:* 21
Elliott Faga	Jonah Arikimoana	Paul Tula	
Ellison Hoasipepe	Jonas Balunga	Samson Amoni	

Obituaries

22 Nov 2014 Manasseh Birahu, aged 59, professed 32 years

Bishop Protector: Rt Revd Alfred Karabongi, Bishop of Hanuato'o

Addresses in the Solomon Islands

Patteson House, PO Box 519, Honiara, Guadalcanal
Tel: 22386 Regional Office tel & fax: 25810
Email: honiarassf@brosgmail.com

St Bonaventure Friary, Kohimarama Theological College, PO Box 519, Honiara, Guadalcanal Tel: 50128

Saint Francis Friary, PO Box 7, Auki, Malaita Province
Tel: 40054

San Damiano Friary, Diocese of Hanuato'o, Kira Kira, Makira Ulawa Province

Michael Davis Friary, PO Box 519, Honiara, Guadalcanal

La Verna Friary/Little Portion, Hautambu, PO Box 519, Honiara, Guadalcanal

Holy Martyrs Friary, Luisalo, PO Box 50, Lata, Temotu Province

Society of St John the Divine

SSJD

Founded 1887

Cottage 252
Umdoni
Retirement Village
PO Box 300
Pennington 4184
KwaZulu Natal
SOUTH AFRICA

Tel: +27
039 975 9552

Emails:
maryevelyncoffee@gmail.com

hil64337@gmail.com

Angelus
& Morning Prayer
8.15 am
follwed by Midday Office

On Saints' Days, Eucharist
4.45 pm
followed by Angelus & Evening Prayer

Compline
7.30 pm

Prayer Time taken privately

The Society has never been a large community, with just sixty professions over a century, and has always worked in Natal. Originally the community ran schools and orphanages. In 1994, after the death of the older Sisters, the four of us who remained moved to a house that was more central in Durban.

We moved to Umdoni Retirement Village in Pennington in 2003. Our involvement outside the village involves being on the Board of Governors of our school, St John's Diocesan School for Girls in Pietermaritzburg, and all our Associates, Friends and Oblates worldwide. Sister Mary Evelyn is a Layminister and exercises her ministry within Umdoni. Sister Margaret Anne is now resident in our Frail Care.

Sister Mary Evelyn SSJD
Sister Margaret Anne SSJD
Sister Sophia SSJD
Sister Hilary SSJD

Oblates and Associates
These are people who are linked with us and support us in prayer.
Oblates: There is one, non-resident, and she renews her oblation annually.
Associates: There are over a hundred, some overseas. They have a Rule of Life and renew their promises annually.
Friends: They have a Rule of Life and like the Associates and Oblates meet with the Sisters twice a year.

Community Publication
One newsletter is sent out each year to Oblates, Associates and Friends in Advent.

Community History and books
Sister Margaret Anne SSJD, *What the World Counts Weakness,* privately published 1987 (now out of print).
Sister Margaret Anne SSJD, *They Even Brought Babies,* privately published.

Bishop Visitor
Rt Revd Rubin Phillip,
Bishop of Natal, Dean of the Province

Office Book
An Anglican Prayer Book 1989 (South African) for Morning & Evening Prayer.
Our own SSJD book for Midday Office & Compline.

Society of St John the Evangelist

(UK)

SSJE

Founded 1866

Email: **superior@ssje.org.uk**

A Registered Charity.

The Society of Saint John the Evangelist is the oldest of the Anglican orders for men, founded at Cowley in Oxford in 1866 by Father Richard Meux Benson. From it grew the North American Congregation and we were also involved in the founding of several other Communities around the world both for men and women. SSJE worked as a Missionary Order in several countries, most notably India and South Africa. In 2012 the English Congregation closed its last House in London and went into retirement where they continue to live out their vows.

FATHER PETER HUCKLE SSJE
(Superior, assumed office 7 March 2002)
Father Peter Palmer
Brother James Simon

The Fellowship of St John: Email: superior@ssje.org.uk
Bishop Visitor: Rt Revd Dominic Walker OGS

Society of St John the Evangelist

(North American Congregation)

SSJE

Founded 1866

The Monastery
980 Memorial Drive
Cambridge
MA 02138
USA
Tel: 617 876 3037

Email: monastery@ssje.org

The Society of St John the Evangelist was founded in the parish of Cowley in Oxford, England, by Richard Meux Benson in 1866. A branch house was established in Boston in 1870. The brothers of the N. American Congregation live at the monastery in Cambridge, Massachusetts, near Harvard Square, and at Emery House, a rural retreat sanctuary in West Newbury, Massachusetts. They gather throughout the day to pray the Divine Office, and live under a modern Rule of Life, adopted in 1997, which is available online at www.ssje.org. At profession, brothers take vows of poverty, celibacy and obedience.

SSJE's guesthouses offer hospitality to many. Young adults (ordinarily 21 to 34) may serve for a year as Monastic Interns. Guests may come individually or in groups for times of silent reflection and retreat. SSJE brothers lead retreats and programs in their own houses and in parishes and dioceses throughout North America. SSJE brothers also serve as preachers, teachers, spiritual directors and confessors. SSJE's ministry occasionally extends overseas to Europe, Israel/Palestine and Africa. Nearer to home, they are engaged in part-time ministries with students and young adults, homeless people, deaf people, Asian-Americans, and people in recovery (12-step programs).

Community History

Eldridge Pendleton, *On the Kingdom: The life of Charles Chapman Grafton, Society of Saint John the Evangelist*, SSJE, 2014.

Morning Prayer
6.00 am
Eucharist
7.45 am
Midday Prayer
12.30 pm
Evening Prayer
6.00 pm
Compline
8.30 pm

(The schedule varies slightly during the week. The complete schedule can be found on the community's website.)

Office Book
BCP of ECUSA, and the Book of Alternate Services of the Anglican Church of Canada

Website
www.ssje.org

Cowley Publications
Websites:
www.cowley.org
&
www.amazon.com
&
www.forwardmovement.org

Bishop Visitor
Rt Revd
Frank T. Griswold, III

BROTHER GEOFFREY TRISTRAM SSJE
(*Superior, assumed office 4 May 2010*)
BROTHER JAMES KOESTER SSJE *(Deputy Superior)*
BROTHER MARK BROWN SSJE *(Assistant Superior)*

David Allen	Curtis Almquist
John Oyama *(in Japan)*	Robert L'Esperance
Bernard Russell	Luke Witewig
John Goldring *(in Canada)*	Jim Woodrum
Jonathan Maury	John Braught
Eldridge Pendleton	
David Vryhof	*Novices:* 2

Obituaries

17 Oct 2014 M. Thomas Shaw, aged 69, professed 36 years, Bishop of Massachusetts 1994-2014

Associates

The Fellowship of Saint John is composed of men and women throughout the world who desire to live their Christian life in special association with the Society of Saint John the Evangelist. They have a vital interest in the life and work of the community and support its life and ministries with their prayers, encouragement and gifts. The brothers of the Society welcome members of the Fellowship as partners in the gospel life, and pray for them by name during the Daily Office, following a regular cycle. Together they form an extended family, a company of friends abiding in Christ and seeking to bear a united witness to him as "the Way, the Truth and the Life", following the example of the beloved Disciple. For further information, or to join the Fellowship, visit the Society's website: www.ssje.org.

Other address: Emery House, 21 Emery Lane, West Newbury, MA 01985, USA Tel: 978 462 7940

Community Publication: *Cowley*: a quarterly newsletter. Available online (www.ssje.org) or in printed form (contact monastery@ssje.org). For a subscription, write to SSJE at the Cambridge, Massachusetts, address. The suggested donation is US$20 annually.

Guest and Retreat Facilities

MONASTERY GUESTHOUSE in Cambridge, MA - 16 rooms.
EMERY HOUSE in West Newbury, MA - 6 hermitages, 3 rooms in main house.
At both houses: US$100 per night standard - US$50 for students; $125 individually guided - $65 for students; $135 program retreats - $65 for students (closed in August).

Society of St Margaret

(Duxbury)

SSM

Founded 1855
(US Convent founded 1873)

St Margaret's Convent
50 Harden Hill Road
PO Box C
Duxbury
MA 0233-0605
USA
Tel: 781 934 9477

Email: sisters@ ssmbos.org

Website
www.ssmbos.org

Morning Prayer
6.00 am

Eucharist 7.30 am

Noon Office
12 noon

Evening Prayer
5.00 pm

Compline 7.30 pm

Office Book
BCP
of ECUSA

The Society of St Margaret is an Episcopal Religious Order of mission-focused sisters living an ancient tradition with a modern outlook. Our lives as Sisters are guided by the principle, "Love first, Love midst, Love last." We take vows of poverty, celibate chastity, and obedience; listening for the voice of God in all circumstances.

Our mission of hospitality calls us to welcome people to our houses for times of refreshment and renewal. Our mission of service calls us to move out beyond our dwelling places to serve those in need, to go where God leads and to share Christ's light. We strive to live a balanced life of active work and contemplative prayer, and are committed to partner with those who share our passion for a world of justice, mercy and peace.

The central work of the community is worship and prayer and the Eucharist provides the pattern for our daily lives. As Jesus took bread, blessed and broke it, so our lives are taken, blessed, broken, and given through our varied ministries. As we work with children, care for the elderly, and do parish work, we seek always to live as Christ's hands and heart in this world.

SISTER ADELE MARIE SSM *(priest)*
(Mother Superior, assumed office March 2011)
SISTER CAROLYN SSM *(Assistant Superior)*

Sr Catherine Louise *(priest)*
Sister Marjorie Raphael
Sister Emily Louise
Sister Gloria
Sister Ann
Sister Claire Marie
Sister Mary Gabriel
Sister Adele
Sister Julian
Sister Christine
Sister Marie Thérèse
Sister Brigid
Sister Promise
Sister Sarah Margaret *(priest)*
Sister Kristina Frances
Sister Kethia

Obituaries
19 Jul 2013 Sister Marion, aged 93, professed 62 years
20 Jan 2015 Sister Marie Margaret, aged 76, professed 48 years

Associates
Associates of one Convent of the Society of St Margaret are Associates of all. They have a common Rule, which is flexible to circumstances. They include men and women, lay and ordained. No Associate of the Society may be an Associate of any other community.

Addresses of other houses

Sisters of St Margaret, 375 Mount Vernon Street, Apt 511, Boston, MA 02125, USA Tel: 617 533 7742 Email: srchristinessm@gmail.com

St Margaret's Convent, Port-au-Prince, HAITI
Mailing address: **St Margaret's Convent, Port-au-Prince, c/o Agape Flights, Inc., 100 Airport Avenue, Venice, FL 34285-3901, USA**
Tel: 011 509 3448 2609 Email: marietheresessm@yahoo.com

Neale House, 50 Fulton Street #2A, New York, NY 10038-1800, USA
Tel: 212 619 2672 Email: annwhitaker1942@gmail.com

Community Publication: *St Margaret's Quarterly*. Historical issues available free on our website or by mail. For information, contact convent@ssmbos.org. Current Community news is shared via e-mail and Social Media. Those needing hard copies should contact us at convent@ssmbos.org.

Community History
Sister Catherine Louise SSM, *The House of my Pilgrimage: a History of the American House of the Society of Saint Margaret,* privately published, 1973.
Sister Catherine Louise SSM, *The Planting of the Lord: The History of the Society of Saint Margaret in England, Scotland & the USA;* privately published, 1995.
Contact convent@ssmbos.org to order. $6 US each, plus $4 US shipping and handling.

Guest and Retreat Facilities
Guest facilities are available for small groups and individuals. Contact the Duxbury convent for more information.

Bishop Visitor: Rt Rev Alan M. Gates, Bishop of Massachusetts.

Society of St Margaret

(Hackney)

SSM

Founded 1855
(St Saviour's Priory 1866)

Website: www.stsaviourspriory.org.uk

St Saviour's Priory is one of the autonomous Houses which constitute the Society of St Margaret founded by John Mason Neale. Exploring contemporary ways of living the Religious life, the community seeks, through a balance of prayer and ministry, to respond to some of the needs that arise amongst the marginalised in East London. The Office is four-fold and the Eucharist is offered daily. The Sisters' outreach to the local community includes: working as staff members (lay or ordained) in various parishes; supporting issues of justice and racial equality; supporting the gay community; Sunday Stall and Drop in Centre; Dunloe Centre for the homeless and alcoholics; complementary therapy; individual spiritual direction and retreats; dance workshops; art work and design. The Sisters also share their community building and resources of worship and space with individuals and groups.

St Saviour's Priory
18 Queensbridge Road
London E2 8NS
UK
Tel: 020 7739 9976
Email: ssmpriory@aol.com

Leader of the community
020 7613 1464

Guest Bookings
020 7739 6775
Fax: 020 7739 1248

(Sisters are not available on Mondays)

Morning Prayer
7.15 am
(7.30 am Sun)
followed by
Eucharist
(12.15 pm on major feasts)

Midday Office
12.45 pm

Evening Prayer
5.00 pm

Night Prayer
8.30 pm

Office Book
Celebrating Common Prayer

Registered Charity
No 230927

THE REVD SISTER JUDITH BLACKBURN SSM *(priest)*
(Leader of the Community, assumed office 26 February 2014)
SISTER ANNA HUSTON & SISTER ELIZABETH CRAWFORD
(Assistant Leaders)

Sister June Atkinson
Sister Frances (Claire) Carter
Sister Pauline (Mary) Hardcastle
Sister Enid Margaret Jealous
Sister Moira Jones
The Revd Sister Helen Loder SSM *(priest)*
Sister Pamela Radford

Associates and Friends

ASSOCIATES make a long term commitment to the Society of St Margaret, following a Rule of Life and helping the Community where possible. An Associate of one SSM house is an Associate of all the houses. There are regular quiet days for Associates who are kept in touch with community developments.

FRIENDS OF ST SAVIOUR'S PRIORY commit themselves to a year of mutual support and friendship and are invited to regular events throughout the year.

Community Publication: *The Orient*, yearly. Write to The Orient Secretary at St Saviour's Priory. Brochures about the Community are available at any time on request.

Community Wares

Cards, books and religious items for sale.

Community History

Memories of a Sister of S. Saviour's Priory, Mowbray, 1904.

A Hundred Years in Haggerston, published by St Saviour's Priory, 1966.

Sister Catherine Louise SSM, *The Planting of the Lord: The History of the Society of Saint Margaret in England, Scotland & the USA;* privately published, 1995.

Guest and Retreat Facilities

Six single rooms for individual guests. Excellent facilities for non-residential group meetings.

Most convenient time to telephone

10.30 am - 1.00 pm (Not Mondays).

Bishop Visitor

Rt Revd Jonathan Clark, Bishop of Croydon

Society of St Margaret (Chiswick)

SSM

Founded 1855

St Mary's Convent & Nursing Home
Burlington Lane
Chiswick
London W4 2QE, UK
Tel: 020 8 994 4641
Fax: 020 8995 9697

Email: stmarysnh@gmail.com

Matins 8.00 am

Eucharist 10.00 am (9.00 am Tue & Sat)

Midday Office & Litany of the Holy Name 12.15 pm

Vespers 4.45 pm

Compline 6.15 pm

Office Book
'A Community Office' printed for St Margaret's Convent, East Grinstead.

Registered Charity: No. 231926

The Convent at Chiswick is one of the autonomous Convents that constitute the Society of St Margaret, founded by John Mason Neale. The Sisters' work is the worship of God, expressed in their life of prayer and service. At Chiswick they care for elderly people in a nursing home and have guests. There is a semi-autonomous house and a branch house in Sri Lanka. There are two Sisters in retirement flats in Uckfield who offer intercessory prayer, spiritual direction, pastoral support and other involvement in the life of the town and parish.

MOTHER JENNIFER ANNE SSM
(Mother Superior, assumed office 2 March 2015)
SISTER MARY CLARE SSM *(Assistant Superior)*
Sister Raphael Mary
Sister Rita Margaret
Sister Cynthia Clare
Sister Lucy
Sister Barbara
Sister Mary Paul
Sister Sarah

Obituaries
19 Sep 2013 Sister Mary Michael, aged 87, professed 51 years

Associates: Associates observe a simple Rule, share in the life of prayer and dedication of the community, and are welcomed at all SSM convents.

Community Publication: The newsletter of St Margaret's Convent and St. Mary's Nursing Home is sent out if requested.

Community History
Sister Catherine Louise SSM, *The Planting of the Lord: The History of the Society of Saint Margaret in England, Scotland & the USA;* privately published, 1995.

Pamela Myers & Sheila White, *A Legacy of Care: St Mary's Convent and Nursing Home, Chiswick, 1896 to 2010,* St Mary's Convent, Chiswick, 2010.

Doing the Impossible: a short sketch of St Margaret's Convent, East Grinstead 1855-1980, privately published, 1984. Postscript 2000.

Most convenient time to telephone: 10am - 5pm.

Bishop Visitor
Rt Revd Martin Warner, Bishop of Chichester

St Margaret's Convent
157 St Michael's Road
Polwatte
Colombo 3
SRI LANKA

Bishop Visitor
Rt Revd Dhiloraj Canagasaby, Bishop of Colombo

SEMI-AUTONOMOUS HOUSES OVERSEAS

The Sisters run a Retreat House, a Hostel for young women, a Home for elderly people, and are involved in parish work and church embroidery.

SISTER CHANDRANI SSM
(Sister Superior, assumed office 2006)
Sister Lucy Agnes
Sister Mary Christine

Obituaries
17 Mar 2015 Sister Jane Margaret, aged 86, professed 59 years

Other address
A children's home: **St John's Home, 133 Galle Rd, Moratuwa, SRI LANKA**

Society of St Margaret

(Walsingham)

SSM

Founded 1855
(Walsingham Priory founded 1955)

The Priory of Our Lady
Bridewell Street
Walsingham
Norfolk
NR22 6ED
UK

Tel: 01328 820340 (Sisters & guests)

Tel: 01328 821647 (Admin)

In January 1994, the Priory of Our Lady at Walsingham reverted to being an autonomous house of the Society of St Margaret. The Sisters are a Traditional Community whose daily life is centred on the Eucharist and the daily Office, from which flows their growing involvement in the ministry of healing, and reconciliation in the Shrine, the local parishes and the wider Church. They welcome guests for short periods of rest, relaxation and retreat, and are available to pilgrims and visitors. They also work in the Education Department and Welcome Centre of the Shrine.

SISTERS MARY TERESA SSM & MARY ANGELA SSM
(Joint leaders, appointed March 2015)

Sister Alma Mary
Sister Francis Anne *(transferring to SSM Chiswick)*
Sister Columba
Sister Carol Elizabeth

Obituaries
16 Mar 2015 Sister Phyllis, aged 79, professed 30 years

Emails:
sisterangela@prioryofourlady.uk.com *(Admin)*
teresa@prioryofourlady.uk.com
bursar@prioryofourlady.uk.com *(bursar)*
Guests@prioryofourlady.uk.com

Website: www.ssmwalsingham.moonfruit.com

Bishop Visitor: Rt Revd Peter Wheatley

Readings & Morning Prayer
7.00 am

Mass 9.30 am
(9.00 am on Thu, with Exposition to 10 am)
(No Mass on Sun in Sisters' Chapel)

Exposition of the Blessed Sacrament
10-30 am-12.30 pm
(except Sun & Thu)

Midday Prayer
12.45 pm

Evening Prayer
5.00 pm

Night Prayer 8.45 pm
(7.00 pm Sun, Tue & Sat)

Associates
There are Associates, and Affiliated Parishes and Groups.

Community Publication: Community booklet, *Wellspring*, published annually in the autumn. Write to the Priory for information. £3.50, including postage.

Community History
Sister Catherine Louise SSM, *The Planting of the Lord: The History of the Society of Saint Margaret in England, Scotland & the USA;* privately published, 1995.

Community Wares
Cards (re-cycled) and embroidered; books; Religious objects (statues, pictures, rosary purses etc).

Guest and Retreat Facilities: St Margaret's Cottage, (self-catering) for women and men, families and small groups. One single room (bed sit, ensuite) on the ground floor, suitable for a retreatant, and three twin rooms upstairs.

Most convenient time to telephone: 10.30 am - 12.30 pm; 2.30 pm - 4.30 pm; 6.30 pm - 8.30 pm.

Office Book: The Divine Office

Registered Charity: No. 25515

Society of St Paul

SSP

Founded 1958

2728 Sixth Avenue
San Diego
CA 92103-6397
USA
Tel: 619 542 8660
Email: anbssp@societyofstpaul.com

Bishop Visitor
Rt Revd
James R Mathes,
Bishop of San Diego

The Society of St Paul began in Gresham, Oregon in 1958. Early ministry included nursing homes, a school, and commissary work in the Mid-East and Africa. In 1959, SSP was the first community for men to be recognized by the canons of ECUSA. The brothers live a life of prayer and are dedicated to works of mercy, charity and evangelism. In 1976, the order moved to Palm Desert, California, providing a retreat and conference center until 1996. In 2001, the brothers moved to St Paul's Cathedral in San Diego. In particular, we are involved at St Paul's Senior Homes and Services, the Uptown Faith Community Services, Inc., Dorcas House, a foster home for children whose parents are in prison in Tijuana, Mexico, and St Paul's Cathedral ministries.

THE REVD CANON BARNABAS HUNT SSP
(*Rector, assumed office 1989*)
THE REVD CANON ANDREW RANK SSP (*Associate Rector*)

Fellowship of St Paul
The Fellowship of St Paul, our extended family, is an association of Friends, Associates and Companions of the Society of St Paul, who live a Rule of Life centered on the Glory of God.

Society of the Sisters of Bethany

SSB

Founded 1866

7 Nelson Road
Southsea
Hampshire
PO5 2AR
UK
Tel: 02392 833498
Email: ssb@sistersofbethany.org.uk

Website: www.sistersofbethany.org.uk

Mattins 7.00 am

Mass 7.45 am
(8.00 am Sun; 9.30 am Wed & alternate Sats)

Terce 9.15 am

Midday Office
12 noon

Vespers 5.00 pm

Compline 8.00 pm

Office Book
Anglican Office book with adaptations

Registered Charity:
No. 226582

The Sisters of Bethany (SSB) are the founding community of a wider Bethany family that includes Associates, Oblates and the Order of Companions of Martha and Mary (OCMM):

Associates are a body of close friends who live in their own homes and accept a simple Rule of Life.

Oblates are a recent development (2014), who also live in their own homes. They have adopted the Rule of Life used by the Sisters, modified appropriately to their own circumstances. Oblates and Sisters live by a spirituality derived from the Salesian Rule of the Visitation Order. They share times of study and ongoing formation.

The Sisters' online ministry using Twitter (**twitter.com@bethanysister**) and Facebook (**facebook.com@sisters.ofbethany**) engages with nearly 8,500 people, meeting them where they are and helping them see God in the 'everyday'.

Each member of the Bethany family makes the offering of herself in the hidden life of prayer, praying daily for the unity of Christians and, by prayer and activity, seeking to share in Christ's mission reconciling the divided Churches of Christendom and the whole world.

The OCMM is a new monastic order (2010). The Sisters live in community under a Benedictine-inspired Rule and are linked to SSB by close ties of friendship, shared activity and prayer intentions under the patronage of the household of Bethany. **OCMM, St Mary's Vicarage, Church Lane, Mellor, Blackburn BB2 7JL**
Website: www.companionsmarthamary.org
Facebook: (CompanionsMarthamary)

MOTHER RITA-ELIZABETH SSB
(Reverend Mother, assumed office 22 October 2009)
SISTER MARY JOY SSB *(Assistant Superior)*

Sister Katherine Maryel
Sister Ruth Etheldreda
Sister Ann Patricia
Sister Gwenyth
Sister Joanna Elizabeth
Sister Elizabeth Pio

Obituaries
12 Jan 2015 Sister Florence May, aged 94, professed 51 years

Bethany family:
SSB, OCMM, Oblates together

Associates, Oblates, contacts

Associates' Sister: Sister Gwenyth
Oblates' Sister: Sister Elizabeth Pio
Order of Companions of Martha & Mary: Amma Sue OCMM

Community Wares: Cards.

Community Publication: Associates' magazine, July and December

Guest and Retreat Facilities

Six guest rooms (one twin-bedded). Individual retreatants can be accommodated. Closed at Christmas.

Most convenient time to telephone:

9.30 am - 11.45 am, 1 pm - 4 pm, 6 pm - 7.45 pm

Bishop Visitor

Rt Revd Trevor Willmott, Bishop of Dover and Bishop in Canterbury

Some other Communities

Asia

Devasevikaramaya
31 Kandy Road, Kurunegala, Sri Lanka Tel: 0094 372 221803
An order for women, founded by the first Bishop of Kurunegala, Rt Revd Lakdasa de Mel, in the 1950s.

The Order of Women, Church of South India
18, CSI Women's House, Infantry Road, Bengaluru, Karnataka 560001, India

Soon after the inauguration of the CSI in 1948, a Religious Order for women was organized under the initiative and leadership of Sister Carol Graham, a deaconess in the Anglican Church before 1948. The Order has both active and associate members. The former take a vow of celibacy, observe a rule of life and are engaged in some form of full-time Christian service. The Order is a member of the Diakonia World Federation. The Sisters are dispersed among the twenty-one dioceses of the CSI.

Order of St Benedict
810-1 Baekrok-ri, Habuk-myon, Yangsan-shi, Kyungnam 626-860, South Korea

Australasia and the Pacific

Congregation of the Sisters of the Visitation of Our Lady (CVL)
Convent of the Visitation, Hetune, Box 18, Popondetta, Oro Province, PNG

Europe

Society of the Franciscan Servants of Jesus and Mary (FSJM)
Posbury St Francis, Crediton, Devon, EX17 3QG, UK

Society of Our Lady of the Isles (SOLI)
Lark's Hame, Aithness, Isle of Fetlar, Shetland ZE2 9DJ, UK (also on Unst)
https://sites.google.com/site/societyofourladyoftheisles/
The two professed Sisters are in the process of moving to the island of Unst. The two Companions will remain on Fetlar.

North America and the Caribbean

Order of the Teachers of the Children of God (TCG)
5870 East 14th Street, Tucson, AZ 85711, USA

Society of Our Lady St Mary (SLSM)
Bethany Place, PO Box 762, Digby, Nova Scotia, BOV 1AO, Canada

Single Consecrated Life

One of the earliest ways of living the Religious life is for single people to take a vow of consecrated celibacy and to live in their own homes. This ancient form of commitment is also a contemporary one with people once again embracing this form of Religious life. Some may have an active ministry, others follow a contemplative lifestyle, some are solitaries, and others are widows or widowers.

In 2002, the Advisory Council (for Religious Communities in the Church of England) set up a Personal Vows group in response to enquiries from bishops and others to advise those who wish to take a vow of consecrated celibacy. In 2011 the Advisory Council approved a constitution for the network, and a leadership team was elected which now provides support for those who have professed this vow and arranges gatherings. In the Roman Catholic Church, this form of living the consecrated life was affirmed by Vatican II, which re-established the Order of Consecrated Virgins (OCV) and now an order of Widows is also emerging.

People exploring this call should be single, widowed, widowered or divorced, mature Christians (men or women) already committed to a life of prayer and willing to undertake a period of discernment before taking a temporary vow which may precede a life vow. An appropriate spiritual director and support from association with a Religious Community or through the Single Consecrated Life network is important to ensure adequate formation. We also have a group of Friends who support us in prayer.

The vow is received by a person's bishop. The bishop (or their appointee) becomes the 'guardian of the vow' and the act of consecration is registered with SCL for the Advisory Council.

SUE HARTLEY *(Coordinating Dean)*
BEVERLEY SMITH *(Dean of Sisters)*
PHILLIP TOVEY *(Dean of Brothers)*

Persons in Life Vows: 32
Persons in First Vows: 6
Seekers: 12

For further information contact:

Sue Hartley SCL,
272 New North Road, Ilford IG6 3BT, UK
Email: suemhartley@btinternet.com

Website: http://singleconsecratedlife-anglican.org.uk/index.html

Directory of dispersed celibate communities

In this section are communities that from their foundation have lived as dispersed communities. In other words, their members do not necessarily live a common life in community, although they do come together for chapter meetings and other occasions each year.

Like traditional communities, they do take vows that include celibacy.

Oratory of the Good Shepherd

OGS

Founded 1913

Website
www.ogs.net

Bishop Visitor
Rt Revd Jack Nicholls

The Oratory of the Good Shepherd is a society of priests and laymen founded at Cambridge (UK), which now has provinces in North America, Australia, Southern Africa and Europe. Oratorians are bound together by a common Rule and discipline; members do not generally live together in community. The brethren are grouped in 'colleges' and meet regularly for prayer and support, and each province meets annually for retreat and chapter. Every three years, the General Chapter meets, presided over by the Superior of the whole Oratory, whose responsibility is to maintain the unity of the provinces.

Consecration of life in the Oratory has the twin purpose of fostering the individual brother's personal search for God in union with his brethren, and as a sign of the Kingdom. So through the apostolic work of the brethren, the Oratory seeks to make a contribution to the life and witness of the whole Church.

In common with traditional communities, the Oratory requires celibacy. Brothers are accountable to their brethren for their spending and are expected to live simply and with generosity. The ideal spiritual pattern includes daily Eucharist, Offices, and an hour of prayer. Study is also regarded as important in the life. During the time of probation which is for two years, the new brother is cared for and nurtured in the Oratory life by another brother of his College. The brother may then, with the consent of the province, make his first profession, which is renewed annually for at least five years, though with the hope of intention and perseverance for life. After five years, profession can be made for a longer period, and after ten years a brother may, with the consent of the whole Oratory, make his profession for life.

Companions and Associates
The Oratory has an extended family of Companions, with their own rule of life, and Associates. Companionship is open to men and women, lay or ordained, married or single.

Community History
George Tibbatts, *The Oratory of the Good Shepherd: The First Seventy-five Years,* The Almoner OGS, Windsor, 1988.

Obituaries
18 Sep 2014 Michael Bootes, aged 78, professed 46 years

PETER HIBBERT OGS
(*Superior, assumed office August 2011*)
2 Blossom Road, Erdington, Birmingham, B24 0UD, UK
Tel: 0121 382 7286

The Community in Australia

KEITH DEAN-JONES OGS
(*Provincial, assumed office 2011*)
St John's Rectory, 294 Victoria Street, Taree, NSW, AUSTRALIA
or PO Box 377, Taree, NSW, AUSTRALIA
Tel: (0) 26552 1310 Email: kdean-jones@ogs.net

Michael Boyle
Trevor Bulled
Robert Braun
Michael Chiplin
Barry Greaves
Charles Helms
Ronald Henderson
Roger Kelly
Kenneth Mason
Kyle Penlaligan
Geoffrey Tisdall
Lindsay Urwin

Probationers: 0

The Community in North America

PHILIP HOBSON OGS
(*Provincial, assumed office August 2005*)
151 Glenlake Avenue, Toronto, Ontario, M6P 1E8, CANADA
Tel: (0) 416 604 4883 Email: phobson@ogs.net

David Brinton
Gregory Bufkin
William Derby
Carlson Gerdau
Michael Moyer
Bruce Myers
Walter Raymond
Edward Simonton

Probationers: 0

The Community in southern Africa

JABULANI NGIDI OGS
(*Provincial, assumed office 2013*)
16660 Luganda Road, Luganda, PO Box 846, Pinetown 3609, SOUTH AFRICA
Tel: +27 (0) 31-7067000 Email: jnigidi@ogs.net

James Mvuba
Thanda Ngcobo
Douglas Price
Thami Shange
Sithembiso Mthethwa

Probationers: 0

The Community in Europe

PETER WALKER OGS
(*Provincial, assumed office August 2013*)
38 Glynde Crescent, Felpham, West Sussex PO22 8HT, UK
Tel: 01243 822 067 Email: pwalker@ogs.net

Peter Baldwin
Michael Bartlett
Alexander Bennett
Michael Bullock
Malcolm Crook
Peter Ford
Nicholas Gandy
David Johnson
Brian Lee
Christopher Powell
John Salt
Dominic Walker

Probationers: 0

Directory of acknowledged Communities

In this section are communities that are 'acknowledged' by the Church as living out a valid Christian witness, but whose members do not all take traditional Religious vows. Some communities expect their members to remain single whilst others may include members who are married: some have both members who remain celibate and those who do not. The specific vows they take therefore will vary according to their own particular Rule. However, communities in this section have an Episcopal Visitor or Protector. Some are linked to communities listed in section 1, others were founded without ties to traditional celibate orders. This section also includes some ashrams in dioceses in Asia.

In the Episcopal Church of the USA, these communities are referred to in the canons as 'Religious communities' - as distinct from those in section 1 of this *Year Book*, which are referred to as 'Religious orders'. However, this distinction is not used in other parts of the Anglican Communion where 'communities' is also used for those who take traditional vows.

Brotherhood of Saint Gregory

BSG

Founded 1969

Brotherhood of Saint Gregory
Saint James' Rectory
2627 Davidson Avenue
Bronx
NY 10468
USA

Email:
Servant@gregorians.org

Website
www.gregorians.org

Office Book
The Book of Common Prayer (1979)

The Brotherhood of Saint Gregory was founded on Holy Cross Day 1969, by Richard Thomas Biernacki, after consultation with many Episcopal and Roman Catholic Religious. The first brothers made their profession of vows in the chapel of the New York monastery of the Sisters of the Visitation (RC). Later that year, Bishop Horace Donegan of New York recognized the Brotherhood as a Religious Community of the Episcopal Church.

The community is open to clergy and laity, without regard to marital status. Gregorian Friars follow a common Rule, living individually, in small groups, or with their families, supporting themselves and the community through secular or church-related employment.

The Rule requires the Holy Eucharist, the four Offices of the Book of Common Prayer, meditation, theological study, Embertide reports, the tithe, and participation in Annual Convocation and Chapter.

The Postulancy program takes a minimum of one year; Novitiate at least two years, after which a novice may make First Profession of Annual Vows. Members are eligible for Life Profession after five years in Annual Vows.

Gregorian Friars minister in parishes as liturgists, musicians, clergy, artists, visitors to the sick, administrators, sextons, and teachers. A number serve the diocesan and national church. For those in secular work the 'servant theme' continues, and many are teachers, nurses, or administrators, sharing the common goal of the consecration of each brother's lifetime through prayer and service.

Community Publications & Wares
The Brotherhood produces a quarterly newsletter titled *The Servant.* Subscription is US$8.00 per year. An order blank is available by mail or via our website.

There are a number of Brotherhood publications - please write or visit our website for further details regarding placing an order.

Community History
Karekin Madteos Yarian BSG, *In Love and Service Bound: The First 40 years of the Brotherhood of Saint Gregory,* BSG, 2009.

Bishop Visitor
Rt Revd Rodney R Michel,
assisting Bishop of Pennsylvania

BROTHER RICHARD THOMAS BIERNACKI, BSG
(Minister General and founder, assumed office 14 September 1969)

Brother James Teets
Brother Luke Antony Nowicki
Brother William Francis Jones
Brother Tobias Stanislas Haller *(priest)*
Brother Edward Munro *(deacon)*
Brother Donovan Aidan Bowley
Brother Christopher Stephen Jenks
Brother Ciarán Anthony DellaFera
Brother Richard John Lorino
Brother Ronald Augustine Fox
Brother Maurice John Grove
Brother Virgilio Fortuna *(deacon)*
Brother Gordon John Stanley *(deacon)*
Brother Karekin Madteos Yarian
Brother William David Everett
Brother Thomas Bushnell
Brother Robert James McLaughlin
Brother Peter Budde
Brother John Henry Ernestine
Brother Francis Sebastian Medina
Brother Aelred Bernard Dean
Brother Joseph Basil Gauss
Brother Mark Andrew Jones *(priest)*
Brother Richard Matthias
Brother William Henry Benefield
Brother Nathanael Deward Rahm
Brother Thomas Lawrence Greer
Brother Enoch John Valentine
Brother Ron Fender
Brother David Luke Henton
Brother David John Battrick *(priest)*
Brother Bo Alexander Armstrong
Brother Francis Jonathan Bullock
Brother James Patrick Hall
Brother Richard Edward Helmer *(priest)*
Brother Eric Shelley
Brother Larry Walter Reich

Novices: 1
Postulants: 4

Gregorian friars meeting in plenary session.

Church Army

CA

Founded 1882

Acknowledged as
a mission community
2012

Church Army
Wilson Carlile Centre
50 Cavendish Street
Sheffield
S3 7RZ

Tel: 0300 123 2113

Email:
missioncommunity@churcharmy.org.uk

Website
www.churcharmy.org.uk

Daily prayers at 12 noon

Community history
Videos and articles about the history of the Church Army can be found on our website here:
http://www.churcharmy.org.uk/pub/aboutus/125/125home.asp

Registered Charity Nos.
No. 226226
and SC040457

Our vision is of a movement of Christ's disciples who are so set on fire by the love of Jesus that they go to the margins of society, beyond the reach of most of the Church, showing that love through both words and actions. It is for people like this that the Church Army Mission Community exists; to be a home for those with a passion for evangelism.

It is a family where they can be resourced and encouraged, a place where they can cry together and laugh together, celebrate God's goodness and stand with each other in the difficulties. It is not an organisation so much as a movement that focuses on relationships rather than rules. It is held together by a commitment to Christ, to the gospel and to holiness of life. Though coming from within the Anglican Church, it has an inclusive ethos and is open to those from other churches.

It is a vision of a community of love sustained by prayer and the grace of God. Our mission flows out from this Mission Community seeing transformed by Christ.

CANON MARK RUSSELL
(Community Leader, assumed office September 2012)
CAPTAIN ANDREW CHADWICK *(Dean of Community)*

Around 250 members

Community Publications
Shareit! Magazine that goes out to individual supporters and churches. It is full of real life stories of the work of the Church Army and our partners.
Inspire This is the UK's biggest reach Christian magazine going FREE to UK churches, with a circulation of 50,000-55,000 and a readership of at least 200,000.
Church Army's daily prayer diary.

Guest and Retreat Facilities
20 single, 10 double rooms. No restrictions.
Rooms are available from £40* a night. (Some discounts available for churches and charities.)

Most convenient time to telephone:
9.00 am - 5.00 pm

Bishop Visitor: Rt Revd Tim Thornton,
Bishop of Truro

Church Mission Society

CMS

Founded 1799

Acknowledged as
a mission community
2008

**CMS
Watlington Road
Oxford
OX4 6BZ**

**Tel: 01865 787400
Fax: 01865 776375**

**Email:
info@cms-uk.org**

Website:
www.cms-uk.org

Bishop Visitor
Rt Revd Dr
Christopher Cocksworth,
Bishop of Coventry

Registered Charity No.
No. 1131655
Company No. 6985330

CMS is a community of people in mission obeying the call of God to proclaim the Gospel in all places and to draw all people into fellowship with the Lord Jesus Christ. The community has developed a life which is focussed on its vocation to mission, participating together in mission, learning together from mission and praying together for mission. CMS has always had a significant community feel about it, being a membership Society, whose members associated together in order to promote and support evangelistic mission. A spread-out network of local members and associations quickly grew up. Some members even refer to CMS as their "family". A transforming community life was also part of CMS mission service, in mission compounds, mission schools and hospitals and the various CMS training colleges.

CMS had a major influence in forming what today is called the Anglican Communion, about two-thirds of whose Churches trace their origins to the missionary movement fostered by CMS or have had CMS contributions to their early growth and development. Over its 200-year existence, CMS has sent out about 10,000 people in mission. Under a new constitution, approved in 2009, community members affirm seven promises, including a commitment to participating in mission service, regular prayer, bible reading, study, reflection, supporting the Church's mission, and mutual encouragement. CMS supports people in mission in over thirty-five countries in Africa, Asia, Europe (including the UK), the Middle East and Latin America.

CHARLES CLAYTON *(Chair of Trustees)*
THE REVEREND CANON PHILIP MOUNSTEPHEN
(Community Leader/Executive Director)
Membership: 2,500+

Community Publications: *Connect*, three times a year, distributed free to members. Occasional monographs on mission themes through the CMS Crowther Centre for Mission Education. See CMS website for more news and information about regular printed publications.

Community Wares: See the website for free resources for prayer, group study and seasons of the Christian year plus books, resources and craft products for sale from the CMS shop: www.shop.org.uk.

Conference Facilities: CMS in Oxford has excellent modern conference facilities for meetings from 2 to 150 people. See www.cms-uk.org/conferencing for details.

Community of the Gospel

CG

Founded 2007

N1582 Midway Road
Hortonville
WI 54944
USA

Email:
dschroeder003
@new.rr.com

Website:
www.
communityofthegospel
.org

Evening Prayer
7pm (Sat)

Bishop Visitor:
The Rt. Rev. Chilton Knudsen, DD

We are a non-residential Monastic Community whose members try to help each other become more Christ-like. We do this by living a monastic life of daily prayer, reflective study, and personal service in the secular world. We seek to demonstrate our faith in unique ways as best we can, while allowing our lives to be transformed by God. Although we are primarily a dispersed community (we live and work in various parts of the world), we travel together as one in spirit with Our Lord. We believe that our purpose is to awaken to God's wisdom and love, and to shape our lives following God's principles. The expression of our personal mission in life is a response to the love of God who made each of us in a unique way. We join together as the body of Christ to share our journey and our resources as we are able, and mutually to encourage each other's faith journey.

BROTHER DANIEL-JOSEPH SCHROEDER
(Guardian, assumed office 30 March 2007)
BROTHER DANIEL-CHAD HOFFMAN *(Deputy Guardian)*

Br Gregory Thomas Schumacher
Sr Margaret Black
Br John Charles Westaway
Br Juan Charles Valles
Br John Kneepkens
Sr Kathryn Elizabeth Scarborough
Sr Catherine Lo Prieno
Oblate Derek Lee
Kelly Keith
Becky Cooper
Sr Julian Sky Welsh
Br John Huebner
Frank Kajfes
Laurie Sandblom
Yossi Lopez-Hineynu
Bill Freeman
Deborah Aronson
Garth Wadleigh
Martha Thomas
Julie Dahl
Oblate Doug Webber
Tony Emling
Louisa Young
Liefe Wheeler
Naomi O'Connor

Novices: 6
Postulants: 8

Friends of the Community

We have a category of "Friends of the Community." These are people who wish to stay connected with the Community, but who do not wish to be engaged in a formal formation process. They prayer for us regularly, as we pray for them, and they are welcome to attend our annual Convocation.

Community of Saints Barnabas & Cecilia

CSBC

Founded 1997

Revd Sister
Sandra Sears CSBC
17 Sixth Street
Gladstone
South Australia
AUSTRALIA 5473

Tel:
Home **(61 8) 8662 2504**
Mobile **0400157709**

Emails:
comsbc@bigpond.com
personal: **srskscsbc@bigpond.com**

Morning Prayer 8.00 am

Midday Office
12 noon

Evening Prayer 5.00 pm

Compline
personal choice

Office Book
A Prayer Book for Australia (APBA)

Taizé: Prayer for Each day

The Community of Ss Barnabas & Cecilia came into being in 1997, when the then Bishop of Willochra in South Australia, the Rt Revd David McCall, called Sisters Jean Johnson and Sandra Sears to Jamestown in the State's mid north to form Community.

Since then the Community house has moved twice - to Peterborough in 1998, and Gladstone in 2011. The community is open to men and women, (the double title reflects that) married and single, who are practising members of any Christian denomination. They live in their own environment, and are free to exercise their own gifts. This means that the Community is dispersed throughout the three dioceses of South Australia. The charism of the Community is 'Encouragement' - of gifts in each other, in our churches and in the wider community.

Vows are renewed every year at our annual retreat at Camp Willochra, near Melrose. They are chastity, simplicity, and obedience to the Bishop under God. Our habit is a grey alb, navy blue scapular, and blue girdle (with three knots). Our cross has fluted tips (redolent of the rose which symbolises St Barnabas) with a raised Celtic harp at its centre (symbolising St Cecilia).

BROTHER MARTYN ROBINSON CSBC
(Spokesperson, assumed office 5 April 2014 for 3-year term)

Revd Sr Sandra Sears	Sr Jeanne Frost
Revd Sr Sal Tatchell	Sr Pauline Treloar
Sr Sue Nirta	Sr Bev Driver
Revd Br John Edwards	Sr Katherine Thorpe
Sr Riccarda Favorito	Sr Cheryl Wiseman

Obituaries

18 Sep 2014 Sister Jean Johnson, aged 85, professed 17 years *(Founding member)*

Community Publication: Quarterly newsletter. No subscription, but donation if possible.

Community Wares: Blank note cards and Christmas cards; Music (eg Southern Flinders Mass setting, various hymns and songs).

Community History: *In a Dry and Thirsty Land*, Anglican Diocese of Willochra, 2015. (A publication to celebrate the centenary of the Diocese.)

Guest & Retreat Facilities
Three double bedrooms (one with a double bed, the others with two singles). Cost - donation. The house is open depending on the movements of Revd Sr Sandra Sears.

Most convenient time to telephone:
0900 – 1700 (Central Standard Time GMT + 9:30 [+/- 1:00 Summer Time]. Mobile number preferred.

Friends
We have Friends of the Community who support us in prayer and in practice.

Bishop Visitor: Rt Revd John Stead, Bishop of the Diocese of Willochra
Chaplain: Fr Bill Goodes (Adelaide)

Community of St Denys

CSD

Founded 1879

contact address:
57 Archers Court
Castle Street
Salisbury
SP1 3WE
UK

Email: junewatt@btinternet.com

Bishop Visitor
Rt Revd
Nicholas Holtam,
Bishop of Salisbury

Registered Charity
No 233026

The Community was founded for mission work at home and overseas. The remaining Sisters live in individual accommodation. The present dispersed community of men and women live with a Rule of Life based on the monastic virtues and a particular ministry towards encouragement in the practice of prayer and active service. There is a Board of Trustees responsible for financial matters.

MRS JUNE WATT, Oblate CSD
(Leader, assumed office October 2010, re-elected 2014)
REVD DAVID WALTERS, Oblate CSD *(Deputy Leader)*

Committed members: 18
among whom the professed sisters are:
Sister Margaret Mary Powell
Sister Frances Anne Cocker *(priest)*

Obtuaries
7 Jun 2013 Sister Elizabeth Mary Noller *(priest)*, aged 86, professed 22 years, Senior Sister 2000-2003

Fellowship
CSD has a fellowship.

Community History
CSD: The Life & Work of St Denys', Warminster to 1979, published by CSD, 1979 *(out of print)*.

Community Publication
Annual *Newsletter* and quarterly prayer leaflet. Write to the Leader (address above). A suggested donation of £5.00 is welcome.

Companions of St Luke, OSB

Founded 1992

Companions of St Luke, OSB
PO Box 861
Plaistow
NH 03865-0861
USA
Email:
csl91.membership@gmail.com

Website
www.csl-osb.org
"Opus Dei":
http://www.cslosb.rhcloud.com/

Office Book
BCP (ECUSA)

Community Publication
The Community has a quarterly newsletter called *Value Nothing Whatever Above Christ Himself.* It is available upon request from csl91membership@gmail.com

Bishop Visitor
Rt Revd William Franklin, Episcopal Diocesan of Western New York

The Companions of St Luke OSB is a Benedictine community as defined by the Canons of the Episcopal Church. As such, it incorporates vowed members and Oblates who may be married or partnered as well as celibates, those who live dispersed and those who are called to live in community. Our stability is in Christ and the Community, and our cloister is in the heart.

From our foundation, it has been the intention of the Companions to live the Benedictine life in a manner consistent with our time under the Benedictine Rule and our vows of Obedience, Stability, and Conversion of Life. Further, we are an intentional hybrid of 'Christian Community' and traditional monastic order, a dynamic tension that informs our commitment to "prefer nothing whatever to Christ, that He may bring us all together to everlasting life" [RB 72]. We are knit together with Christ and each other through our commitment to pray regular, daily Offices, spending time in contemplative prayer, and ongoing study. We live in the world, working to frame our secular lives around our love of God and our prayers.

ABBOT ROBERT COTTON OSB
(Abbot, assumed office October 2010)
BROTHER DAVID GERNS OSB *(Dean)*

Brother Matthias Smith
Sister Anna Grace Madden
Brother Camillus Converse
Sister Martha Lamoy
Brother Luke Doucette
Sister Mary Francis Deulen
Brother Kenneth Maguire
Brother Bede Leach
Brother Basil Edwards
Br Stephan Francis Arnold
Sister Helena Barrett
Sister Veronica Taylor
Brother Dunstan Townsend
Brother Thomas Anthony Goddard
Brother Victor Bullock
Sister Kate Maxwell
Brother Anskar Nonken
Brother Peter De Franco
Brother Anselm King-Lowe

Novices: 4 *Postulants:* 5

Oblates and Companions: The Companions of St Luke has an Oblate program. Oblates are considered by this community to have a 'full and authentic' vocation with its own formation. Oblates sit with their vowed counterparts in the Office, have voice and seat in Chapter.

Community Publication: Brother David Gerns OSB (ed), *Reflections on Benedictine Life in the Modern World* - a small booklet of reflections on Benedictine Life in a dispersed community by members of the Companions of St Luke. It is available upon request from csl91membership @gmail.

Company of Mission Priests

CMP

Founded 1940

Warden's address:

St Mary Magdalene's Vicarage
Wilson Street
Sunderland
SR4 6HJ
Tel & Fax:
0191 565 6318
Email: frskelsmm@btinternet.com

Website : www.missionpriests.com

Associates
Laymen closely associated with the Company in life and work may be admitted as Associates.

Community Publication:
Occasional Newsletter

Office Book:
The Divine Office (Vincentian calendar)

Bishop Visitor
Rt Revd
Lindsay Urwin OGS

The Company of Mission Priests is a dispersed community of male priests of the Anglican Communion who, wishing to consecrate themselves wholly to the Church's mission, keep themselves free from the attachments of marriage and the family, and endeavour to strengthen and encourage each other by mutual prayer and fellowship, sharing the vision of Saint Vincent de Paul of a priesthood dedicated to service, and living in a manner prescribed by our Constitution, and with a Vincentian rule of life. For many years the company, although serving also in Guyana and Madagascar, was best known for its work in staffing 'needy' parishes in England with two, three, or more priests who lived together in a clergy house. Although this is rarely possible nowadays, because of the shortage of priests, we encourage our members who work in proximity to meet as often as practicable in order to maintain some elements of common life. The whole company meets in General Chapter once a year, and the Regional Chapters more frequently.

We were among the founding members, in the year 2000, of the Vincentians in Partnership, which works in accordance with the principles established by St Vincent de Paul, to support and empower those who are poor, oppressed, or excluded.

FATHER BERESFORD SKELTON CMP
(Warden, assumed office 2012)

Michael Whitehead
Anthony Yates
Allan Buik
John Cuthbert
Peter Brown
Michael Shields
David Beater
Michael Gobbett
Ian Rutherford
Andrew Collins Jones
Tim Pike
Philip North
Mark McIntyre
Alan Watson
Simon Atkinson
Peter Bostock
Robert Martin
Christopher Buckley
Kevin Palmer
Andrew Welsby
Derek Lloyd
Alexander Lane
James Hill
Peter Garvie
Benjamin Eadon
Peter Bolton
Andrew Horsfall
Andrew Hammond
Adrian Ling
Simon Sayer

Probationers: 0
Aspirants: 3

Contemplative Fire

CF

Founded 2004

Registered Office:
16 Chorley Avenue
Saltdean
Brighton BN2 8AQ
Tel: 077 099 55091
Email:
contemplativefire@btinternet.com

Website: www.contemplativefire.org

Office Book
Each local CF community develops its own liturgical pattern and provision, with a variety of resources drawn upon.

Community Wares
Cards,
'Rhythm of Life Resources'
Sheer Sound" CD,
"Sacred Posture" DVD,
"Seeking Stillness" booklet.

Bishop Accompanier/ Visitor:
Rt Revd Paul Bayes
Bishop of Liverpool

Senior Accompanier:
Sister Rosemary SLG

Registered Charity No: 1106392

Contemplative Fire is a network community having a Trinitarian rhythm of life of prayer, study and action, or being, knowing, doing. *Contemplative Fire: Creating a community of Christ* at the edge was established in the Oxford Diocese in 2004 by Philip Roderick as one of the Diocese's "Cutting Edge Ministries". It then became one of the first generation of the national initiative, Fresh Expressions of Church. *Contemplative Fire* was welcomed as an Acknowledged Community in November 2013.

The call and charism of *Contemplative Fire* seeks to hold in creative tension contemplation and engagement, the hidden and the apostolic. *Contemplative Fire* is increasingly geographically dispersed. Companions on the Way are those who are drawn to become "members" of *Contemplative Fire.* Currently, we have 115 Companions in the UK, (29 in Canada and 1 in Maui, Hawaii).

As a whole community rhythm we currently have, for those who are able to attend, an annual *Contemplative Fire* retreat, a Community Weekend and four Wisdom on the Way days each year. In addition, there are opportunities for Companions at local, regional or national level, to facilitate, attend events, and design, or receive online, *Contemplative Fire* resources on different aspects of prayer and contemplative discipleship.

PHILIP RODERICK
(Founder & Community Leader, assumed office 2004)
115 Members/Companions on the Way

Community Books

Philip Roderick, 'Dynamic Tradition: Fuelling the Fire' in Louise Nelstrop and Martyn Percy (eds), *Evaluating Fresh Expressions,* Canterbury Press, Norwich, 2008.

Tessa Holland & Philip Roderick, 'Contemplative Fire: Creating a Community of Christ at the Edge' in Steven Croft and Ian Mobsby (eds), *Fresh Expressions in the Sacramental Tradition,* Canterbury Press, Norwich, 2009.

Tessa Holland, 'A Rhythm of Life: Critical Reflections' & Philip Roderick, 'Connected Solitude: Re-Imagining the Skete', both in Graham Cray, Ian Mobsby and Aaron Kennedy (eds), *New Monasticism as Fresh Expression of Church,* Canterbury Press, Norwich, 2010.

Little Sisters of Saint Clare

LSSC

Founded 2002

Mother Guardian
19334 King's Garden Dr. N., Shoreline WA 98370 USA
Tel: 206 533 0884
Email: motherguardian@gmail.com

LSSC Office Mail and Seattle Chapter House, St. Andrew's Episcopal Church, 111 Northeast 80th Seattle WA 98115 USA

Website: www.stclarelittlesisters.org

Services at St Andrew's Episcopal Church. Call for times.

Office Books
BCP, SSF Office for Franciscan saints, Holy Women, Holy Men Celebrating the Saints

The Little Sisters of St. Clare is a dispersed women's Franciscan community that seeks to live a contemporary expression of the rule of St. Clare in the world. We desire to live a simple and consecrated life but do not live in a common house. We strive always to be mindful of our vocation to contemplative and intercessory prayer, carefully maintaining the challenging balance between secular and Religious life. Our first focus is to order our own lives to live under a common Rule. Each of us is responsible for our own financial support and livelihood. We support ministries to the poor in our local communities and serve in our local parish churches within the Diocese of Olympia, Washington, USA.

We use our discernment and formation program to encourage and equip women who are called by God to our community. Our formation program is designed from our experience living the Gospel. It provides a supportive study program, time for reflection and conversation about Christian living and spiritual practices. Our curriculum is offered to all members in our local Chapters. They are all within a 100 miles from Seattle.

Sister Dorothy-Anne Kiest, LSSC
(Mother Guardian, assumed office October 2007)
Sister DedraAnn Bracher, LSSC *(Deputy Guardian)*

Sisters:
Sr Mary-Agnes Staples
Sr Mary-Louise Sulonen
Sr Marie-Elise Trailov
Sr Karen-Anne Williamson
Sr Kathryn-Mary Little
Sr Mary-Olivia M. Stalter
Sr Brigid Kaufmann
Sr Julian Ortung
Sr Grace Teresa Grant

Companions:
Tovi Andrews
Nancy Jones
Patricia Roberts

Novices: 4
Marcia Bracher
Patrice O'Brien
Laura Carroll
Judith Kenyon

Associates LSSC: 6

Obituaries
11 May 2014 Nora Blum, aged 88, Companion for 3 years

Community Book
We have self published a little book called *Holy Weavings - A Tapestry of Reflections* by The Little Sisters of Saint Clare. We offer this to others for a donation of $15 to cover our costs and shipping. Write: LSSC, % St. Andrew's Episcopal Church (see address above).

Episcopal Visitor: Rt Revd Sanford Z K Hampton, *retd*

Companions and Associates
We have various categories of membership. Companions are welcomed as they take a service role working closely with the Sisters. Associate membership is a way to stay connected with the community intercessory prayer requests. Companions and Associates may elect to participate in our Chapter formation program. This is an opportunity to spend time in prayer and learn about spiritual practices that are central to the Franciscan ethos and contemplative living. Inquiries may be made to Sister Julian Ortung, Vocations Guardian at srjulianortung@gmail.com

Guest and Retreat Facilities
No retreat facilities. Spiritual direction available. Call Mother Guardian.

Most convenient time to telephone:
Pacific Time, USA : 9.00 am - 11.30 am, 2.00 pm - 4.00 pm

Order of Anglican Cistercians

OCist

Founded 2010

Chepynge Saint Bernard
47 Park Road
Chipping Norton
Oxfordshire
OX7 5PA
UK

Email:
ocist@talktalk.net

Website:
www.ocista.webs.com

Vigils *(at dawn)*

Lauds

Midday Office

Vespers

Compline

The Order of Anglican Cistercians consists of uncloistered and dispersed professed men of eighteen years or over; laity who are confirmed and communicant Anglicans, and priests. The Order is open to celibate, single or married men who live within the jurisdiction of an Anglican diocese in Great Britain. Our way of life is lived according to our Rule, and in substantial conformity with that mapped out in the *Rule of Saint Benedict* and thus we are part of the Benedictine family. Our lives are dedicated to seeking union with God through Jesus Christ, whilst living a dispersed and uncloistered form of monasticism. The day is balanced between the *Opus Dei*, work, reading and study. We aspire to a life-long desire to seek God through silence, contemplation, *Lectio* and the daily Offices. We live under the three vows of Stability, Conversion of Character, and Obedience, and we aim to live this out by the grace of God.

Brother Geoff van der Weegen OCist
(Prior, elected 12 May 2010)
Brother Philip Barratt OCist *(Sub-Prior)*
Brother □lred Partridge

Novices: 2 *Postulants:* 2

Office Book
The Divine Office (Anglican Cistercian Calendar).

Bishop Visitor
Rt Revd Tony Robinson, Bishop of Wakefield

Order of the Community of the Paraclete

OCP

Founded 1971
Reformed at Chapter of Pentecost 1991

Ordinary People Living Extraordinary Lives

Community of the Paraclete@ St. Dunstan's Episcopal Church 722 N. 145th Street Shoreline WA 98133 USA

Website
www.theparacletians.org

Monthly gatherings at St Dunstan's Church, Shoreline, WA & St Michael's Episcopal Church, Yakima, WA

Eucharist, meal, study & fellowship, every first Friday 5.30 pm - 9 pm

Office Book: BCP

The Community of the Paraclete is an apostolic community offering an authentic Religious life of prayer and service. We were recognized by the Episcopal Church in 1992. The Paracletians are self-supporting women and men, lay and ordained, who have committed themselves to live under the Paracletian Rule and constitution. Our vision: we are a network of Paracletian communities learning how to grow spiritually and exercising our gifts in ministry. We stand with and serve anyone who is broken in mind, body or spirit. See our website for current ministries.

BROTHER JOHN RYAN OCP
(Minister, assumed office June 2009)
Email: BrjohnPastoralServices@gmail.com
BROTHER MARVIN TAYLOR OCP *(Vice-Minister)*
Brother Richard Buhrer
Brother Douglas Campbell
Sister Ann Case
Sister Susanne Chambers
Brother Carle Griffin
Sister Barrie Gyllenswan
Sister Patricia Ann Harrison
Brother Timothy Nelson
Sister Martha Simpson
Sister Suzanne Waldron
Novices: 2

Associates 3; *Friends* 10; *Companions* 24

Friends, Associates and Companions
FRIEND: any baptized Christian, with the approval of chapter.
ASSOCIATE: confirmed Episcopalian, active member of an Episcopal parish, or church in communion with the Episcopal Church or the Episcopal See of Canterbury; six months' attendance at local chapter, and the approval of chapter.
COMPANION: Any person who is a benefactor of the Order.

Other Addresses: Members are in the states of Arizona, Florida and Washington, USA.

Community Publication: *Paracletian Presence*, free

Bishop Visitor
Rt Revd Nedi Rivera, Bishop of Eastern Oregon

The Order of Mission

TOM

Founded 2003
Acknowledged as a Religious community 2013

Postal address:
c/o St Thomas Crookes, Nairn Street
Sheffield
S10 1UL

Tel: c/o 0114 2671090

Email:
admin @missionorder.org

Website:
www.missionorder.org

Bishop Visitor
Most Revd John Sentamu, Archbishop of York

Registered Charity No.: 1100206

The Order of Mission (TOM) is a dispersed global covenant community of Missional Leaders. We take vows to live in Simplicity, Purity and Accountability and make a commitment to live according to the TOM Rule of Life, a set of practical tools for missionary living grounded in biblical insights.

We are a family on mission committed to hearing the call of God on our lives and responding in obedience and faith.

REVD KELD DAHLMANN
(Senior Guardian, assumed office March 2015)
REVD CANON MICK WOODHEAD (UK)
REVD ERIC TAYLOR (USA)
REVD MALCOLM POTTS (Australia)
REVD THOMAS WILLER (Scandanavia)
(Regional Chairs of Guardians. TOM has a global membership. Each region is served by a small team of Guardians headed by a Chair.)

Permanent Members 216 (110 in UK)
Temporary Members 283 (78 in UK)
Explorers 78 (25 in UK)
Associates 85 (67 in UK)

Associates
Associate members are those who support the value, calling and work of the Order and seek to live according to the pattern of the community but do not feel called to take vows to become either Permanent or Temporary Members.

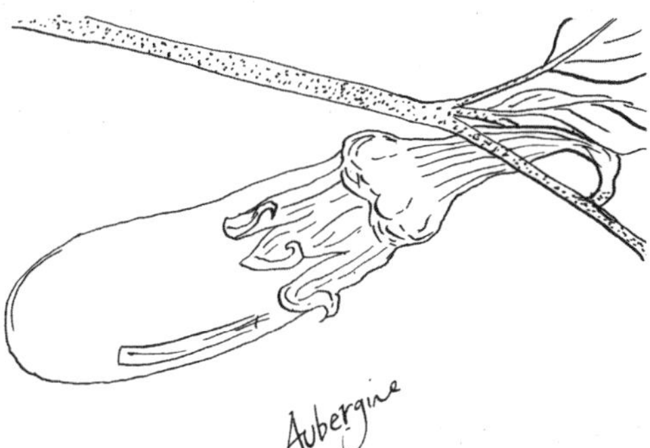

Aubergine

The Sisters of Jesus

Founded 2000

34 Eaton Road
Bowdon
Altrincham
Cheshire
WA14 3EH
Tel: 0161 233 0630 (evenings)

E-mail:
(Foundation Sister)
susangabriel@btinternet.com

Website:
www.sistersofjesus.org.uk

Bishop Visitor
Rt Revd
Richard Blackburn,
Suffragan Bishop of Warrington

Registered Charity No.:
The Gettalife Project.
Charity number 1131341.
See the Sisters of Jesus website for more information
and the website
www.gettalife.org.uk

The core of our vocation is the call to the Religious Life, not living in community but in the midst of everyday circumstances. It is to have our first priority a search for the reality of the living God as Ignatius of Loyola put it, to 'know God in all things' and to live out a life of kinship based on this call of our shared life in Christ and therefore Sisters of him and of each other.

The first vows were taken by the Foundation Sister before Bishop Christopher Mayfield, the Bishop of Manchester, on the festival of St Michael and All Angels, 2000. The community was acknowledged by the Advisory Council in July 2011. At present, this pilot light, newly-acknowledged dispersed community comprises three Sisters, two in temporary vows. The Foundation Sister took permanent vows in 2007. We now have an affiliated Sister possibility. At present, there are three core Sisters and four people exploring.

REVD DR SUSAN GABRIEL TALBOT
(Foundation Sister)
CLAIRE SHERMAN *(Assistant)*

Novices: 1 *Postulants:* 4

Office book
We have developed our own liturgies for Morning and Evening worship as well as our use of the traditonal Compline liturgy.

Associates and Friends
It is possible to join as an Affiliated Sister or Friend should that be appropriate for the candidate and according to our Constitution. There are guidelines for an Affiliated Sister which can be discussed with the Foundation Sister.

Guest and Retreat Facilities
It is possible to stay for a time of quiet at the main house,which is a period terrace with one guest room. The 24 hour or 48 hour stay would be as the Foundation Sister's guest. It can be directed or just 'time-out' (women only). Costs, depending on circumstance, but full board for 24 hours £25-30. £15 for a day with soup, bread and cheese lunch.

Sisters of Saint Gregory

SSG

Founded 1987
as the Companion Sisterhood of Saint Gregory by the Brotherhood of Saint Gregory.
Achieved autonomy in 1999 as The Sisters of Saint Gregory.

Contact address for the Treasurer, who receives and routes all communications:
Sister Susanna Bede Caroselli, SSG
505 Allenview Drive
Mechanicsburg
PA 17055
Tel: (717) 697 7040

Email:
SCAROSEL @messiah.edu

Website:
www. sistersofsaintgregory.org

The Sisters of Saint Gregory is a women's community canonically recognized by the Episcopal Church. The community is comprised of lay and clergy, young and old, regardless of marital status. Called together by God to the vowed life in the world, we live intentionally dispersed, some individually and some with our families, supporting ourselves and the community through secular or church-related employment performed in a spirit of service. Sisters are also encouraged to serve their parishes and dioceses and other church-sponsored or civic outreach programs. We follow a Rule of Life that requires the Daily Offices in the *Book of Common Prayer*, prayer and meditation, the Holy Eucharist, Embertide reports, a tithe, and participation in an annual convocation and chapter for retreat, business, fellowship and worship. The formation program includes a one-year postulancy and two-year novitiate with spiritual and theological study. After five years in annual vows, a Sister may elect to make life profession.

Sister Laurie Joseph Niblick, SSG
(Leader)
Sister Mary Catherine Robertson, SSG
(Administrator)
Sister Lillian-Marie DiMicco
Sister Helen Bernice Lovell
Sister Susanna Bede Caroselli
Sister Carin Bridgit Delfs *(priest)*
Sister Connie Jo McCarroll *(deacon)*
Sister Eugenia Theresa Wilson *(deacon)*
Sister Michael Julian Davidson

Novices: 1
Postulants: 1

Office Book: Book of Common Prayer (1979)

Community Publication: *The Dove*

Bishop Visitor: Rt Rev. Laura J. Ahrens,
Bishop Suffragan of Connecticut

Society of the Community of Celebration

SCC

Founded 1973

809 Franklin Avenue
Aliquippa
PA 15001-3302
USA
Tel: 724 375 1510
Fax: 724 375 1138

Email: mail@ communityof celebration.com

Website: communityof celebration.com

Morning Prayer
8.00 am

Noonday Prayer
12.30 pm

Evening Prayer
5.30 pm

Compline (seasonal)
9.00 pm

Conventual **Eucharist** is celebrated on Saturdays at 5.30 pm and Saints' days as applicable. Monthly service Taizé worship (except February) Sunday at 7.30 pm.

The Community of Celebration is a life-vowed, contemporary residential community whose roots stretch back to the renewal of the Church of the Redeemer, Houston, Texas, in the 1960s. Today the Community resides in Aliquippa (near Pittsburgh), Pennsylvania. Members are women and men, single and married, lay and ordained. Following the *Rule of St Benedict*, members live a rhythm of prayer, work, study, and recreation.

Our ministry is to be a Christian presence among the poor, responding to the needs around us by offering safe, affordable housing; serving with neighborhood organizations concerned with the revitalization of Aliquippa, and providing hospitality, retreats, sabbaticals, and conferences. We provide various chaplaincies, supply clergy, liturgical consultants, worship leadership and speakers for conferences.

BILL FARRA
(Primary Guardian, assumed office 1995)
JAMES VON MINDEN *(Assistant Guardian)*

Mimi Farra	Joe Beckey
Revd Steven McKeown	Revd Phil Bradshaw
May McKeown	Margaret Bradshaw

Associates: Companions of the Community of Celebration follow the Rule of Life for Companions.

Other address
UK house, c/o Revd Phil Bradshaw, 35 Cavendish Road, Redhill, Surrey RH1 4AL, UK
Website: ccct.co.uk

Guest Facilities: We offer a chapel, meeting and dining spaces, and overnight accommodation for 11-13 people (one guesthouse can be self-catering for 4-5 people). We welcome individual retreatants and groups, men and women. For further information contact Celebration's hospitality director by mail, telephone or email.

Most convenient time to telephone:
9.00 am - 12.00 pm Eastern Time (Mon-Fri)

Community Wares: Music and worship resources, including CDs, songbooks, liturgical music, children's music, *A Pilgrim's Way* study manual (English & Spanish) - see website store.

Office Book: Book of Common Prayer

Bishop Visitor: Rt Revd C. Christopher Epting

Community Publication: *News from Celebration* - once a year. Contact Bill Farra for a free subscription.

Community books

W Graham Pulkingham, *Gathered for Power*, Hodder & Stoughton, London, 1972
Michael Harper, *A New Way of Living*, Hodder & Stoughton, London, 1972
W Graham Pulkingham, *They Left their Nets*, Hodder & Stoughton, London, 1973
Betty Pulkingham, *Mustard Seeds*, Hodder & Stoughton, London, 1977
Faith Lees with Jeanne Hinton, *Love is our Home*, Hodder & Stoughton, London, 1978
Maggie Durran, *The Wind at the Door*, Kingsway Publications/Celebration, 1986
David Janzen, *Fire, Salt, and Peace*, Shalom Mission Communities, 1996
Phil Bradshaw, *Following the Spirit*, O Books, 2010
Betty Pulkingham, *This is my story, this is my song*, WestBow Press, 2011

Society of St Luke SSL

Founded 1994

32b Beeston Common
Sheringham
NR26 8ES
Tel: 01263 825623

Emails
ssluke@btinternet.com
andrewssl@me.com

Morning Prayer & Eucharist 8.30 am

Midday Prayer & Meditation 12.15 pm

Evening Prayer 5.00 pm

Night Prayer 9.00 pm

Registered Charity No.: 1107317

The Society of St. Luke was established by the Christian Deaf Community (CDC) of the Middle East. CDC is an Anglican Religious Community within the Province of Jerusalem. Initially SSL focused upon the two schools for deaf youngsters situated in Beirut (Lebanon) and Salt (Jordan.) Times have changed since those roots were set down. The Society today, while remembering the schools in prayer and where possible giving financial support to them, has broadened its mission. It became a charity in 2004 with its primary aims of providing 'prayer for the suffering world' and 'relief and support to those who come for help and counsel.' These aims reflect the Anglican Church's mission of 'care and prayer'.

Father Andrew Lane SSL
(Superior, assumed office 18 October 1994)
Sister Julie Wiseman
Sister Penny Daniels

Associates: 25 Associates (Oblates) who take vows of Simplicity and to keep the Aims of the Society.

Community Publication
Newsletter at the Feast of St Luke, Christmas & Easter. Contact the Community; donations invited.

Community Wares: Notelets, marmalade & pickles.

Most convenient time to telephone:
Any time as answer phone is available.

Office Book: Common Worship

Bishop Visitor
Rt Revd Graham James, Bishop of Norwich

Society of Saint Anna the Prophet

SSAP

Founded 2005

SSAP Chapter House
1655 Rainier Falls Drive NE
Atlanta, GA 30329
USA

Mailing Address:
SSAP, PO Box 15118
Atlanta, GA 3033
USA

Email *(superior)*:
nancyjuliabaxter@gmail.com

Website:
annasisters.org

Centering Prayer
12.30 pm Mon through Fri at the Chapter House

Eucharist: Mon through Thu (in elder care facilities); Annas are in their own parishes on Sundays

Office Book
St Helena Breviary

SSAP is a vowed religious community of elder women, both lay and ordained, in the Episcopal Church USA. The mission of the SSAP is Godly aging and ministry with the old and young, particularly those who are not able to participate in a parish. The Society ministers with and to elders living in care or in senior living communities, celebrating Holy Eucharist and offering pastoral care.

In addition to the corporate ministries of the Society, individual ministries within Episcopal parishes and in the workplace fulfill the sisters' call to serve old and young. Several of the Annas are care-giving grandmothers. Some of the Annas are retired and focus on a more contemplative life. A few are living in care.

The SSAP is a dispersed community (Annas live in their individual homes), and sisters are single, widowed, married, and partnered. Their ages range from 54 to 89. Embracing vows of **simplicity, creativity, and balance**, the Annas are committed to their own Godly aging and the challenge of being a prophetic presence as elders in the Church and in the world. Each sister creates her personal rule of life or *regula* which structures her day-to-day spiritual disciplines.

Community Wares

None at present. We do knit prayer shawls which are given as gifts to elders in care.

Community History

A history of our first ten years is currently being written. There is a brief history entitled *Beginnings*.

Guest Facilities

The Chapter House has four bedrooms for brief overnight stays by out of town Annas.

Overnight hospitality may be offered to members of other religious communities (women only) if space is available. Donations accepted.

Most convenient time to telephone

Communication by email or post is preferred; however, phone calls may be received between 6.00 pm – 8.00 pm (Eastern Standard Time) at 404-373-4666

Bishop Visitor

Rt Revd Anne Hodges-Copple, Suffragan Bishop of North Carolina

REVD NAN BAXTER, SSAP
(Founder and Superior, assumed office 2005)
KATHERINE MITCHELL, SSAP
(Assistant Superior)

Life Vows:
Julia Bottin
Peggy Courtright
Revd Eloise Hally
Revd Ruth Healy
Revd Katharine Hilliard-Yntema
Marilyn Hughes
Revd Lori Lowe
Jane Moser
Laura Pittard
Eleanor Pritchett
Revd Lily Anne Rein
Revd Katherine Roberts

Annual Vows:
Sally Addis
Elizabeth Allan
Gwen Bottoms
Marjorie Chandley
Alice Davidson
Maggi Ewing
Revd Cynthia Hizer
Joyce Hunn
Adair Maller
Revd Patricia Merchant
Revd Mary Moore
Ann Ottesen
Revd Joan Pritcher
Revd Barbara Ryder
Karen Swenson
Linda Claire Snyder
Lynn Tesh
Revd Carolynne Williams

Novices: 0 *Provisionals:* 2

Obituaries: Mary Ann Neale

The Third Order, Society of Saint Francis

The Third Order of the Society of Saint Francis consists of men and women, ordained and lay, single or in committed relationships, who believe that God is calling them to live out their Franciscan vocation in the world, living in their own homes and following ordinary professions. Like the First Order Friars and Sisters and Second Order Nuns, The Third Order members, (called Tertiaries) encourage one another in living and witnessing to Christ through a Rule of Life that includes prayer, study and work. The Third Order is worldwide, with a Minister General, and five Ministers Provincial to cover their respective Provinces.

TSSF

KENNETH E. NORIAN TSSF
(Minister General, assumed office September 2011)
45 Malone Street, Hicksville, NY 11801, USA
Tel: +1 917 416 9579 Email: ken@tssf.org

Founded:

1920s
Americas

1930s
Europe

1975
Africa

1959
Australia / Asia Pacific

1962
Aoteoroa-New Zealand

Statistics for the whole community

	Professed	*Novices*
Americas	413	44
Europe	1837	103
Australia/ Asia Pacific	314	80
Africa	101	30
NZ-Aoteoroa	187	45
Total	**2852**	**302**

Office Book

Each of the five Provinces has different norms regarding the Offices used. Common to all is the 'The Community of Obedience'. Members are encouraged to use this in the context of Morning and Evening Prayer. This may be from: Provincial Books of Common Prayer; Daily Office SSF; CSF Office Book

Bishop Protector General
The Rt Reverend J. Jon Bruno, DD, Episcopal Diocesan of Los Angeles, CA, USA

PROVINCE OF THE AMERICAS

REVD TOM JOHNSON TSSF *(Minister Provincial)*
214 Leafwood Way, Folsom, CA, USA
Tel: +1 916 987 1711
Email: tjohnsonret@gmail.com

Website of Province: www.tssf.org

Statistics of Province

Professed: 413; *Novices:* 44; *Postulants:* 33

Associates of the Society of Saint Francis
Welcomes men and women, lay or clergy, single or in committed relationships, young and old, to join us as Associates in our diverse Franciscan family.

Provincial Publication
The Franciscan Times. Available online at www.tssf.org/archives.shtml

Bishop Protector: Rt Revd Gordon P. Scruton

PROVINCE OF EUROPE

AVERIL SWANTON TSSF *(Minister Provincial)*
11, The Grange, Fleming Way, Exeter EX2 4SB, UK
Tel: +44 1392 430355
Email: ministertssf@franciscans.org.uk

Administrator: **HOWARD MCFADYEN, Les Standous, La Fontade 46300, Gourdon, FRANCE** **Email: handjmcfadyen@gmail.com**

Website of Province: www.tssf.org.uk
Statistics of Province: *Professed:* 1837; *Novices:* 103

Provincial Publication
The Little Portion (twice yearly), also available on TSSF Website
Third Order News (three times a year); Contact: ton@tssf.org.uk

Bishop Protector: Rt Revd Stephen Cottrell, Bishop of Chelmsford

PROVINCE OF ASIA PACIFIC

RT REVD GODFREY FRYER TSSF *(Minister Provincial)*
9 Stonebridge Place, Aspley, QLD 4034, Australia.
Tel: +61 (0)7 31226541
Email: provincial.minister@tssf.org.au

Website of Province: www.tssf.org.au
Statistics of Province:
Professed: 314 *Novices:* 80

Provincial Publication: *Quarterly Newsletter* - available on request from the website www.tssf.org.au/Newsletter/

Community History: Denis Woodbridge TSSF, *Franciscan Gold: A history of the Third Order of the Society of St Francis in the Province of Australia, Papua New Guinea and East Asia: Our first fifty years: 1959-2009.* Available from the Provincial Secretary.

Bishop Protector: Rt Revd Garry Weatherill, Bishop of Ballarat

PROVINCE OF AFRICA

ELECTION PENDING *(Minister Provincial)*
Website: www.tssf.org.za

Statistics of Province

Professed	*Novices*
109	34

Bishop Protector: Rt Revd Daniel Yinka Saro, Ghana

Provincial Publication

Pax et Bonum (published three times a year). Available free of charge from provincial Publications Officer: Alan Rogers TSSF Email: alanrs@telkomsa.co.za
Or the Newsletter Editor: The Rev Canon Roy Snyman TSSF
Email: fr.roy@telkomsa.net

Pacific Province

Revd John Hebenton TSSF *(Minister Provincial)*
15 Farm Street, Mt. Maunganui, New Zealand
Tel: 07 575 9930 (home); 07 578 7916 (work); 021679202 (mobile)
Fax: 07 574 0079
Email: john.hebentontssf@gmail.com

Website of Province: www.franciscanthirdorder.godzone.net.nz

Statistics of Province

	Professed	*Novices*
New Zealand	101	10
Melanesia	88	35
TOTAL	**189**	**45**

Provincial Publication: *TAU* Available from the Provincial Secretary:
Terry Molloy Email: tharmolloy@xtra.co.nz

Community History: Booklets by Chris Barfoot: *Beginnings of the Third Order in New Zealand 1956-74;*
Peace and Joy : Part 2 of the History of the Third Order, Society of St Francis in New Zealand

Bishops Protector

Rt Revd Philip Richardson, Bishop of Waikato
Rt Revd Richard Naramana, Bishop of Ysabel *(for Melanesia)*

The Worker Sisters and Brothers of the Holy Spirit

WSHS & WBHS

Founded 1972 (Sisters) & 1979 (Brothers)

Contact addresses:

Sr Deborah WSHS (Canadian Director)
711 McMurtry Road
Midland, ON
CANADA
L4R 0B9
Tel: 647 965 3196
Email: strdeborah @hotmail.com

Sr Christine WSHS, (American Director)
528 First Street
Windsor
CO 80550
USA
Tel: 970 686 7135
Email: casturges @gmail.com

Website: www. workersisters.org & www. workerbrothers.org

The Worker Sisters and Brothers of the Holy Spirit is a Covenant Community which seeks to respond to God's call through the power of the Holy Spirit, participate in Jesus Christ's vision of unity, become his holy people, show forth Fruit, and in obedience to his command, go forth into the world. It offers women and men, regardless of marital status, a path for individual spiritual growth through a life commitment to a Rule which provides an opportunity to experience prayer, worship, becoming, discovery, belonging, relating, commitment and mission. Membership is made up of:

First Order: Sisters - Lay Workers and Lay Sisters;
Second Order: Brothers - Lay Workers and Lay Brothers;
Third Order: Clergy Sisters and Clergy Brothers;
Companions: Lay and Clergy Persons;
Friends: Lay and Clergy Persons

The first three Orders are bound together under a Life Commitment to a common Rule which is Benedictine in orientation. Members do not live together, yet are not separated by geographical boundaries.

SISTER DEBORAH WSHS *(Canadian Director)*
SISTER CHRISTINE WSHS *(American Director)*
(Co-Directors, assumed office April 2010)

Members: 133
Novices: 1 *Postulants:* 3

Obituaries

26 Feb 2013	Sister Beverley Edith, professed 16 years
21 Aug 2013	Brother Richard Wooda, professed 13 years
17 Dec 2013	Sister Margie Veronica, professed 31 years
7 Jan 2014	Sister Bette Patrick, professed 29 years

Companions and Friends

COMPANIONS make a Life of Commitment to a Rule of Life. FRIENDS share in the prayer and spiritual journey of the Community.

Other Address

Sister Kathleen Rachel WSHS, Director of Admissions,
2601 Sungold Dr, Las Vegas, NV 891134, USA

Office Book: Book of Common Prayer

Community Ecclesiastical Visitors

CANADA: Rt Revd Philip Poole, Friend WSHS/ WBHS, Diocese of Toronto

USA: Rt Revd Barry Howe, Friend WSHS/ WBHS, Diocese of West Missouri, *(retired)*

Ashrams & other Communities

Bethel Ashram

Warickadu, Kuttapuzha P.O., Tiruvalla, Pathanamthitta District, Kerala, India Tel: 09562 335401

The Ashram is a part of Madhya (Central) Kerala Diocese, CSI. Located in Warickad, since 1926 the Ashram has run a school, looked after orphans and run a dispensary. Today its ministry includes a small geriatric care ward, a retirement home for monastic sisters of the Church of South India, and a boarding school. It is also used as a place of retreat for the diocese.

Christa Kulu Ashram

Tirupattur, Vellore, Tamil Nadu 635602, India

The Christu Kula Ashram was among the earliest Christian Ashrams, starting in 1921. It aimed to promote equality between Europeans and Indians, and to give an Indian presentation of Christian life and worship. It is in Vellore Diocese, CSI, and is linked to the National Missionary Society of India.

Christa Prema Seva Ashram

Shivajinagar, Pune - 411 005, India Tel: 20 553 9276

Founded as the Ashram for the Christa Seva Sangha in 1922 by Jack Winslow to create a community of Indian and British members living in equality, the original community ceased in the early 1960s. Some members of this group were influential in the formation of the Third Order SSF *(see entry elsewhere)*. The Ashram is now the focus of a non-celibate community.

Christa Sevakee Ashram

Karkala, Karnataka, India

Started in 1950 in Karnataka (Southern) Diocese, CSI, this Ashram runs a home for aged men and two homes for aged women, altogether caring for fifty elderly people, who are deserted, poor or without relatives. This Ashram is also functioning as a self-employment training centre, a centre for retreats and conferences, and as a short-term stay home for deserted women or women in distress.

Community of St Stephen

4 Rajput Road, Delhi 110 054, India Tel: 11 2396 5437

St Stephen's Community, for women, began as St Stephen's Home in 1871 and formally became a community in 1886. In the 1940s, it came to consist of those Indian and English women who wished to live together as a community under a simple rule of prayer and life.

Christavashram

Manganam P.O., Kottyam District, Kerala 686 018, India
Email: christavashram@gmail.com
Website: manganam.tripod.com/ashram/index.html

Christavashram (Society of St Thomas) is an active Christian community for service, founded in 1934. It is in Madhya (Central) Kerala Diocese, CSI. The Community consists of 120 people, including members, staff and children of the Kerala Balagram, staff and trainees of the Gurukul Ecumenical Institute and Peace Centre staying in the campus, and 30 Associate members living outside

Some other communities

This section includes communities, either monastic or acknowledged, that whilst not Anglican in ecclesiastical allegiance are in communion with Anglicans.

There is also here a community in the USA, inter-denominational in its origins, which includes Lutherans as well as Anglicans, as the ELCA is now in full communion with the Episcopal Church of the United States.

The Sisters of Christa Sevika Sangha (page 31) help lay the foundations of their new building.

Mar Thoma Syrian Church

Mar Thoma Dayaraya

Founded 1996

Plachery PO
(Kalayanad)
Punalur 691 331
Kerala, INDIA
Tel: 04742222282
Email: rev.alexa@gmail.com

Night Prayer & Morning Prayer 5.00 am
3rd Hour 9.00 am
6th Hour 12 noon
9th Hour 3.00 pm
Evening Prayer 6.00 pm
Night Prayer 9.00 pm

This is one of four monastic communities of the Mar Thoma Syrian Church (a Church in Full Communion). It is a part of a monastic movement that goes alongside the better-known Ashram movement. There are six brothers and their monastery is in the hill ranges of Kerala. They live on a rubber plantation donated to the church by Captain Thomas Alexander in 1929 to run an orphanage of 30 boys now managed by the brothers. Their life is one of contemplative prayer and witness to those around by service in the orphanage and outreach in mission parishes in the local villages. They also take in ordinands and aspirants for ordination for experience of the life of prayer.

FATHER ALEXANDER ABRAHAM
Acharya (Abbot)

Brother Isaac Matthew
Father P Philip
Brother Sanil Alexander
Brother Reji Kuriakose
Brother Anish Thomas

Office Book
The Community uses a reformed version of the Shimtho in Malayalam.

Guest facilities: There is a guesthouse with five rooms as well as facilities for larger groups for a day.

MAR THOMA SANYASINI SAMAOHAM
Elanthor P.O., Pathanamthitta District, INDIA Tel: 0468 2361972
Sister P.T. Mariamma *(Superior)*

CHRISTA PANTHI ASHRAM
Darsani P.O., Sihora - 483 225, INDIA Tel: 07624 260260
Christa Panthi Ashram, Sihora, was established in 1942 under the leadership of Revd K T Thomas, Mr John Varghese and Mr M P Mathew, who both later became ordained. Today there are more than forty members, including permanent workers and volunteers. In addition to Gospel work, the activities of the Ashram include hospital work, village schools, a home for the destitute, agricultural work and a rural development programme.
Revd James Idiculla *(Acharya)*

CHRISTA MITRA ASHRAM
P.B. No. 3, Ankola P.O., North Kanara, Karnataka - 531 314, INDIA
Tel: 08388 230392, 230287 (0)
Started in 1940, an ashrams of the Mar Thoma Evangelistic Association.

Christu Dasa Ashram
Olive Mount P.O., Palakkad - 678 702, India Tel: 0492 272974
Started in 1928 as an Ashram with celibate members, it is located in the north- east-ern part of Kerala near the Tamil Nadu border.

Miss Mariyamma Thomas *(Superior)*

Santhigiri Ashram
11/488, Edathala North, Aluva, Kerala - 683 564, India
Tel: 0484 2639014, 2839240
Email: santhigiriasram@yahoo.co.uk Website: www.santhigiri.in/index.html
This is a holistic healing and meditation centre.

Suvartha Premi Samithi
Munsiari, Ranthi P.O., Pithorragarh, Uttar Pradesh, India
Revd A K George and two lady workers went to Tejam and Munsiari on the border of Tibet and started work among the Bothi community. The Bhotias used to trade with Tibet until the 1949 invasion by China. The missionaries hoped to reach Tibet with the help of the Bhotias. Some from the Bhotia community accepted the Gospel and congregations have been founded at Munsiari and Tejam. At present, two groups are working here.

Communities in Churches who have signed the Porvoo agreement

Porvoo created a community of Churches, the members of which have signed an agreement to "share a common life in mission and service". Anglicans in the British Isles and Iberia are currently members, with Lutherans from Denmark, Estonia, Finland, Iceland, Lithuania, Norway and Sweden.

There are a number of established Religious communities in the Church of Sweden, entries for which can be found in the following pages with the addresses of others below.

Community of the Holy Trinity Founded 1993
Mount Foundation, 795 91 Rättvik, Sweden Tel. 0248 79 7170

Mary Magdalene Sisters
Henriksdalsringen 9, 4th floor, 131 32 Nacka, Sweden Tel. 08 714 7751

Sankt Sigfrid Sisters
Sjöborgen, Old Växjövägen 5, 360 44 Ingelstad , Sweden Tel 0470 30128

The Risen Saviour sisterhood
Overselo Abbey Farm, 640 61 Stallarholmen, Sweden Tel: 0152 41116

Congregation of Daughters of Mary of the Evangelical Way of Mary

Founded 1958

Mariadöttrarna
Mariagården vid
Vallby Kyrka
SE - 745 98
Enköping
SWEDEN
Tel & Fax:
0046 (0)171 811 47

"Quiet Time"
for sisters only
6.30 am

Prayer at noon
9.30 am

Vespers
3.00 pm

Compline
9.00 pm

The Holy Communion
Wed 9.00 am
Fri 5.30 pm
Sun 10.00 am

The establishment of the Evangelical Way of Mary is a work of God. He found an instrument that was willing to listen and obey, so that he could speak, act and create. Her name was Paulina Mariadotter (Gunvor Paulina Norrman 1903-1985). She belonged to the Evangelical-Lutheran Church of Sweden. As a young woman, Paulina Mariadotter dedicated herself to Christian social work. She became aware of the need of the single woman and she received a message from God: "Jesus Christ both can and wants to deliver the single woman's energy of life to the Service of His Love's Life."

Paulina Mariadotter lived this message in her own life and other women came and experienced that this was something from God. God could create "a new congregation, religious life in the midst of the world". Our mission is to live and pray for unity. We also have a mission to make the Lord's Mother Mary known, loved and honoured also in the Evangelical-Lutheran part of the Church of Christ.

The spiritual content for the Evangelical Way of Mary was received between 1938 and 1949. As Birgitta Laghé (Doctor of Theology) sums up: "The vision of the designation 'the Visitation' (1949) constitutes the foundation for both the Lutheran and the Roman Catholic branches of the Daughters of Mary." In 1958, the first sisters gave their perpetual vows and received the blessing by a priest. In connection with this the sisters began using a habit.

There is also a branch in the Roman Catholic Church, the Daughters of Mary OSB at Vadstena, Sweden. The movement into the Roman Catholic Church was taken in deep unity in 1988.

The Lord's Mother Mary is the Mother of the Congregation. The possibility for the Daughters of Mary to live without a visible Mother is that each sister has devoted herself to the vocation so that gives the engagement for her to subject herself by her own free will to what the Lord had spoken about the Evangelical Way of Mary.

We are 26 sisters, ranging in age from 25 to 91 years old. We are of four nationalities: Swedish, Danish, Finnish and German. Besides Paulina Mariadotter, 20 sisters of the first generation have already left the life here below.

Bishop Visitor & Chaplain

Bishop: Ragnar Persenius Chaplain: Bertil Murray

Other Address

Mariadöttrarna, Mariagarden, Østerskovvej 38, Kollund, DK-6340 Krusaa, DENMARK Tel & Fax: 0045 74678898

Community History

Birgitta Laghé, *Den Evangeliska Mariavägen till enhet: En studie i Paulina Mariadotters spiritualitet*, Artos & Norma bokförlag, 2004. Summary in English, translated title: *The Evangelical Way of Mary to Unity: a study of the spirituality of Paulina Mariadotter.*

Yvonne MariaWerner (editor), *Nuns and Sisters in the Nordic countries after the Reformation: a female counter-culture in modern society*, The authors and the Swedish Institute of Mission Research, printed by X-O Graf, Uppsala, 2004.

Mariadöttrarna, P*aulina Mariadotter HERRENS Redskap*, Verbum förlag, 1990. This biography by the sisters is translated into German, Danish and Finnish.

Guest & Retreat Facilities

To live with us in our open home, we welcome women. In groups that visit over the day, we welcome both men and women.

Most convenient time to telephone: 10.00 am – 12 noon, 4.00 pm – 6.30 pm

---

Östanbäcks kloster

under the

Rule of St Benedict

Heliga Korsets och Profeten Elias kloster i Östanbäck

Östanbäcks kloster
SE– 733 96 Sala,
SWEDEN

Tel: +46 224 25088, 251 80, 251 88

After ten years of preparation for monastic life for men in the Church of Sweden, with much initial help and inspiration from the (Anglican) Society of St Francis, five years as students in varying noviciates or small fraternity experiments, 5 as a more regular community in a vicarage outside the city of Västerås involved in the life of the parish, the community settled in an old village (Östanbac) 40 kms to the north and adopted the *Rule of St Benedict.*

The declarations and the constitution written before the solemn dedication of the monastery in 1975 by the bishop emeritus Bengt Sundkler, formerly of Bukoba, Tanzania, describes a life, where priority is given to the liturgical prayer and to manual labour as well as to the reception of guests (for retreat, re-orientation in life e.g. after a divorce, general spiritual guidance, refugees, lonely persons looking for fellowship).

The search for visible unity in diversity of all Christians, including acceptance of the Roman ministry of Peter, has received a symbol in the 'Church of Unity' dedicated in

Email: munkljus@munkljus.se
or
caesarius@swipnet.se

Vigils
4.00
(Sundays & red letter days 3.55)

Lauds
4.35 (5.00)

Mass
6.15 (8.30)

Terce
9.00 (8.00)

Sext
1.15

None
14.00

Vespers
17.30

Compline
19.40

Bishop Visitor
Bishop Anders Arborelius
Roman Catholic Bishop of Stockholm,

assisted by
Bishop Björn Fjärsted, emeritus Bishop of Visby,
Church of Sweden

2012 with broad participation from different churches. The community was affiliated with the Dutch Benedictine Congregation from 1994 and now, after its dissolution, with the Congregation of the Annunciation.

CAESARIUS CAVALLIN
(Father, assumed office 2 April 1983)
NILS-OLOV LINDSTRÖM *(Vicar, ställföreträdare)*

Johannes (Ove) Lindell
Birger Johannes Nielsen
Anders Zetterberg-Stormgaard
Boris Pahlm
Alf Almkvist Forsman
Poul Exner
Knut Klaveness Heidelberg

Oblates
There are around 20 secular Oblates now. Contact through the Father of the monastery.

Community Publication
Irregular newsletters to those who want by email or post in Swedish, English, German and French.

Community History
Sven-Erik Brodd, *Evangeliskt klosterliv i Sverige,* Uppsala, 1972.
Articles in *Erbe und Auftrag* and other reviews through the years.
References in Petà Dunstan, *This Poor Sort,* DLT, London, 1997.

Community Wares
Candles, candlesticks, wood and metal crafts, devotionals, cards etc.

Guest & Retreat Facilities
Guest rooms: 7, men only. Married couples also possible. No payment required but a gift of Sw Cr 290 (E30) per day would cover costs.

Most convenient time to telephone
9.30 am – 10 am weekdays

Sisters of the Holy Spirit in Alsike kloster

Helgeandssystrarna

Founded 1965

Alsike Kloster
SE - 741 92
Knivsta
SWEDEN

Tel: 46 (0) 1838 3002

Emails:
systrarna@ alsikekloster.org
or
syster.marianne @gmail.com

Website:
www.alsikekloster.org

Lauds 7.00 am

Terce 9.00 am

Midday prayer
12 noon

None 3.00 pm

Vespers 6.00 pm

Compline/Vigils
8.00 pm

The monastic family of the Holy Spirit Sisters at Alsike Kloster is one of the fruits of the re-awakening of monastic life which started in the first half of the 20th century in the Reformation churches in Europe. This movement touched the Swedish Church in the 1940s-1950s.

In 1948, Sister Marianne Nordström was invited by the Order of the Holy Paraclete to test her vocation. Having returned to Sweden in 1954, she and Sister Ella Persson started a common life in the Diocese of Stockholm, moving to Uppsala in 1856 on the invitation of the then Dean, Olof Herrlin (later Bishop of Visby) to take up work among the university students. In 1964 the community moved to Alsike, twenty kilometres south of Uppsala, continuing their life of prayer and hospitality in the old schoolhouse close to the parish church. During this period novices came and went. In 1983, Sister Karin Johansson was received as a postulant and made her final profession in 1995. By then, Archbishop Gunnar Weman had succeeded Bishop Herrlin as Visitor, and the community, having become involved in refugee work since 1978, was declared the Sanctuary of the diocese by him. The years of crisis in the Swedish Church brought them into contact with the Evangelical Lutheran Church of Kenya, where they have found a response for their way of life and a new hope of growth. There are now plans to erect a kind of monastic village for work with refugee children, students and mission.

SISTER MARIANNE NORDSTRÖM
(Prioress, assumed office 1965)
Sister Ella Persson
Sister Karin Johansson

Community Publication
Meddelande till S:t Nicolai Vänkrets (twice a year)

Guest & Retreat Facilities
According to plans for the "monastic village", there will be five rooms, free of charge.

Most convenient time to telephone: between Offices.

Oblates and Friends
The community has Oblates and 'Friends of St Nicolas'.

Office Book: adjusted Benedictine Office

Bishop Visitor: Rt Revd Göran Beijer

Chaplain: Rt Revd Gunnar Weman

Sisters of Saint Francis

Helige Franciskus Systraskap

Founded 1979

Klaradals kloster
Lindåsvägen 22
SE 443 45 Sjövik
SWEDEN
Tel:+46 302 43260

Email:
porten@ klaradalskloster.se

Lauds
6.45 am

Sext
12 noon

Vespers
5.30 pm

Compline
8.30 pm

Mass
Tuesday 6.30 pm
Thursday 8.00 am
Friday 8.00 am

Helige Franciskus Systraskap (Sisters of Saint Francis) is a community in the Swedish Lutheran Church. We follow an adapted version of the Catholic Rule for the Third Order Regular of St Francis.

Our convent is situated 40 kilometres north east of Göteborg. Our life has its center in prayer, community life and meeting others either in our guest house, in the village or when invited to parishes, prayer groups, networks and other gatherings.

SISTER INGER JOHNSSON
(Leader, assumed office 13 January 2011)

Sister Lena Pettersson
Sister Hanna Söderberg
Sister Gundega Petrevica

Guest & Retreat Facilities
Five rooms.
For organized retreats we welcome both men and women, otherwise women only.
We take guests in periods, normally two weeks per month.
Guests leave a gift for food and lodging.

Most convenient time to telephone
Weekdays 9.30 am -11.30 am

Bishop Visitor
Rt Revd Biörn Fjärstedt (retired bishop of Visby)

Brothers of Saint John the Evangelist (OSB)

EFSJ

Founded 1972

PO Box 782
Freeland
WA 98249
USA
Tel: 360 320 1186
Email:
efsj@whidbey.com

Website: www.
brothersofsaintjohn
.org

Most convenient time to telephone: 10 am - 12 noon, 2 pm - 3 pm

Morning Prayer
8.45 am

Noonday Prayer
12 noon

Vespers 5.30 pm

Office book: BCP

Bishop Visitor
Rt Revd
Sanford Z K Hampton

The community strives to promote interest, study and understanding of the vocation to the Religious life, and to sustain a Religious community on South Whidbey Island, WA. This monastic community is guided by the venerable *Rule of St Benedict.*

The Ecumenical Fellowship of Saint John was founded in Los Angeles in the spring of 1972 by five men - clergy and lay - from the Episcopal, Lutheran and Roman Catholic Communions of the Church. On Saint John's Day 1973, four of the founding group (two Lutherans and two Roman Catholics) made Promises of Commitment at Saint John's Episcopal Church in Los Angeles. After some years in Fallbrook, San Diego County, the Community moved to Whidbey Island in 1990. In 2000, we were blessed with the gift of 10 secluded and wooded acres, with an additional 10 added in 2013, donated by Judith P Yeakel of Langley. Here the monastic house was built, and blessed on Holy Cross Day 2003. The 'Called to Common Mission' declaration of ELCA and TEC made it easy for Lutherans and Episcopalians to become one. We were officially recognised as a canonical Religious community at the Diocesan Convention 2010.

BROTHER RICHARD TUSSEY EFSJ
(Superior, assumed office December 1973)
BROTHER DAVID MCCLELLAN EFSJ *(Prior)*

Sister Julian of Norwich DiBase Obl/OSB
Brother Aidan Shirbroun Obl/OSB
Brother Thomas Langler Obl/OSB
Sister Frideswide Dorman Obl/OSB
Sister Hildegard Babson Obl/OSB
Sister Agnes Steele Obl/OSB
Brother Columba Johnson Obl/OSB

Associates: We currently have three Associates.

Community Publication: *Benedicite.* Contact us via email or post; no charge other than freewill offering.

Community Wares: "Tanglewood Treats": jam, pecan pie, etc. (Tanglewood is the name of our monastery.)

Guest and Retreat Facilities: No overnight guests at present. We do have a building fund.

Remembering and thanksgiving

The new Oratory at OSB Salisbury.

Wendy Robinson (1934-2013)

Wendy Robinson was known to - and appreciated by - many Anglican Religious communities, whose members she was ever ready to help, advise and serve and to whom she proved a good friend. Here, Sister Katharine, a novice sister at SSC, who knew her well and lived alongside her in the last years of her life, remembers the contribution Wendy made to many in their Christian journey.

Wendy Pannell Robinson (née Flintoff) was born in Barnsley, North Yorkshire, on 1 July 1934 and spent her early childhood on a farm on the moors. After gaining a BA in English at the University of Bristol, she qualified as a teacher and subsequently as a psychiatric social worker. Whilst working in East Africa, she met Edward Armitage Robinson and they were married in Lusaka, Zambia in 1964. Back in the UK in Oxford and with a family of three sons, Wendy resumed her career as a psychotherapist. She also became involved in training counsellors and therapists in London, taught pastoral psychology to Anglican ordinands at Cuddesdon, and worked with groups, such as the staff at ASSP's St Helen's Hospice.

Her work and questing was very demanding and required an equally robust and deep faith life. Her journey to the Orthodox Church in the 1980s had had several wayside inns – the Methodist chapel of her childhood, the evangelical Christianity of university days, the silence and social action of the Quakers, the sacramental tradition of the Anglican Church. Her quest led her to find support and wisdom in the life and worship of the Sisters of the Love of God, Oxford, and she turned to Mother Jane SLG for spiritual guidance, as well as becoming a Companion in 1971.

Wendy took up work with many Religious communities (apostolic and enclosed contemplatives), both Anglican and Roman Catholic in the UK, Ireland and Norway. She had a deep belief that the lives of Religious were essential to the well-being of all. Therefore she was aware of the importance of enabling the members of these communities to deepen their self-understanding and the gifts and shadows inherent in living together. She worked closely with the novice guardians at their conferences as well as providing teaching for the novices themselves.

Wendy was a great note-maker and communicator who rarely wrote up her work, preferring to present it live. Thankfully, some of her thoughts were written down and published by SLG Press (notably *Exploring Silence*, recently reprinted). It was as if for her there was no overall dogmatic answer only "the personal particular of answers and encounters." Metaphor remained key to her way of participating in life, both in worship and at work – never closing off the potential for new insight and new life. To the end there remained in Wendy a strong, determined, humorous streak of 'Yorkshire common sense' that transcended any limiting approach to life. She was faithful to her family and her friends and revelled in being a grandmother. She died on 12 December 2013.

Abbot Michael King OSB (1942-2014)

Michael King was the founder and first superior, then Abbot, of the Benedictine community, first based in Fitzroy and in later years at Camperdown. A chorister in his young days at St Paul's Cathedral, Melbourne, he learned to play the organ and the piano and this led to a life-long appreciation of music. He learned too the Anglo-Catholic tradition and became an expert in liturgical practice. But these were accompaniments to his life's work: a ministry of prayer and pastoral care.

Ordained in the 1960's, the second parish where he became Vicar was St Mark's, Fitzroy, a church that was likely to be closed. But Father Michael's energy and commitment brought it back to life with inspiring liturgy and a deep care for the people that lived there, including the poor, the elderly and the sick. To support the witness and the work, he founded a Religious community that maintained the daily Office and Mass in church, whilst engaged in apostolic work. A visit by Father Michael to the Benedictines at Three Rivers in the USA in 1979 led to the decision for the small community to adopt formally *The Rule of St Benedict* and concentrate on monastic life. This meant leaving the parish in Fitzroy much to the dismay of the bishop as well as the congregation.

Once settled in their new home at Camperdown, the community grew slowly, including women from the early 1990s, and Michael was elected its Abbot in 2002. He was a fine preacher and also a great listener, a gentle, patient man, much sought out for his counsel and friendship. He had indifferent health for many years but continued unbowed through the tiresome irritations that it brought. He died in the early hours of 28 August 2014 at the age of 72, much mourned by all those whose lives he touched.

Sister Mary Philip Bloore OSB (1927-2014)

Sister Mary Philip was born on 26 November 1927 and educated in Staffordshire, UK, at a convent school. After a degree in social work at the University of Birmingham, she specialised in psychiatric social work, for which she gained a diploma at the London School of Economics. After a decade working in different places in England, she felt called to try her vocation at the Benedictine Abbey at West Malling, entering on 26 May 1962. She was solemnly professed on 30 November 1966. Twenty-five years later, she accepted the invitation, along with another Sister, to help broaden the men's community at Camperdown in Australia to include women. Sister Mary Philip had never visited Australia and so this was a huge step for a Benedictine nun who had vowed her stability in another country. An initial year was followed by a further two-year commitment, after which her companion sister returned to Malling. Mary Philip stayed and transferred her stability.

She became a mainstay of the monastery, working in many different ways in the kitchen, the sacristy and the laundry and being the Oblate Sister. In all these activities, she gave her utmost and did all jobs with cheerfulness and dedication. She will be best remembered by many for her work receiving guests, her loving smile, helpfulness and willingness to listen being a personification of Benedictine hospitality.

In her last years, Sister Mary Philip became frailer and in her last six months she resided at a care home, where her needs could be met more easily. She settled in her new surroundings contentedly but in late September she was taken to hospital, dying peacefully in the early hours of 3 October 2014.

Brother (Bishop) M Thomas Shaw SSJE (1945-2014)

Marvil Thomas Shaw III was born in Battle Creek, Michigan, on 28 August 1945. After reading for degrees in theology, he was ordained a priest in 1971, after a diaconal year spent at a parish in Northamptonshire, UK. He returned to the USA to be Vicar of St James's, Milwaukee, before trying his vocation at SSJE in 1975. A year after his life profession in 1981, he was elected superior. During his ten years as leader, the community found confidence to pursue fresh initiatives to renew its life and ministries. He initiated the eight-year process of discernment that led to a new version of the Rule of Life of SSJE, the result being a unique contemporary monastic rule. He encouraged the development of a retreat ministry at Emery House and established the Cowley publishing imprint for books on prayer and spirituality. The Community also renewed its commitment to at-risk children through Camp St Augustine. Brother Tom also found himself in demand as a preacher and spiritual director all over the USA.

Two years after his term as leader of SSJE ended, he was called to the episcopal bench, being consecrated on 24 September 1994, and succeeding as 15th Bishop of Massachusetts the following January. He was active in this role in raising funds, ministering to young people, travelling internationally, and was fearless in standing up for the disadvantaged and underprivileged in society. His mischievous sense of humour and charismatic charm helped him reach out to many people in his diocese and beyond.

Amidst his busy schedule, he remained faithful to his monastic witness of prayer, continuing to reside at the Society's monastery in Cambridge, Massachusetts, so that he did not lose touch with his community and his Religious vocation.

In January 2013, Brother Tom announced his intention to retire from his see in 2014. However, a few months later he was diagnosed with brain cancer. He valiantly continued through his struggle with the illness, resigning on 13 September 2014 on the consecration of his successor. He died a month later on 17 October aged 69. In his last days, he told his brothers of how 'very thankful' he was for the life God had given him, 'the many wonderful people he had met, for the opportunities and challenges he had faced, and for the amazing grace he had experienced throughout his life.'

Sister Kathleen Frideswide CJGS (1916-2015)

Sister Kathleen Frideswide led an interesting and varied life. As a young person, she travelled abroad and found work as a nanny in Germany. She became fluent in German and could remember speaking to one of the more important German military officers when out walking her charge on one occasion. On the outbreak of the Second World War, her father was much alarmed and insisted she came home immediately or he would fetch her back himself. Her employers understood and she managed to return to England.

She taught in various primary schools and then found her vocation in CJGS, being professed in annual vows on 1 December 1959. She continued to teach at Sandleford Priory, Newbury, UK, and then went to the community's school in Barbados. She returned to the UK to Sandleford again and then Falkland St Gabriel, (also Newbury) before a second stint in the Caribbean in Antigua. In later years, she looked after guests at West Ogwell, Devon, CJGS's mother house, and did some teaching in Torquay.

By 1996, the Community's numbers had dwindled and so sisters could no longer be involved in schools. CJGS moved to live alongside the Community of St John Baptist at Windsor, where Sister Kathleen helped in the infirmary wing as health permitted. She went with CSJB/CJGS on the move to Begbroke but it became clear she required more support. After several falls, she transferred to St John's Home, Oxford, where she was given excellent care and increasing help as needed. Towards the end of her life, she developed dementia but remained cheerful. She died peacefully on 8 January 2015 aged 98.

Father Laurence Eyers SSM (1912-2015)

Father Laurence Eyers SSM died on 24 January 2015 at the age of 102. He had been professed in the Society of the Sacred Mission for 64 years.

Born in the Melbourne suburb of Canterbury on 11 October 1912, Frederick Thomas Eyers was ordained in 1939, priested a year later, and served a curacy at Christ Church, South Yarra. With the Second World War raging, he enlisted as a chaplain, serving with the 2nd Australian Imperial Force. He ended up in the UK where he joined SSM when on leave, being professed in 1950. His life in community was lived in various houses in many locations. He served in parishes in the UK and in Australia he was at different times in Adelaide, Perth and Canberra, before a stint as Prior at Diggers Rest.

He was loyal and reliable whatever he was asked to do. In his last years he commented that: 'I have always had the feeling that wherever I was or whatever I was doing was appropriate - putting me here or there was the Lord's job.' He was consequently a model for how a Religious can serve in many different ways through a long life. He was an attentive and caring listener, especially to those in trouble, and was an encouraging presence to his brethren and those for whom he had pastoral care. From 2006 he lived in retirement at Broughton Hall, Camberwell, where he once again fitted in to the rhythm of life around him, content to be where God placed him.

Sister Scholastica CSC (1912-2015)

Sister Scholastica CSC died on 16 February 2015, 13 days after her 103rd birthday and after 78 years in profession. Born in Adelaide, Violet Ferris attended St Peter's Collegiate Girls' School, which had been founded by the Sisters of the Church in 1894, and where she developed her sharp intellect. She distinguished herself in sports too: a champion runner, captain of hockey and the St Peter's interschool sports team. She was also a prefect and a House Captain. This illustrates her confidence and infectious energy from a young age, qualities which became hallmarks of her long service both to her community and to education.

She joined the Community of the Sisters of the Church in 1932, spending the years 1937-47 after profession in England. On her return to Australia, aged 35, she stepped into the role of Principal at her old school. She made significant decisions in the next eight years, relocating the school from Kermode Street to the outer suburbs of Adelaide at Stonyfell. This allowed the school to grow and develop purpose-built facilities. With entrepreneurial vision, she ignored those who called for financial restraint and thereby launched the school into a new era. Her brave decisions meant the St Peter's could evolve to be the leading independent school it is today.

In the 1960s, Scholastica took the same spirit into her work at St Michael's Grammar School, Melbourne, also founded by CSC in the 1890s. She was Principal there, a role she held alongside being the Sister Provincial for the sisters. At St Michael's, she argued for rebuilding on a large scale and her "Give for the Love of Mike" campaign raised a quarter of a million dollars in twelve weeks. She pioneered the building of a science block, a new hall, a library and a chapel.

In later years, Schol worked in the Solomons, helping to establish CSC in that country, and then after further time in Australia, she spent her last years in the UK, much loved by her sisters and all who met her. But she will always be best remembered for her influence on several generations of Australian children. They recall her as a 'no-nonsense' head, yet very caring, a role model for many students, and especially as a good listener. She had a wicked sense of humour and was capable of surprises – most notably when she hitched up the long skirt of her habit and demonstrated a faultless hurdling technique over the St Michael's rubbish bins!

Many will give thanks for her legacy both to education and the Religious life for many years to come.

Organizations

SSJD sisters in Toronto walk the labyrinth

AUSTRALIA

Advisory Council for Anglican Religious Life in Australia

The Council consists of:

Rt Revd Garry Weatherill, Bishop of Ballarat *(Chair)*

Further information about the bishops and secretary of the Committee had not been received at the time of going to press.

The Brother Robin BSB	Sr Carol Francis CHN	Sister Eunice SSA
Mother Rita Mary CCK	Brother Wayne LBF	Br Christopher John SSF
Sister Sue Nirta CSBC	Fr Keith Dean-Jones OGS	Father Christopher SSM
Sister Linda Mary CSC	Sister Juliana SI	

NEW ZEALAND

Conference of Anglican Religious Orders in Aotearoa New Zealand (CAROANZ)

Membership consists of: Rt Revd Victoria Matthews *(Chair)*
with representatives of: Associates of the Holy Cross; CSN; SLG; Associates of Southern Star Abbey, Kopua; Order of St Stephen; First Order SSF; Third Order SSF; Urban Vision.

EUROPE

Advisory Council on the Relations of Bishops & Religious Communities (commonly called 'The Advisory Council')

Rt Revd David Walker, Bishop of Manchester *(Chair)*
Rt Revd Jonathan Clark, Bishop of Croydon
Rt Revd Tony Robinson, Bishop of Pontefract
Rt Revd Humphrey Southern, Principal of Cuddesdon Theological College

Communities' representatives (elected Dec 2010 for 5-year term):

Sister Anita Cook CSC	Sister Mary Stephen Packwood OSB
Brother Damian SSF	Father Peter Allan CR
Sister Elizabeth Pio SSB	Sister Rosemary Howarth CHN
Sister Joyce Yarrow CSF	Abbot Stuart Burns OSB
Sister Mary Julian CHC	

Co-opted:
Revd Canon Chris Neal
Revd Ian Mobsby *(Moot Community and representing new and emerging communities)*

ARC representative: Dom Simon Jarrett OSB
Conference of Religious Observer: Abbot Richard Yeo OSB
Hon. Secretary: Father Colin CSWG Email: father.colin@cswg.org.uk

Conference of the Leaders of Anglican Religious Communities (CLARC)

The Conference meets in full once a year.
Hon. Secretary: Father Colin CSWG Email: father.colin@cswg.org.uk

General Synod of the Church of England

Representatives of Lay Religious

Sister Anita OHP (Elected 2006, re-elected 2010)
Brother Thomas Quin OSB (Elected 2010)

Representatives of Ordained Religious

Revd Sister Rosemary CHN (Elected 2002, re-elected 2005 & 2010)
Revd Thomas Seville CR (Elected 2005, re-elected 2010)

Anglican Religious Communities in England (ARC)

ARC supports members of Religious Communities in the Church of England. At present its membership is the entire body of professed members of communities recognised by the Advisory Council *(see above)*. It has held occasional conferences when members can come together both to hear speakers on topics relevant their way of life and to meet and share experiences together. A news letter is sent out 2 or 3 times a year to all houses. ARC represents Anglican Religious Life on various bodies, including the Vocations Forum of the Ministry Division of the CofE, The Advisory Council and the *Year Book* editorial committee. Some limited support is also given to groups of common interest within ARC who may wish to meet. Its activities are coordinated by a committee with members elected from Leaders, Novice Guardians, General Synod representatives and the professed membership. The committee usually meets three times a year.

A meeting was held in 2012 to review the future of ARC. It was in favour of ARC continuing but in favour of radical change, enlarging the membership to include possibly Acknowledged and maybe other communities.The idea of holding a large conference every 4 to 5 years was also suggested. The committee are working towards these aims.

Prior Simon OSB & Sister Sue CSF *(representing Leaders)*
vacancy (representing General Synod Representatives)
Sister Beverley CSF *(representing Novice Guardians)*
Sister Hilda Mary CSC *(Chair)*, Sister Anne CSJB *(Vice-Chair)*,
Sister Pam OHP & Sister Mary John OSB *(representing professed members)*

More information about Anglican Religious Life (in England) or about ARC itself, may be obtained from:

The Anglican Religious Communities, c/o The Secretary to the House of Bishops,
Church House, Great Smith Street, London SW1P 3AZ

Email: info@arcie.org.uk Website: www.arcie.org.uk

Conference of Anglican Religious Orders in the Americas (CAROA)

The purpose of CAROA is to provide opportunities for mutual support and sharing among its member communities and co-ordinate their common interests and activities, to engage in dialogue with other groups, to present a coherent understanding of the Religious Life to the Church and to speak as an advocate for the Religious Orders to the Church. CAROA is incorporated as a non-profit organization in both Canada and the USA.

Brother Jude Hill SSF (*President*)
Father David Bryan Hoopes OHC (*Vice-President*)
Sister Margaret Howard CSC (*Secretary-Treasurer*)
The Revd Dr Donald Anderson (*General Secretary*)
PO Box 99, Little Britain, Ontario K0M 2C0, CANADA
Tel: 705 786 3330 *Email: dwa1319@gmail.com*

House of Bishops Standing Committee on Religious Orders in the Anglican Church of Canada

The Committee usually meets twice a year, during the House of Bishops' meeting. Its rôle is consultative and supportive.

Rt Revd Linda Nicholls, Suffragan Bishop of Trent-Durham *(chair)*
Most Revd Fred J Hiltz, Archbishop & Primate of Canada
Rt Revd Michael Bird, Bishop of Niagara
Rt Revd Philip Poole, Suffragan Bishop of York-Credit Valley
The Superiors of CSC, OHC, SSJD & SSJE
Revd Dr Donald W Anderson, General Secretary of CAROA
The Ven Paul Feheley, Principal Secretary to the Primate (*Secretary*)

General Synod of the Anglican Church of Canada

Religious Synod members:

To be announced

National Association for Episcopal Christian Communities (NAECC)

The NAECC is an inclusive association that shares and communicates the fruits of the Gospel, realized in community, with the church and the world. It is primarily a forum for those who are living or exploring new or continuing models of religious commitment within the context of community.

Bill Farra SCC *(President)*
Masud Ibn Syedullah TSSF *(Secretary)*
James Mahoney *(Treasurer)*

Website: naecc.us

Glossary and Indices

A prayer sculpture by Beryl Maw at Burnham Abbey on the day of its blessing.

Glossary

Aspirant

A person who hopes to become a Religious and has been in touch with a particular community, but has not yet begun to live with them.

Celibacy

The commitment to remain unmarried and to refrain from sexual relationships. It is part of the vow of chastity traditionally taken by Religious. Chastity is a commitment to sexual integrity, a term applicable to fidelity in marriage as well as to celibacy in Religious Life.

Chapter

The council or meeting of Religious to deliberate and make decisions about the community. In some orders, this may consist of all the professed members of the community; in others, the Chapter is a group of members elected by the community as a whole to be their representatives.

Clothing

The ceremony in which a postulant of a community formally becomes a novice, and begins the period of formation in the mind, work and spirit of the community. It follows the initial stage of being a postulant when the prospective member first lives alongside the community. The clothing or novicing ceremony is characterised by the Religious 'receiving' the habit, or common attire, of the community.

Contemplative

A Religious whose life is concentrated on prayer inside the monastery or convent rather than on social work or ministry outside the house. Some communities were founded with the specific intention of leading a contemplative lifestyle together. Others may have a single member or small group living such a vocation within a larger community oriented to outside work.

Enclosed

This term is applied to Religious who stay within a particular convent or monastery - the 'enclosure' - to pursue more effectively a life of prayer. They would usually only leave the enclosure for medical treatment or other exceptional reasons. This rule is intended to help the enclosed Religious be more easily protected from the distractions and attentions of the outside world.

Eremitic

The eremitic Religious is one who lives the life of a hermit, that is, largely on his or her own. Hermits usually live singly, but may live in an eremitic community, where they meet together for prayer on some occasions during each day.

Evangelical Counsels

A collective name for the three vows of poverty, chastity and obedience.

Habit

The distinctive clothing of a community. In some communities, the habit is worn at all times, in others only at certain times or for certain activities. In some communities, the habit is rarely worn, except perhaps for formal occasions.

Novice

A member of a community who is in the formation stage of the Religious Life, when she or he learns the mind, work and spirit of the particular community whilst living among its members.

Oblate

Someone associated closely with a community, but who will be living a modified form of the Rule, which allows him or her to live outside the Religious house. Oblates are so-called because they make an oblation (or offering) of obedience to the community instead of taking the profession vows. In some communities, oblates remain celibate, in others they are allowed to be married. A few oblates live within a community house and then they are usually termed intern(al) oblates. The term oblate is more usually associated with Benedictine communities.

Office/Daily Office/Divine Office

The round of liturgical services of prayer and worship, which mark the rhythm of the daily routine in Religious Life. Religious communities may use the services laid down by the Church or may have their own particular Office book. The Offices may be called Morning, Midday, Evening and Night Prayer, or may be referred to by traditional names, such as Mattins, Lauds, Terce, Sext, None, Vespers and Compline.

Postulant

Someone who is in the first stage of living the Religious life. The postulancy usually begins when the aspirant begins to live in community and ends when he or she becomes a novice and 'receives the habit'. Postulants sometimes wear a distinctive dress or else may wear secular clothes.

Profession

The ceremony at which a Religious makes promises (or vows) to live the Religious Life with integrity and fidelity to the Rule. The profession of these vows may be for a limited period or for life. The usual pattern is to make a 'first' or simple profession in which the vows are made to the community. After three or more years a Life Profession may be made, which is to the Church and so the vows are usually received by a bishop. In the Anglican Communion, Life Professed Religious can usually be secularized only by the Archbishop or Presiding Bishop of a Province.

Religious (as in 'a Religious')

The general term for a person living the Religious life.

Rule

The written text containing the principles and values by which the members of a community try to live. The Rule is not simply a set of regulations, although it may contain such, but is an attempt to capture the spirit and charism of a community in written form. Some communities follow traditional Rules, such as those of St Benedict or St Augustine, others have written their own.

Tertiary/Third Order

This term is usually associated with Franciscan communities, but is used by others too. A Third Order is made up of tertiaries, people who take vows, but modified so that they are able to live in their own homes and have their own jobs. They may also marry and have children. They have a Rule of Life and are linked to other tertiaries through regular meetings. In the Franciscan family, the Third Order complements both the First Order of celibate friars and sisters and the Second Order of contemplative Religious.

Vows

The promises made by a Religious at profession. They may be poverty, chastity and obedience. In some communities, they are obedience, stability and conversion of life.

Index by dedication / patron saint

Index by location

Index of Community Wares & Services for Sale

CHURCH LINEN & NEEDLEWORK, EMBROIDERY & VESTMENTS

CRAFTS & RELIGIOUS ARTEFACTS

Index of Communities by Initials